THE SPEAKING STONE

THE SPEAKING STONE

Stories Cemeteries Tell

Michael Griffith

UNIVERSITY OF CINCINNATI PRESS

About the University of Cincinnati Press

The University of Cincinnati Press is committed to publishing rigorous, peer-reviewed, leading scholarship accessibly to stimulate dialog among the academy, public intellectuals and lay practitioners. The Press endeavors to erase disciplinary boundaries in order to cast fresh light on common problems in our global community. Building on the university's long- standing tradition of social responsibility to the citizens of Cincinnati, state of Ohio, and the world, the Press publishes books on topics that expose and resolve disparities at every level of society and have local, national and global impact.

The University of Cincinnati Press, Cincinnati 45221
Copyright © 2021

Published in 2021

ISBN 978-1-947602-30-4 (paperback)
ISBN 978-1-947602-31-1 (e-book, PDF)
ISBN 978-1-947602-29-8 (e-book, EPUB)

Library of Congress Cataloging-in-Publication Data

Griffith, Michael, 1965– author.
The speaking stone : stories cemeteries tell / Michael Griffith. Stories cemeteries tell
Cincinnati : University of Cincinnati Press, 2021. | Includes bibliographical references and index.
LCCN 2020020102 | ISBN 9781947602304 (paperback) | ISBN 9781947602298 (epub) | ISBN 9781947602311 (pdf)
LCSH: Spring Grove Cemetery & Arboretum (Cincinnati, Ohio)—Ancedotes.
| Cemeteries—Ohio—Cincinnati—Ancedotes. | Sepulchral monuments—Cincinnati (Ohio). | Griffith, Michael, 1965—Ancedotes. | Cincinnati (Ohio)—Biography—Ancedotes.
LCC F499.C562 G75 2021 | DDC 977.1/7800222—dc23
LC record available at https://lccn.loc.gov/2020020102

Designed and produced for UC Press by Julie Rushing
Typeset in Kepler Std and Trajan Pro
Printed in the United States of America
First Printing

For Nicola and Bix

Contents

A STATE OF UNGRESS: COMPOSING AS RAMBLING | 3

THE ABSENT GUEST: LEON VAN LOO | 17

BAKE VISIBLY!: ERNST HUENEFELD | 21

"A GREAT AWKWARD BUNGLEHOOD OF WOMAN": FANNY WRIGHT | 31

INTERLUDE: THE BANK-SHOT UNMEMOIR | 47

"DEATH'S TAXICAB": WILLARD HESS AND MARTIN HALE CRANE | 51

ACCIDENTAL CHARON:
JACOB STRADER, DRED SCOTT, AND BODY-SNATCHING | 69

"DUE ALLOWANCE FOR FOAM":
MARTHA MCCLELLAN BROWN AND THE OHIO WOMEN'S CRUSADE | 75

"ANOTHER WELL-PICKED SKELETON": HOMUNCULI, MAIL-ORDER TREE STUMPS,
PETRIFIED LOGS, AND THE MANY, MANY CHARLES MILLERS | 93

OUTLOOK HAZY: LAURA PRUDEN, HARRY HOUDINI,
AND ARTHUR CONAN DOYLE INTERROGATE THE SPIRITS | 117

GHOSTS OF THE WALLDOGS: GUS HOLTHAUS | 127

INTERLUDE: THE CRYPTO AUTO-OBITUARY | 150

"AND THEY DID KILL HER BY INCHES":
THE STRANGE CASE OF CARRIE ELDER | 153

THE SCULPTOR, HIS SON, THE ODD FELLOWS, AND THE WEIRD ASSASSIN:
LOUIS REBISSO(S) AND OSCAR MUNDHENK | 169

SIX DEGREES OF JONATHAN CILLEY | 191

THE PERMEABLE EARTH | 221

Acknowledgments | 223

Notes | 225

Image Credits | 233

Index | 235

THE SPEAKING STONE

A STATE OF UNGRESS
COMPOSING AS RAMBLING

I'VE LONG BEEN AN AVID READER OF OBITUARIES. They're the only kind of story in the newspaper—in the whole hot-take mediasphere, for that matter—that features a completed arc, with beginning and end, rather than being a chaotic dispatch from the middle of things. Obituaries follow a stately, near-universal template, one that's elegantly improvised upon and compressed, a strict poetic form: the ghazal of a life, the sonnet. Especially since the rise of obituaries about ordinary people—a form that took on special poignancy in the aftermath of 9/11—obituaries can offer the reader a sense, too, of the multifariousness of the paths not taken, of the range of occupational choices and ways of contributing to (or wrecking) humanity.

One day a couple of years ago, for example, I recall reading an obit for Leo Hulseman, inventor of the red Solo Cup, enabler of Toby Keith songs and college Greek scenes. Alongside him that day were Marilyn Sachs, the author of, among other books for young people, the classic *A Pocketful of Seeds*, about a young Jewish girl in occupied France whose parents are taken away by the Nazis; George S. Irving, voice of the Heat Miser from Rankin/Bass's unkillably wonderful/awful stop-motion special *The Year Without a Santa Claus*; Debbie Reynolds, the Unsinkable Molly Brown herself, sunk by a stroke just one day after the sudden death of her daughter, Carrie Fisher; and Tyrus Wong, the Chinese-born artist who, by channeling Song Dynasty landscape paintings, gave *Bambi* its spare, haunting, distinctive look (but was for decades deprived of the credit).

As Marilyn Johnson points out in her book *The Dead Beat*, all you have to do to find synchronicities and compelling links on the obituary page is to pay attention, maybe squint a little.[1] The messy partisanships and envies of daily life make "only connect" a hard motto to live by; but note how quickly death whisks away the obstacles, how efficiently the conventions of the obituary speed the path to reconciliation. Among their other accomplishments, three of the dead that day were luminaries of animated films: Irving, not only the red-faced "Mr. Hundred and One"[2] but also the narrator of *Underdog*; Reynolds, who contributed in the holiday hokum category, too, as Rudolph the Red-Nosed

Reindeer's mom, and who also, unforgettably, gave voice to E. B. White's philosopher-spider Charlotte A. Cavatica; and the great cel artist Wong.

Let's claim Irving for the lighter side of kids' entertainment (leaving aside Underdog's penchant for collateral damage, the Heat Miser's tragic Midaslike tendency to melt things in his clutch). And, sure, we'll stipulate that Hulseman will be remembered not for his business acumen, or for saving noses and laps from coffee-scorching with his "Traveler Lid," but for his status as Patron Saint of Tailgating, Dark Lord of Beer Pong. (No one's dignity could survive Toby Keith's par-tay anthem "Red Solo Cup," with its opening rhyme of "receptacle" with "testicles," then its beeline into the chorus of "Red solo cup I fill you up/ Let's have a party let's have a party.")

The other three, though, make up a mini-pantheon of Death in Children's Entertainment. Sachs, who built her best-known novel around collaboration and the Holocaust. Reynolds, who as the minuscule heroine of *Charlotte's Web* taught Wilbur the pig, Fern the flinty farmgirl, and the rest of us a hard lesson about mortality (and who as consolation left 514 eggs, a legacy that seems almost cruel in the context of Reynolds's death, since—an awful reversal of the "natural" order—she was immediately preceded in it by her daughter). And Wong, a man in large part responsible for the tone and power and terrible beauty of the first, most desolating screen death I ever witnessed. Lesson of the day's death notices? Red Solo Cup, I fill you up with anguish.

But what I like best about obituaries, as about most of the fiction I love, are not the plot elements (feats and honors, in this case) but the pungent oddities that peek up between and around them: quotations, anecdotes, details offered as synecdoches for a whole life. These are the elements that give the reader, having invested just two or three minutes, something of a person's tone and timbre. Obituaries are miniatures that, in the hands of a sly, resourceful, above all empathetic writer, don't just transcend the form's limitations but are in some basic way *about* showing how obnoxious and deficient linearity is as a way of viewing a life. They give a useful reminder: the real life lies between the lines.

When the work is going well, I love my attic writing space: the slanted walls, the low ceiling crazed with cracks, the perpetual semi-dark, the walls a sickly blue like an aquarium's inside. But when the work is a struggle, as it was at the start of last September, the roof looms low, the gloom condenses, and it starts to feel like a coffin.

Alexander Courage

Which simile was a bit too apt, since the book I was working on was a novel about an obituary writer (and a puzzle deviser, but that's a story for another time). I can say with certainty when that book began percolating: May 31, 2008. That day, the *New York Times* ran a notice by the wonderful Margalit Fox about Alexander "Sandy" Courage, who'd died two weeks earlier at eighty-eight. Courage was a prolific Hollywood music director and composer, but, as often happens in the career of an artist, one of his compositions came to swamp, dwarf, nearly obliterate all the others. In 1965, Courage was asked to compose the theme for a science fiction TV pilot. The show's creator, scorning what he called "space music," wanted something with more grandeur, so Courage crafted a lush hybrid, with symphonic bombast to spare but also featuring a wavering soprano and, behind it, the whooshing sounds (voiced by Courage himself) of . . . who knows, maybe Velocity? Mystery? The

Shimmering Void? In her obituary, Fox summed up the theme of *Star Trek* as "an exquisite combination of pomp and cheesiness, Valhalla and Vegas in equal measure." It became not only a near-ubiquitous tune but a cultural touchstone, one that fifty-plus years later is still hummed in hallways, quoted on TV and in film, piped into elevators and malls, even performed in orchestra halls.

Gustave Flaubert once suggested that the biographer should write as if taking revenge for his subject, and here, Margalit Fox embraced the role. She reported that the show's creator, Gene Roddenberry, had insisted on splitting songwriting credit with Courage, and so had jotted down some words to accompany the tune. These were never used, were never (it seems) even intended for use, but their existence guaranteed Roddenberry fifty cents of every dollar the song would ever earn. Fox didn't content herself with the story of Roddenberry's greed. She went instead for scorched-earth retribution, quoting—in their entirety, as I recall—the spectacularly vapid lyrics he had written, which began with one of the laziest rhymes in all poesy, plus the humiliating metrical-guide apostrophe common to doggerel auteurs who are just starting out: "Beyond the rim of the star-light/ My love is wand'ring in star-flight."[3] In an obituary of maybe fifteen column inches, Fox devoted three or four to this brilliant bit of vengeance. There was also delicious irony in the *form* the payback took: over the years, Roddenberry had been paid millions for public use of the theme music, his contribution to which was heretofore invisible; Fox was simply letting him, for once, fully earn the royalty he'd been collecting.[4]

You may have noticed the phrase "as I recall" above. It's necessary because, as I discovered when I lost the clipping I'd dragged around for a few years and went to print the obituary from the newspaper's online archive, Fox's revenge has been expunged from the record. Gone the anecdote, gone the lyrics. One can't perhaps know for *certain* why this is, but I'd venture a wild guess that the offending passage was sent to wander "beyond the rim of star-light," invisible to human eyes, by the Roddenberry estate's lawyers.

From Fox's version of Courage's life emerged an idea for a novel, to be set against the backdrop of the dying American newspaper industry in the late 1990s, about a crusading obituarist who takes Flaubert's injunction in deadly earnest, and who eventually becomes a kind of vigilante, roaming the city to set right the wrongs done in life to the newly dead.

A dumb idea? Yes, sure, but one I grew attached to and kept hacking away at for several years. Which leads back to the frustrations of late last summer.

Some radical tree-hugger

Dr. Thomas Fogarty with President Obama after accepting
the National Medal of Technology & Science in 2014

The Fogarty
catheter

The Eisenhower Executive Office Building, 1981

Louise McLaughlin, vase, 1880

In times of frustration or anxiety, I've always tended toward compulsive motion. So when the novel's flow slowed and nearly halted, the cheap evasion I hit upon (I mean the *strategy I devised*) was to prime the pump every morning with an hour-long cemetery walk.

It's my good luck to have, just half a mile from home and in the middle of the city of Cincinnati, one of the first and, at about 750 acres, one of the largest garden cemeteries in the world, Spring Grove Cemetery and Arboretum. Founded in 1845, it's an astonishingly beautiful place, with serpentine roads rising generally from front to back; spectacular vegetation, including more than twelve hundred varieties of trees and shrubs; fourteen ponds; wildlife including swans, geese, coyotes, foxes, owls, hawks, turkeys, deer, and more; and among its tens of thousands of markers, mausoleums, and crypts a virtual encyclopedia of nineteenth- and early-twentieth-century architecture and funerary custom.

But before I get to Spring Grove, I should confess that there was another thing driving me away from the desk and toward my cemetery walks, a bit of anxiety and insecurity that needed working out before I could make real progress on the novel.

My writing space is in the attic of our house, a narrow brick Victorian from 1895—a modified shotgun, really, very tall but just one room wide. When my wife and I arrived in Cincinnati in 2002, we found a business card tucked into the front door. It bore the name of Thomas Fogarty, a professor of cardiac surgery at Stanford, who had scrawled across it, "Grew up in this house!" Presumably Dr. Fogarty had dropped by to look at the old place in the month between the closing and our move to the city. We were intrigued by this information but not quite sure what to do with it, so we clipped the card to the fridge, where everything soon takes on a mantle of invisibility. We forgot about it.

A decade later, on a Saturday afternoon in spring, my wife and I were out in our postage-stamp front yard, trying to dismantle a tree. Our lone little hardwood had died the year before, and we'd done nothing about the corpse through the spring and summer. In fall, to make the tree's skeleton look less like blight than like something intended—a jaunty bit of art rather than the bare coatrack of laziness—we'd bought half a dozen rolls of fluorescent-patterned duct tape and let our five-year-old decorate its trunk. This helped some, and enabled us to sputter our way through winter, during which the tree looked no deader than anything else. Now spring had come again, and with it the exhaustion of our stall tactic. And so, using a borrowed rechargeable chainsaw not meant for tasks of this scale, I was disassembling the twenty-foot tree piece by piece.[5] Braced between branches halfway up, leaning back to grind my way through a thick limb, I couldn't help noticing that a van had pulled up to the curb, not fifteen feet away.

No one got out. It was as if they'd seen an idiot intent on death by sparagmos or headfirst fall and decided it would make a fine Saturday's entertainment. After ten minutes or so, the silent and motionless audience started freaking me out. My wife cautiously approached the van, the window rolled down, and a conversation started. The driver was the friend and attendant of her passenger, an elderly woman who had grown up in our house in the 1930s and 1940s, and who liked to drive by now and again to see how the old place was faring in our slightly down-at-the-heels neighborhood in this more than slightly down-at-the-heels city. Nicola chatted with her for a couple of minutes, and the old woman told a couple of stories and then asked whether, the next time her brother Tom came to town from California, they might drop by and take a look around.

I was away for the first half-hour of Thomas Fogarty's visit to the house, and for the balance of his stay split my time between amusing our daughter and attending his sister, who didn't feel up to risking the stairs and so contented herself with soaking in the slanted morning sun of the dining room. Dr. Fogarty told my wife all kinds of stories, covering family history—the father who died when Tom was eight, the boy's subsequent role as, if not man of the house, at least handyman of the house—and the quirks of the place. There was the clawfoot tub buried in the garden; the stained glass he'd scavenged and replaced (sorry!) on the cheap before moving out; the worn blond picture-frame floors, now buffed down to near nonexistence, refinished (the floor guys had warned us) for the last time; the financially necessary move the Fogartys had made to divide the house into a two-family and take in a boarder. Fogarty explained, too, the source of the nine semicircular dents we'd noticed in the attic's main wooden support. That had been his space, his retreat, and to vent frustrations he'd gone at the beam with a baseball bat, a peewee Samson banking on his inability to bring down the house.

But the remarkable thing was what he'd done up there later. In his twenties, Thomas Fogarty—in the same room where I was trying now to push through self-doubt and write my ridiculous novel about a vigilante obituarist—had begun a medical revolution.

As a boy Tom was a gifted tinkerer, able to fix almost anything, but an indifferent student. In eighth grade, to help with family finances, he took a job cleaning medical equipment at Good Samaritan Hospital. Soon he was promoted to scrub technician, and by his senior year in high school he'd grown interested in a medical career and had become the private scrub tech of Dr. Jack Cranley, the vascular surgeon who would become Fogarty's mentor and would help put him through college.

At the time—the 1950s—surgery to extract clots from limbs was a gruesome, dangerous business. The prevailing method was to cut the artery down its length to find the clot, then to use forceps to remove it. This might require hours under general anesthesia, and because of the long-term interruption of blood flow, amputation was frequently called for afterward. Fogarty set himself the task of devising a better way. In his attic eyrie, he experimented with a urethral catheter and balloons of various kinds and thicknesses. His idea was that the catheter was strong and flexible enough to push through the clot; if he could figure out a way to attach it to a balloon, he could make a tiny incision, string the catheter down the artery, then gently inflate it with saline solution.

The engineering turned out to be tricky. First there was the question of the balloon. The ones Fogarty tried tended to burst when inflated, or when he dragged the catheter through glass tubes filled with gelatin—his homemade simulations of arterial clots. Eventually, though, he discovered a promising mix of durability and flexibility in the cut-off fingertip of a latex surgical glove. The next challenge was how to connect the catheter and the balloon, as there existed at the time no glue capable of binding vinyl to latex. Fogarty's solution was to use his manual dexterity and the fishing skills of his boyhood, and essentially to make the device into an exotic trout fly.[6]

In 1960, even before Fogarty finished his MD at the University of Cincinnati, his embolectomy catheter became the first device designed for minimally invasive surgery. That innovation led to balloon angioplasty (in fact the first such procedure, in 1965, was done using a Fogarty catheter), to a whole host of modern surgical techniques . . . and to a paradigm shift in the way surgery was conducted.

So another reason to escape my writing space was to throw off the killing weight of Fogarty's example. He had accomplished something actually *important* here, and what was my goofy nonsense to that? Every time I made another pun or devised another ridiculous hink-pink puzzle (for example, "1990s prop comedian, now policing European polecats? Hinkily pinkily"— answer "Carrot Top, ferret cop") and leaned back and looked around the room for the affirmation I seemed to need, I was forced to confront the unpleasant realization that what I was doing here didn't much matter.[7]

I'd like to think that I don't suffer delusions of grandeur; certainly I know that my books aren't going to make me what Hegel would call a World-Historical Individual. But one of the preconditions of writing, at least for me, has always been a basic, tentative agreement with myself to write *as if* these creaky bits of wordplay and heaped-up absurdities might matter. I didn't need anyone else to care, but *I* needed to. Fogarty, damn him, was harshing my mellow. By God, I had come up with "Glass receptacle, located in a Tanzanian archipelago, for money to help a former *Who's the Boss?* star now down on his luck (hinkily pinkily)." Couldn't "Zanzibar Danza jar" be enough to justify a life? No?

In order to get going in the novel, I needed to cease my irritable reaching, to cry uncle. The cemetery promised an escape from an absurd home-office ego battle in which I would always get drubbed. It also offered "perspective," a term we little people use to drag our betters down so that we can better tolerate our fates. At Spring Grove, as in many cemeteries, people try vainly to insist on carrying over their worldly status. The brewer orders an extra foot of concrete so that his phallic obelisk outpoints that of the yeast magnate next door. Families pay premiums for spots that overlook lakes or abut the most-traveled paths and intersections. Some spring for opulent materials, unusual ornaments, engraved biographies, even a miniature Gothic cathedral. But nowhere does striving, or pride, look more laughable. In the boneyard there's only one level that matters, and it's mostly underfoot, beneath the squishy trails of the burrowers: the one equality that awaits us all. If you're looking for a curb to your vanity, you could do far worse than walking the cemetery beat—or covering the obituary one.

One morning in early September, walking a road I'd walked or biked a hundred times, I noticed to my left an eccentric Art Nouveau font, an artist's-palette-shaped headstone, and I stopped, pulled out my phone, punched the deceased's name into Google. There I plunged into a story that involved Ulysses S. Grant and William Tecumseh Sherman, early photography, a ghost-hosted dinner party . . . and I headed down a rabbit hole into which I suppose I am now—come on in?—inviting you.

Within days I was embarked on another book, another kind of book. Or, rather, another of more or less the same kind. My last, the novel *Trophy*,[8] which takes place in the instant of its protagonist's death and features his desperate, meandering ploys to extend that moment, is also about rambling—rambling as existential necessity, since as soon as Vada Prickett's life stops flashing before his eyes, it's over. Digression, I've always thought, gets a bad rap. The word implies that there's a proper *gress* from which one has strayed, that every life is a line. But surely linearity is something we impose only afterward, when it's time to make a narrative, when it's time to comb out our gresses and untangle them into something we can call *progress*. We are poor, forked animals who live most of our lives, and thank God, in a state of ungress, regress, circumgress. Many people live lives packed with incident— but whose has a *plot*?

I found myself extending those morning walks in Spring Grove. This was a literalization of what I'd been doing in *Trophy*: more amblings, more attempts to find narrative where I stumbled upon it or tangled myself up in it. I tried to suppress my fear that these were not constitutionals but unconstitutionals—just a way of shirking my duty to work on the new novel. Soon I was wandering (or wand'ring) the cemetery every day, learning to read it, seeing what caught my eye (odd stones, epitaphs, frills or follies, genres of marker, plantings), jotting down names and locations, and then going home to explore in a different way the idiosyncrasies I'd noticed. I tried to undertake the work, or "work," in the spirit of an obituary reader: curious, sympathetic, alert for connections.

Much of the pleasure of writing this book has derived from the chance to experience narrative as a product of impetus and accident. What details will be thrown into conversation or juxtaposition as I walk? Sheepishly, I've begun thinking in terms of rhapsodomancy, the ancient mode of divination that involves flipping open a manuscript of poems at random, or its cousin stichomancy, which takes the Bible as its revelatory text. My chosen form, it seems, is graveyard-walk-omancy.

I have tried to be faithful to this principle of chance, which means that a lot of the best-known denizens of Spring Grove won't appear here. No Miller Huggins, manager of the "Murderers' Row" New York Yankees of 1927 (and, in playing days, awarded for his fielding range one of baseball history's great nicknames, "Little Everywhere"). No George Reeves, TV's first Superman, for whom in real life the pectoral S seemed to stand for snakebit. (He was temporarily interred here.) No Alfred Mullett, a longtime favorite of mine who after the Civil War rose quickly from an "obscure draftsman" to U.S. Supervising Architect, in which position he was responsible for designing and executing more than forty fireproof federal buildings. Many of these were massive, expensive, lavishly ornamented architectural mashups. Perhaps most storied among them are the New York City Hall Post Office and Courthouse, "Mullett's Monstrosity," which was razed in 1939; and the Eisenhower

Executive Office Building, still the workplace of many White House staffers. Mullett was a taskmaster and a crank. The *New York Sun* called him "the most arrogant, pretentious, and preposterous little humbug in the United States." In 1890, his reputation under siege, his health declining, and amid mounting debts, he committed suicide. And yet his work has hung on, outlasting the carpers, enduring the vicissitudes of critical opinion over more than a century, and now is enjoying a renaissance. The wildly overblown Executive Office Building, provides a counterpoint, as Francis Clines memorably put it a couple decades ago, to "the gleaming idealism" of much federal architecture, projecting instead "the Republic's flamboyant, mongrel heart," and it's now considered a loud treasure—sort of the nineteenth-century architectural equivalent of the 1970s pimpmobile. It's a great melting (or melted?) pot of a building.

Likewise—because theirs were graves I didn't stumble across—no Mary Louise McLaughlin, painter and pioneer ceramicist, one of the principals in a legendary rivalry (with Maria Longworth Storer of Rookwood) that helped drive the American art pottery movement. No Levi ("President of the Underground Railroad") and Catherine Coffin, who among their many exploits in 1853 assisted twenty-eight intrepid slaves in the largest-scale escape of the era by helping them masquerade as a funeral retinue of free blacks on the way to a service at my neighborhood's *other* big cemetery, Wesleyan—the only one in the city that allowed the burial of blacks. The group proceeded past the graveyard, up one side of College Hill, and from there to freedom. Nor—closer to our time—could I include Kimberly Walker, the young African American soldier who was murdered by a boyfriend in 2013 and whose gravestone—in the shape of her favorite cartoon character, SpongeBob SquarePants (and accompanied by a matching monument for her twin sister)—became the flashpoint in a controversy about "proper" cemetery tone and dignity. Eventually the SpongeBob-shaped stones stayed, but with full granite walls behind to shield them from passersby. And so on.

In a cemetery of such immensity, that I missed these graves is no surprise. Consider, á la Jorge Luis Borges's "Garden of Forking Paths,"[9] the bewildering multifariousness of available routes, the old but easy-to-forget truth that there's no one inevitable form for material to take, that the writer's job is to find not *the* way through the maze but *a* way. The result of all this, I hope, will be a book fundamentally about the role of retracing and coincidence and surprise connection, whether in a walk or in rereading any familiar text or landscape. Day to day, neither the scape nor its reader remains the same.

There are new conditions of light, new angles of vision or vagaries of mood. (Shoe need tying? Back trouble making you wince and slump? Clinging to a hedge in driving rain? All these will bring different things into view.) Trees grow, flowers bloom, leaves fall and mat underfoot; you may follow a fox or a wisp of thought over a hill and into an undiscovered glade.[10] You may read a surname on a welding-shop signboard, or the side of a building, and then glimpse it on a stone the next day.

Am I claiming to do something fresh? Dear God no. Others figured out the link between walking and storytelling millennia ago, at least as far back as Plato's strolls in the groves of the Academy, and wandering was a major part of the Romantic poets' philosophy and practice too, and and and. But for me the work of these last months has *felt* like a new mode of composition, one that's about the conversion of one vector of motion to another. As a high jumper translates speed to altitude, ramble becomes essay . . . and then it turns out that all along, digression wasn't an *avoidance* of narrative—duh, you fool— but a subgenre of it.

Because no matter what the spaghetti-ish map of one's wanderings may look like—the loops and eddies, the backtrackings—they turn out, in retrospect, to describe a path. John Barth once wrote of postmodernism's alleged disdain for narrative that it's nothing to fret about: "We live in an ocean of story," he wrote, and wherever one drops one's bucket it will come up overflowing.[11] It's been a pleasure to rediscover how right Barth is, and to find, gratefully, that in whatever route one happens to take there seems already inscribed some plan or order. Lately it's occurred to me that for all these years I may have misunderstood the diviners of old, the readers of teacup lees or goat intestines or randomly chosen passages. The object of their faith needn't be God. In the theology Barth implies (or that Marilyn Johnson does in her book on obituaries), when we take the jump into apparent randomness it's not fate that delivers us; it's narrative. There's nothing we can't make into a story. There's nothing that isn't already one.

THE ABSENT GUEST
LEON VAN LOO

LEON VAN LOO WAS A BELGIAN-BORN PHOTOGRAPHER AND ART COL-LECTOR. In 1875 he invented a new technique he called "Ideal Photography," which featured an image printed in zinc oxide applied to blackened sheet-iron. This produced a pearly, translucent upper layer.

An example of his work: in early March 1864, in Washington, DC, Abraham Lincoln promoted Ulysses S. Grant to general-in-chief of the Armies of the United States. Grant then traveled to Nashville to transfer his former command to William Tecumseh Sherman, and the two native Ohioans traveled north together to Cincinnati, which was on Grant's way back to DC. With what the *Cincinnati Enquirer* called "throngs of sight-seekers" massed around the hotel, and with sentries at the door, they holed up in a second-floor salon of the Burnet House for a day-long strategy session about which Colonel S. M. Bowman, a Sherman staffer, would later offer this modest assessment: "[B]ending over their maps, the two generals, who had so long been inseparable, planned together that colossal structure . . . and, grasping one another firmly by the hand, separated, one to the east, the other to the west, each to strike at the same instant his half of the ponderous death-blow." Presumably during that five-day sojourn in Cincinnati (March 18–23), Grant posed for an albumen portrait by Van Loo—the first known photograph taken of the future president after he earned his third star and became commander of the Union Armies.

Another sample of Van Loo's art is a lovely advertising card for his studio. The man was a portly popinjay (note the white piping on his jacket!), and oh, did he know how to bestride a chair.

In 1890, Van Loo was one of the thirteen founding members—make that fourteen, as the group superstitiously enrolled a pet dog—of the Cincinnati Art Club. The club in those early years included an impressive roster of artists, including Frank Duveneck, the portraitist of Native Americans Henry Farny, and Winsor McCay, the cartoonist best known for *Little Nemo*, but also a pioneering animator whose short films include *Gertie the Dinosaur*, the prototype for green-screen interactive human-toon adventures like *Who*

Framed Roger Rabbit? (My favorite of McCay's works, though, is the phantasmagorical newspaper strip *Dream of a Rarebit Fiend*, which depicts the vivid nightmares suffered by a serial overindulger in the cheese-on-toast dish Welsh rarebit.)

Van Loo was Cincinnati Art Club president from 1894 to 1896 and again in 1903–04, and he left money in his will—$250—for a fancy dinner to be held for 150 club friends. (The group had expanded rapidly in those early years.[1]) If it was possible to make it back from the other side to attend his own memorial soirée, the photographer promised, "the boys" could count on him.

He was, alas, a no-show.

Ulysses S. Grant, photo by Leon Van Loo, 1864

Leon Van Loo, on a card advertising his photography studio
on West 4th Street in Cincinnati

BAKE VISIBLY!

ERNST HUENEFELD

WHEN MY DAUGHTER WAS A TODDLER, we occasionally packed a picnic and headed to Spring Grove to give her parents a change of scenery (with alfresco meal) and Bix room to roam and to spill. One of our favorite spots was a still, dark-water lake surrounded by cypress trees exuding their tannins, and nearby was a mausoleum. Our daughter loved walking its ledges, snaking between and hiding behind its columns, but I never paid any notice to the name engraved above—just another wealthy person who could spring for Doric flutes.

Fast-forward five years. My daughter is now attending the School for the Creative & Performing Arts downtown. Every morning—my favorite ritual of the day—I drive her there by way of Spring Grove Avenue, which just west of the cemetery swings past my neighborhood (Northside), under Interstates 74 and 75 and the Ludlow viaduct, then passes under a railroad trestle. There the formerly bustling industrial corridor sputters out, becomes mostly a landscape of shuttered, graffiti-scarred or -enlivened buildings (depending on your taste), and vacant brownfields repurposed into parking: a vast yellow Van Gogh–like field not of sunflowers but of school buses, and just south of that the city's main impound lot. Every morning we pass a defunct bar across from the defunct sausage factory, and I recall that around 2003, before the latter's demise caused the former's, I went with a couple of friends into the Stockyard Café and Beer Garden. Inside a door no longer shaded by its shredded green awning was a sprawling mess. Every surface of every table was piled high—six inches? eight?—with Ziploc-bagged carnival swag and cheapo tchotchkes. We paid two bucks for our beers, then chose a booth and, before setting the bottles down, had to clear space by mounding up small stuffed animals, Chinese finger traps, those paddles with balls attached by an elastic band that's designed to snap in sixty seconds, plastic jacks sets, etc. Much of the merchandise looked dusty and slightly damaged, though it was hard to tell what was just shopworn, or rather tavern-worn. Had the proprietors bought and ended up warehousing a giant odd lot that didn't pan out as they'd hoped? In any case, the future didn't look bright. The Stockyard

Café's head had been cleavered off, and this, apparently, was its pell-mell run around the barnyard. Cut off from its source of customers, isolated by the railyard just west and I-75 just east, it wouldn't survive long.

Which is why I was shocked when, the better part of a decade later, I noticed as I drove my daughter past that the place seemed to be, well, extant. Not humming, but grimly hanging on. So one day I slowed to a crawl and discovered, looking at the front window, that they'd come up with a new survival ploy—pole dancing.

I believe the wavy orange emphasis that crosses the center of the "Dance Pole Rules" sign (shown on next page) is not underscoring but an extension cord, and I don't want to contemplate the incident or incidents that occasioned the hand-scrawled prohibition about jewelry; shot-and-a-beer bars outside meat-packing plants no doubt would have long acquaintance with grisly accidents. But not even no-strip stripper poles—with gender rules that, as one who's trodden those uneven floors and seen the unplumb walls, I'll bet might spring from structural-integrity concerns as well as sexist ones— could save the Stockyard Café. Soon after, it closed.

Farther down the street, alongside an auto parts warehouse, sits an Ohio historical marker that when I first spotted it struck me as almost comic. This was a shrine that wouldn't have made the cut in Chicago or New York, I thought, and it seemed especially forlorn here, in this four-lane wasteland: FIRST GLASS DOOR OVEN.

Eventually I pulled over on the way home one morning to examine it more closely. The text reads, in part:

> The first full-size glass door oven was invented and manufactured here by Ernst H. Huenefeld of The Huenefeld Company in 1909. Specially designed and patented sheet metal frames in the door allowed for expansion and contraction of the glass. The large window, guaranteed against steaming up or breaking from heat, allowed users to view their baking without opening the oven door. . . . A standard feature in homes today, the glass door oven was a technological breakthrough in 1909.

The company's end in the 1960s, when many of the city's former mainstays were foundering, seemed sad, especially on this stretch of road, a wind tunnel of vanished heavy industry. And though it was impressive to consider that, almost exactly a century earlier, this now-desolate place had been a hub of innovation, there was something poignant and pleading about that last sentence, with its undernote of a whine: "Hey, skeptic, this was imporrrrrrtant."

Dance Pole Rules at the old Stockyard Café

Spring Grove Avenue, looking north—Glass Door Oven historical marker in foreground.

Ad for the Boss Glass Door Oven, circa 1918

And of course it *was* important. The first ovens, I gather, date back more than *thirty thousand years*, and were installed in yurts on the central Asian steppe, where they were used to tenderize and smoke mammoth meat. For thirty millennia, people had grappled with how to know when their food was fully cooked without opening the oven and letting out heat, and right here, in this unlikely spot, someone had at last engineered a solution to that problem—a breakthrough so effective that it's become ubiquitous and thus invisible.

Ernst Huenefeld was born in Westphalia (now west-central Germany) in 1838. He emigrated, landed in Cincinnati, and in 1872 bought into an existing enterprise—a supplier of tinplate and roofers' supplies—run by John Schroer. Eventually the new company, carrying Huenefeld's name, expanded into stoves and ovens, washing machines, and other metal products including toys like wagons and scooters. Huenefeld became a hotelier as well, buying the Burnet House downtown, where Grant and William T. Sherman had convened (see "Absent Guest" essay) to plot the Union's endgame strategy in the Civil War. Huenefeld was also a generous benefactor of charitable causes, and in 1908 he donated his estate in the Clifton neighborhood to Bethesda Hospital for use as a convalescent and retirement home. He died in 1931.

The history of the stove is long and tangled—also smoke-choked—and I won't enter into it deeply here. But the near-immediate success of Huenefeld's Boss Glass Door Oven in the 1910s and beyond owes a lot to timing and cultural context. Since the time of the vestal virgins, those chaste attendants to the Goddess of the Hearth who (literally) tended Rome's home fire, never letting it sputter out, and were venerated for their work, hearth and home and cookfire have been deeply connected in myth and in fact. America has since its beginnings been a hotbed of innovation in this area—from Benjamin Franklin's famous 1745 stove, which utilized a serpentine pipe and a baffle to transfer more heat and less smoke into the room, but which still, once the convolutions were negotiated, vented its soot indoors; to Count Rumford's amazing innovations in temperature control and chimney design (accomplished after he, a loyal Tory, fled his native shores for England on the eve of the American Revolution). Gas was relatively scarce and expensive in the United States for most of the nineteenth century, so it was rarely used as a cooking fuel. But when electric light began to take hold, that commodity dropped in price and became more appealing for cooking purposes. Gas had several advantages over other fuels beyond the ones we think of in twenty-first-century contexts: gas stoves didn't require tending and banking, and they didn't smoke, didn't blacken the room with soot that could build up dangerously, and didn't belch out embers that could spark fires.

Another difference was that old-style ovens were essentially architectural—huge, immovable, built into the house's fireplace—whereas stoves became pieces of furniture, and could be situated where the homeowner wanted. They didn't require a bulky storage bin for wood or coal, and they were light enough to be set on legs. The shapely, decorative oven-gams—ever more pinup-worthy as time passed—were an effort to make the newfangled technology more attractive to women, and the stove remains a prime example of the male-created "breakthrough" offered up as salvation for women . . . but viewed by the target audience, understandably, with some ambivalence or puzzlement.

Huenefeld relied on the relatively new field of national magazine advertising, and the approach varied over the years. A 1918 ad featuring a soldier and his family, for example, touted the glass-door oven's ability to keep food from being burned and thrown away: "Spoiled Food Is a National Waste. Help Stop It. *Bake Visibly.*" Immediate postwar ads tried to counter the surge of nostalgia for the old-style hearth by touting the Boss Oven as a uniter of families, sometimes featuring a child standing on a kitchen chair peering into the oven and saying "I'll tell you when they're done, Mother." The family that bakes together . . .

The link between the grand mausoleum my toddler liked to explore and the bombed-out postindustrial stretch of Spring Grove Avenue with the historical marker that begged the viewer not to find it faintly absurd was of course Huenefeld, but I never made the connection until one day last September, wandering past his wee Greek temple, when I thought, "That name is familiar. But why?"

Is it possible for an innovation, or for a kind of presiding ghost or *genius loci*, to become so much a part of the fabric of one's life that you cease to notice it, and in fact if forced to notice tend to think, "Well, sure, but so what?"

It is. Which is why Ernst Huenefeld seems simultaneously like a quaint and distant figure . . . and also the hearth around which we've been sitting for my daughter's whole life, basking in its ambient heat. I should have been thinking of him every time my daughter and I squatted together before the oven, pulled aside the dish towel, and checked to see if the brownies were plumping right.

A side-note to Huenefeld on a half-ton escape artist:

My first trip to Cincinnati was for a job interview in winter 2002. I tried to get a read on the city by poking through the paper and watching local news . . . and that week, the city was berserk over the story of the Runaway Cow.

On February 15, 2002, apparently sensing imminent doom, a 1,050-pound Charolais scaled (that's the verb I'm going with) a six-foot-plus fence at Ken Meyer Meats in Camp Washington—near the Stockyard Café, and just two blocks off Spring Grove Avenue. The cow cut a swath of herbivorous destruction across town, uprooting lawns as it made its way under the interstate, through a neighborhood, across a corner of Cincinnati State Technical and Community College, and up the slopes of Clifton to the hilltop park at Mount Storm, about two miles from her starting point.

With the help of heavy tree cover, steep slopes, and a timely hailstorm, she managed day after day to elude traps, tranquilizer darts, helicopters, and

Cinci Freedom (aka Golda Meir, aka Charlene Mooken, aka Bossy), circa 1995–2008

dogs. Gradually the ex-livestock became a folk hero—in a city once known as Porkopolis, whose biggest employer even today, Procter & Gamble, got its start making soap and candles from the byproducts of slaughter. She was an undercow bucking the system, and folks loved her. I recall a TV news story during my visit about parents packing their schoolkids into the car and trolling the streets of Clifton for a sighting of Moo-dini (another of her hundred names). Children cried on camera as they contemplated the fate she had narrowly averted.

Or hadn't. It was unclear at that point whether the narrative being written was *Smokey and the Bandit*, featuring a clean getaway, or O. J. Simpson's Bronco chase—though come to think of it, O. J. Simpson's Bronco chase ended up having the same plot as *Smokey and the Bandit*, except that the getaway was uglier and more protracted, and lacked a truckload of Coors and a Jerry Reed soundtrack. What I meant to say was that it wasn't clear, in the early days of the saga, whether the cow, variously known in the media as Bossy, as Golda Meir (for her tenacity rather than her Judaism, presumably), and even—I'd guess on account of her elusiveness rather than her status as hunted enemy combatant—as Moosama Bin Laden, was simply postponing the inevitable. But with each passing day, her legend growing, meat became a less likely fate for her. Media came from all over the world, disseminating her story ever more widely.

On February 26—after *eleven days* of evading what Vladimir Nabokov called, in another context, the "farcical gendarmes"—she was roped and then tranquilized on the lower slopes of Mount Storm . . . though even here she was underestimated, and managed to drag her pursuers through another fence and into a backyard before a second dart knocked her out.

At this point the cow's fame had saved her; there was no way she could be returned to the abattoir. She'd been offered a key to the city by the mayor, a place to graze by former Cincinnati Reds owner Marge Schott,[1] a starring role in a bank commercial. But finding a long-term home was trickier. The zoo declined to house her, out of disease concerns and with a wry nod to her escape abilities.

Enter pop artist Peter Max, who offered the local SPCA $180,000 worth of paintings to auction off. In exchange he would get custody of the cow, whom he renamed, a bit mawkishly, Cincinnati Freedom. CF was awarded the key to the city and named honorary grand marshal of the annual Cincinnati Reds Findlay Market Opening Day Parade in early April, but—it had been a terrifying few months—she was too "jumpy" to wear the key and ride in the procession. She balked, stoutly refused to go onto the trailer . . . and how to blame the girl for trust issues, given her first excursion up the ramp?

Soon thereafter, Peter Max—himself a refugee, his parents having fled Berlin for Shanghai in 1938, when he was a toddler—had her moved to the Farm Sanctuary's shelter in Watkins Glen, New York, where she lived a further six years.

In late December 2008, the Artist formerly known as Charlene Mooken had her rear legs give out suddenly. She was diagnosed with spinal cancer, a quick and painful fatal illness in cows, and the decision was made to euthanize her. The entire herd of fellow rescues gathered around in her final hours, with one of the steers licking her face and one of the older females soothing her by licking her back until she took her last breath.

Her companions stayed alongside until she was buried, even chasing away a tractor driver the first time he came to remove her body.

"A GREAT AWKWARD BUNGLEHOOD OF WOMAN"

FANNY WRIGHT

A FEW YEARS AGO, I WROTE AN ESSAY FOR *THE GUARDIAN* THAT BEGAN, "In many ways, literary Cincinnati and Anthony Trollope share a mother." That mother was Frances Trollope, who after an unhappy few years in Cincinnati took her revenge upon fair Porkopolis in *Domestic Manners of the Americans* (1832), a witty and brutal takedown of not only Americans' reeking, offal-strewn streets, foul habits, and general uncouthness but also—and especially—their hypocrisy about slavery.[1]

Trollope's book can also be read as a tart corrective of an earlier work, by the remarkable friend whose powers of myth-making and persuasion brought her to the United States in the first place. That book, *Views of Society and Manners in America: A Series of Letters from That Country to a Friend in England, during the Years 1818, 1819, and 1820, by an Englishwoman* (1821), was in part a gushing praise-song to the young country (or, as James Fenimore Cooper less charitably called it, "nauseous flattery"). Its author was Fanny Wright, who would become one of the earliest, most important—and most reviled—advocates for women in American history.

Frances "Fanny" Wright was born in Scotland in 1795. Early on she fell under the spell of American ideals of liberty. Her father had been investigated for sedition in 1794 for printing and distributing Thomas Paine's *The Rights of Man*, and his daughter took the revolutionary principles underpinning Paine's work deeply to heart. Bereft of most of her family (both parents died by the time she was two) and dismayed by Britain's stultifying conventions of gender and class, Wright decided in 1818, at twenty-two, to undertake a trip across the Atlantic with her sister. Even when her guardian hurried to the embarkation point at Liverpool to plead with her (America was chaotic, wild, sketchy—no place for two young women of means to travel), she would not be dissuaded.

In New York, Wright seized her chance to have a play she'd written back in Scotland—about Swiss insurgents fighting for freedom—produced at a grand theater on what even then was known as Broadway. The play's authorship had to be obscured, lest her gender spark a scandal . . . but word of its authorship soon leaked out, and the play, which had drawn 2,400 people on its opening night and received a standing ovation, closed within a week.

Fanny and her sister Camilla took to the road, seeing as much as they could of the vast new country, interviewing the people they met. The result, eventually, was her book. In it, Wright observes her surroundings in minute and perceptive detail, and follows her ceaseless inquisitiveness where it leads. She was a booster and an enthusiast, yes, but this was not a whitewash, nor the work of a naïf. She had harsh criticism for the abomination of slavery, for one thing, and she lamented that America's lively, resourceful, high-spirited young girls were domesticated into sullen consorts held together, in the upper reaches of society, with hatpins and whalebone corsets. But the tone that dominated was idealistic celebration.

> The Americans are very good talkers and admirable listeners; under-stand perfectly the exchange of knowledge, for which they employ conversation, and employ it solely. They have a surprising stock of information, but this runs little into the precincts of imagination; facts form the groundwork of their discourse. They are accustomed to rest opinions on the results of experience, rather than on ingenious theories and abstract reasoning. . . . The world, however, is the book which they consider most attentively.[2]

Underneath the rhapsody, one may detect a faint condescension here. Wright's appreciation is more of American ingenuousness than of American ingenuity; these are simple folk, too occupied with real-world problems to be tempted to entertain high-flown Ideas. But there's admiration, too, for the energy and industry of Americans, and for the ideals she sees the young nation as representing, ideals she would soon start propounding herself as she beseeched America to fulfill its promise. There's a fascinating tension in the passage, too. Wright was attracted to America in part by its pragmatic, cash-on-the-barrelhead ethos: "this runs little into the precincts of imag-ination; facts form the groundwork of their discourse." But her perspective is not American but European, born of an educated outsider's "abstract rea-sonings"—note that she translates American horse sense immediately back into metaphor, making the world not merely a world but a book. The tensions between the founding ideals of liberty and egalitarianism that were easiest to believe in when she wasn't in the United States and the grinding, dispiriting reality principle that was a crucial element of Americanness can be said to have dominated the rest of Fanny Wright's life.

In 1824, when President James Monroe invited America's great European benefactor and Revolutionary War ally, the now elderly Marquis de Lafayette, to make a farewell tour through the States, Fanny Wright—by now Lafayette's friend and acolyte—accompanied him. This provided her entrée to a rarefied world, and she had the chance to meet and to befriend elder statesmen like Thomas Jefferson and James Madison as well as the current generation of leaders, including Andrew Jackson and Henry Clay.

On her trip, Wright visited New Harmony, Indiana. The town had been labored over by a German American sect for ten years, and, now complete, had recently been purchased by Robert Owen, a Welshman who had chosen this as the place to conduct an experiment in utopian socialism. Owen's idealism and politics were congenial to Wright; the place was beautiful; and the project was in its full first flush of optimism.

By the time Lafayette sailed home in 1825, Frances had taken advantage of liberal U.S. immigration laws and become a naturalized citizen. Soon she embarked upon the project that would make, and then ruin, her name: Nashoba. Inspired by New Harmony, and by the sense instilled by her travels through the South that slavery was an institution being perpetuated, despite the reservations and regrets she heard from liberal southerners, through a combination of economic exigency and moral inertia, Wright decided to buy a large parcel and make her own try at a utopian community. She would buy or otherwise acquire enslaved people, provide them with education, and after five years of training and of service to their cooperative community they would be manumitted and could make good lives for themselves where they chose. She pitched her plan to the statesmen she'd met through Lafayette, and all but Madison offered at least verbal support. Jefferson's response is especially fascinating:

> At the age of eighty-two, with one foot in the grave, and the other uplifted to follow it, I do not permit myself to take part in any new enterprises, even for bettering the condition of man, not even in the great one which has been through life that of my greatest anxieties. Every plan should be adopted, every experiment tried, which may do something towards the ultimate object. That which you propose is well worthy of trial. . . . You are young, dear Madam, and have powers of mind which may do much in exciting others in this arduous task. I am confident they will be so exerted, and I pray to Heaven for their success, and that you may be rewarded with the blessings which such efforts merit.

There seems to be real goodwill in this response, but also a hint of patronizing skepticism. On the one hand, Jefferson was quintessentially an American of Fanny Wright's kind: an erudite idealist, but one dedicated to creating real-world institutions to accommodate and to embody that idealism. On the other, he was old and weary, and well aware too of the ways in which, over a long life, his and the country's ideals had foundered and his and the country's morals shattered on the shoals of race.

Andrew Jackson, at the time a senator but soon to become president, suggested that Wright buy land in Tennessee, which was more freewheeling and less densely populated than the coastal South. She would be less likely to excite serious local opposition in a remote spot in the southern state most amenable (or least unamenable) to abolitionist arguments. He suggested a densely wooded tract of two thousand acres east of Memphis (the site of the present-day suburb of Germantown), and—another wince-inducing irony here, the history of America being full of wince-inducing ironies that we don't quite know what to do about, beyond the wincing—a tract that was available because of his recent forcible ejection of the Chickasaw nation from it. Wright was entranced by the acreage of "good and pleasant woodland, traversed by a good and lovely stream," though she would later have reason to wish that her response to the suggestion had run more to pragmatic/American nouns and less to abstract/European adjectives. In October 1825, she bought the land and named the settlement-to-be Nashoba, a Chickasaw word for wolf.

Wright now penned a tract called "A Plan for the Gradual Abolition of Slavery in the United States without Danger of Loss to the Citizens of the South." One can't help noting the delicacy and even cajolery of this title, clear indication that she was absorbing what southern friends like Jefferson were telling her about the difficulty of achieving her aim. She advertised in abolitionist magazines; she purchased slaves, spent a large sum on supplies, and the experiment began in earnest in early 1826. The work proceeded fairly well at first, and during that year Fanny made occasional trips to an apparently thriving New Harmony to bolster her confidence. She came to relish the vision of herself as a self-sufficient pioneer, "with a bearskin for her bed and a saddle for her pillow." But problems began to mount. Only one fellow settler had farming expertise, and she found it impossible to attract teachers and artisans. Furthermore, the land was swampy, malarial, and prone to flooding, which was presumably why the Chickasaw had used it as a hunting ground rather than a settlement.

In early 1827, Wright traveled again to New Harmony, only to find that the community was imploding; its early promise had degenerated into back-biting chaos. Soon after her return to Nashoba, she fell violently ill, and eventually she had to be rushed to New Orleans by wagon and litter and put on a ship back to Great Britain. She arrived in Europe battered and weakened, perhaps even a little chastened—but she began immediately to restore her stocks of idealism and resolve.

Meanwhile, back in Nashoba, one of the community leaders, James Richardson, sent a fateful report to the abolitionist magazine *Genius of Universal Emancipation*. Wright had billed Nashoba first and foremost as an experiment in ending slavery, but emancipation was not her only "radical" notion. It was part of a nexus of egalitarian ideals that included not only full equality of the races and the sexes but free mixing among and between them; the rejection of organized religion; an attack on greed and the concentration of wealth; and a celebration of sexuality and erotic expression. These ideals were shared by many of her fellow Nashobans, and Richardson, speaking in what he may have thought was an echo chamber of the like-minded (this the precursor, then, of many a Twitter or Facebook fail), seemed to forget how explosive and iconoclastic those ideas were. And one most of all: in his essay, Richardson reported that he was living with a black woman, and the blowback was immediate. Suddenly, Nashoba was a free-love experiment, a cathouse, a den of miscegenation, even a circle of hell.

Fanny Wright, back in England slowly recuperating in body and in spirit, contacted other progressive women to see whether they might be recruited to return with her to Nashoba. One she approached was Mary Shelley, who, intrigued, invited Wright for a week-long visit. The two became fast friends, but Shelley could not be persuaded to decamp to a fetid American backwater. She recognized, too, that beneath Wright's grandiloquent confidence lay doubt and vulnerability—no surprise, perhaps, that the author of *Frankenstein* would be attuned to the idea that the things we've created and taken pride in might also haunt and hunt us. To Dale, the son of Robert Owen who would be accompanying Wright back to the New World, Shelley wrote that Fanny was "neither so independent or so fearless as you think." Shelley came to see Wright off and collected a lock of her hair, which she would keep for the rest of her life.

The one like-minded person who did decide to accompany Wright to Nashoba was Frances Trollope. She headed westward at age forty-eight in part because she was swayed by Fanny's ardor for the New World and the

Frances Wright, by John Chester Buttre,
circa 1835

Detail, Wright gravestone

The Bloomer suit, as rendered
by Currier & Ives, 1851

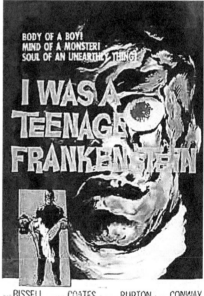

Poster for the 1957 film
I Was a Teenage Frankenstein

cause of abolition, but also because she had creditors to dodge. She was a woman unaccustomed to privation, as might be indicated by her decision to rough it in the swamps of Tennessee with several of her children in tow, and with a brace of household servants. The dank discomforts of the transatlantic passage quickly made clear to Trollope that Wright had embroidered a bit in her descriptions of America, and conditions when they reached Nashoba would have disabused her of any remaining romantic notions. Food was scant, morale dismal. Trollope soon moved on to the bustling frontier city of Cincinnati and a career for a while as a museum impresario, and afterward as proprietor of the doomed and mismanaged Bazaar, a "queer, unique, crescented Babel" that was in essence the first department store.

Fanny Wright hunkered in and doubled down, publishing a full-throated defense of Nashoba—on the voyage she read part of a draft aloud to (baffled?) sailors—that didn't tamp down the controversy but embraced it. Then, back at New Harmony for July 4, she gave a stem-winding oration and began the career that would bring her most fame, or notoriety. One of the most controversial elements of her philosophy was her belief that sexuality was the "strongest and the noblest of human passions." At New Harmony, she became the very first woman in America to espouse such ideas in a large, mixed crowd—a "promiscuous assembly," as her detractors put it.

The cultural backdrop in the late 1820s was explosive. One argument for abolition in the puritanical North, seldom made explicitly, held that its evil was tempting male slaveholders (including Jefferson, infamously) into a further outrage, the sexual license—today it would get a blunter, four-letter name—eventually to be known as "miscegenation." This period marked, too, the peak flowering of a period of evangelical zeal and conversion, especially among women, and one element of the so-called Second Great Awakening was its appeal to emotion and openness to the supernatural. Decades before P. T. Barnum, Trollope would exploit the American susceptibility to hocus-pocus in her wax-figure multimedia shows at Cincinnati's Western Museum. The first, "The Invisible Girl," featured her son Henry, spouting Latin and Greek gibberish, as the voice of the disembodied girl. When she created her Dante spectacle, "Infernal Regions," Christians looking to scare themselves straight by visiting Trollope's version of hell were so prone to freak out and maul the valuable mannequins that Trollope had the figures wired to give a nasty shock.

A decade or two later, in part thanks to Fanny Wright, another offshoot of the Second Great Awakening would be the women's suffrage movement . . .

but for now she was swimming, or flailing, against a flood-tide of disapproval. Wright's first lecture tour had a more immediate backdrop, too: the bitter 1828 presidential race between incumbent John Quincy Adams and her old ally Andrew Jackson, a campaign in which lewd allegations against the candidates, and especially their wives, would get plenty of attention.

Whether the auditor was inclined to rage or approval, Wright's style and stagecraft were galvanizing. Sometimes carrying notes (rarely consulted) and sometimes just with a copy of the Declaration of Independence, she usually appeared amid a phalanx of up to thirty women. She was tall and redheaded, and she developed a style of dress, including a loose bodice and pantaloons that stretched to the ankle, that would later get adopted and adapted by feminists like Amelia Bloomer and Elizabeth Cady Stanton . . . yes, atop her other iconoclasms, Fanny Wright was the first American woman to wear pants in public.

Like many outspoken women, Wright was ridiculed for being mannish, accused of being insufficiently or inauthentically female. Catharine Beecher, elder sister of Harriet Beecher Stowe, heard her speak in Cincinnati in 1829, and years later wrote:

> Who can look without disgust and abhorrence upon such an one as Fanny Wright, with her great masculine person, her loud voice, her untasteful attire, going about unprotected, and feeling no need of protection, mingling with men in stormy debate, and standing up with bare-faced impudence, to lecture a public assembly . . . with brazen front and brawny arms, attacking all that is venerable and sacred in religion, and that is safe and wise in law, all that is pure and lovely in domestic virtue.

Perhaps the most colorful phrase here is "with brazen front and brawny arms," and of course the overall tenor is vicious. But the clause that fascinates me is "going about unprotected, *and feeling no need of protection.*" Those last six words aren't required by logic, and rhetorically are an interruption. Am I wrong to see grudging awe beneath the abhorrence? Where, Beecher seems to be wondering, does this monster of confidence come by her surety?

Barely a decade earlier, another radical woman, putting the words in the mouth of a creature despised and disdained, had written: *Beware, for I am fearless and therefore powerful.* That woman had seen Wright off for America barely a year earlier, had collected a lock of the firebrand's hair before she went.

A DOWNWRIGHT GABBLER,
or a goose that deserves to be hissed_

"A Downwright Gabbler," cartoon by James Akin Philada, 1829

Wright's appearances were mobbed, and sometimes worse than mobbed. But she was unfazable. In New York she gave a series of six lectures, and people clamored in the streets to get in. In one case, when a saboteur cut off the gas line to the hall, Wright proceeded first in darkness and then by flickering candlelight. Later, she would brazen her way through a talk despite toxic smoke billowing from a turpentine barrel ignited by a protester; still later, she would press on even amid spraying window glass and the ricocheting stones that had broken it. Her fame and infamy grew. She was denounced as the Great Red Harlot, the Priestess of Beelzebub, the Whore of Babylon, a Downwright Gabbler.

(A couple of side-notes about the cartoon illustrated here, which dates from her triumphant 1829 tour: Wright is depicted as somewhat less radical and terrifying than she must have seemed in reality—which makes one wonder whether this caricaturist hadn't actually seen her, or whether he had and was trying, for the sake of visual or intellectual simplicity, to make the threat she posed seem more conventional and thus more easily dispatched. Fanny the Goose is wearing a dowdy, unfashionable dress; reading from a prepared text; and she's alone on the stage except for a docile, overly polite man who is holding her traditional bonnet—and resting his hand inside his waistcoat, Napoleonically. The message seems clearly directed at men, who are failing to shout her down and give her the hissing she "deserves.")

It was a heady moment for Wright, who left no idol unsmashed, no conventional wisdom unexploded. She gloried in wounding male virtue: Men, she said, "are incomprehensible animals. . . . They walk about boasting of their wisdom, strength, and sovereignty, while they have not sense so much as to swallow an apple with the aid of an Eve to put it down their throats." She had become a symbol of all things new and disruptive, and "Fanny Wrightism" became the bugbear of polite society. In 1830, the slate of candidates of the Working Men's Party became known as the Fanny Wright ticket; they even won a seat in the New York state legislature.

Wright was not immune to delusions of grandeur. Around this time, her old companion and rival Trollope observed to Wright's mentor the Marquis de Lafayette that "[Fanny] anticipates confidently the regeneration of the whole human race from her present exertions." Is there envy in that? Perhaps. Sneering? Certainly—one can see the dry-ice chill billowing. But Trollope, by this point writing her own, more truculent book about America, also admired Wright's stores of energy and optimism, and her rhetorical gifts. After one Cincinnati lecture, Trollope wrote:

> I knew her extraordinary gift of eloquence, her almost unequaled command of words, and the wonderful power of her rich and thrilling voice. . . . [A]ll my expectations fell far short of the splendor, the brilliance, the overwhelming eloquence of this extraordinary orator. . . . Her tall and majestic figure, the deep and almost solemn expression in her eyes, the simple contour of her finely formed head, unadorned, excepting by its own natural ringlets; her garment of plain white muslin, which hung around her in folds that recalled the drapery of a Grecian statue, all contributed to produce an effect, unlike any thing I have ever seen before, or ever expect to see again.

That combination of affection and derision (brilliantly captured, by the way, in Edmund White's 2003 novel *Fanny*, in which Frances Trollope narrates Fanny Wright's story)[3] defined their relationship. One American value that Trollope understood, absorbed, and even advanced was the huckster spirit, and she had discovered both the liberation and the danger in feeling contempt for one's customer. By this point, Trollope had the carnival barker's cynicism toward rubes, but her friend—against all odds, and at enormous personal cost—resisted cynicism. Wright was, echoing another strand of the American character, a true believer. An entertainment like "Infernal Regions" required recognizing religious zeal and draining it off into entertainment (the American way!). If the believer got zapped by a booby-trapped waxwork, that was the price for seeking comfort in hell. Meanwhile Fanny Wright mounted the dais day after day and mustered genuine rage, didn't just rattle tin pans in the wings but hurled thunderbolts whose reality she *believed* in.

Wright wanted nothing less than to save America from error, to replace false righteousness with true. Her lectures were designed to fit into—but also to break from—the tradition of sermonizing. In her secular religion, churches would be supplanted by Halls of Science, but those halls would be not a repudiation of the religious impulse but a purer, better home for it.

In William Gass's "Emerson and the Essay," he writes that one leaves a Ralph Waldovian production—on the page or in person, the essence of the essay being performance—inspired, with one's heart riding higher. But . . .

We have scarcely gotten home, our feet wet and chilly from the snow, or our chest asweat from the deep summer heat like a heavy coat we can't remove, when our children's sneezes greet us, skinned knees bleed after waiting all day to do so. There is the bellyache and the burned-out basement bulb, the stalled car and the incontinent cat. The windows frost, the toilets sweat, the body of our spouse is one cold shoulder, and the darkness of our bedroom is soon full of the fallen shadows of our failures. Now the quiet night light whispers to us: You are unloved—unlovely—you are old. These white sheets rehearse the corpse they will cover. None of our times change. We are the same age as our essayist. Wrinkles squeeze our eyes shut, and we slide into sleep like a sailor from beneath his national flag. Tomorrow our tumescence must be resumed. Tomorrow, Emerson realizes, he must again be a genius.[4]

To me this passage gets to the nub of Frances Trollope's, and my, esteem for Fanny Wright. In Gass's piece, all the frailties of the auditor apply as well to the lecturer. Mary Shelley saw this vulnerability in Wright and reported it in her letter to Robert Dale Owen. Tomorrow one must once again be a genius, and the price of that genius is a belief in the world's perfectibility. Unless we can muster idealism, unless we can gin up a conviction that things really could and should be better, what's the point? But the world throws up too many barriers against that belief for an intelligent person to hang on to it. Most days, if you're paying any attention at all, you have to be a perfect idiot—*idiot* in its original sense of someone so enmeshed in her own head, her own circumstances, as to be paying no attention to external reality—to believe that the world cares what you think, or that you can make a difference. Over the coming years, Fanny Wright's idealism would be taxed again and again, would waver and need resuscitation again and again.

One realizes, reluctantly, that the preceding paragraph has essentially the same narrative as the video for Bon Jovi's "Wanted: Dead or Alive," in which we see the hard-working hair band post-concert, drained. They may have seen a million faces and rocked them all, but there is always a tomorrow, containing new faces to be rocked. Believing that what you think or do is of world-altering importance is of course a delusion, but it's a hopeful delusion, one that gives humanity more credit than it deserves rather than less. And that's by far the more likable, though also the more mystifying, kind of delusion. But still, even for Fanny Wright or John Francis Bongiovi Jr., there comes the night, the doubt, the exhaustion, and the "white sheets rehearse the corpse they will cover," and "every day it seems we're wastin' away." The world is a colossal buzzkill.

Nashoba reached a breaking point in 1830, and Wright had no choice but to admit defeat. The president of Haiti had offered to help, so she chartered a boat and accompanied thirteen formerly enslaved persons and their eighteen children to western Hispaniola. After helping arrange housing and work for the refugees, Wright returned to New York amid renewed controversy; a newspaper editor accused her of profiting (in the form of a sack of gold coins Haitian president Jean-Pierre Boyer had bestowed upon her for "expenses") from what she'd touted as a moral obligation. Wright wrote a point-by-point refutation, but promptly disappeared from the limelight. She was pregnant, and knew that a child out of wedlock was exactly the scandal her detractors had been looking for. She returned to Europe, secretly married her baby-to-be's father (I would argue that there's no hypocrisy in this: what makes a tyranny is its power to make one submit), and bore her child, a daughter she named Sylva. When a second child died in infancy, she would give Sylva that child's birthdate to provide cover from rumor-mongering.

Fanny Wright spent the 1830s bouncing between the United States and Europe. Neither her marriage nor her domestic situation in Europe was happy. The quiet, retired life wasn't for her, not least because she had no patience for or skill in the things her culture considered properly motherly or huswifely. "And make my Soule thy holy Spoole to bee," as Puritan poet Edward Taylor had urged in his hymn to submission? No thanks. Hapless Fanny and her querulous husband were often ill, and she felt isolated, beleaguered, bedraggled. She and her husband seldom lived together after the mid-1830s, and soon afterward came Fanny's bitter estrangement from Sylva, which would haunt her later years.

In 1834, Wright traveled to London to lecture, but after the first date, attendance plummeted. Indifference was a phenomenon she'd never met with before. The next year she ventured back to the United States. When, after the race riots of 1836 in Cincinnati, she decided to speak and try to calm the waters, she discovered that no one much attended to the substance of what she said. Much as would happen to twentieth-century female icons from the movies—Mae West or Marilyn Monroe, say—her notoriety had hardened into caricature, except that she was pegged not as sexpot but as the Great Red Harlot: "a great awkward bungle of womanhood," one 1830s reviewer wrote, "about six feet in longitude, with a face like a Fury, and her hair cropped like a convict." Wright is one of the first examples of a distinctly American phenomenon: the prison-house of celebrity. To be known by the public is to be owned by it. If Britney Spears earns a PhD in astrophysics, it will enter her obituary only after the underwearless crotch-shot caught on film by a paparazzo, the new Mickey Mouse Club alongside Justin Timberlake, "Hit Me Baby One More Time."

As Norman Mailer (hard to imagine a less likely ally for Wright!) put it in *Armies of the Night*, with typical vainglory but also insight, the celebrity lives in "the sarcophagus of his image": "At night, in his sleep, he might dart out, and paint improvements on the sarcophagus. During the day, when he was helpless, newspapermen and other assorted bravos . . . would carve ugly pictures on the living tomb of his legend."[5] This was Wright's plight in the 1830s. The public felt it had her number, so they lost interest. The country had pressing economic crises, too; the Panic of 1837 would ruin many and spark a recession that lasted eight years. Wright's crowds grew scanter and sadder, and they seemed to be listening to a distant after-echo of her. She was a curiosity, an arena band now consigned to playing dive bars, and being urged to play only her hits, so that they could be simultaneously sung along to and ironized.[6]

Wright's indomitability had always derived from her determination to persist in idealism despite all discouragement. Toward the end, though, she lost the ability to believe with any consistency the sentiment articulated by her fellow abolitionist Theodore Parker, then paraphrased a century later by Martin Luther King Jr. and forty years after that by Barack Obama: "The arc [of the moral universe] is a long one, my eye reaches but little ways; I cannot calculate the curve and complete the figure by the experience of sight; I can divine it by conscience. And from what I see I am sure it bends towards justice." Instead, Wright wrote, she now saw society as "a complicated system of errors."

Wright's health failed again and repeatedly in her final years. Her finances were strained. She went through a tempestuous divorce, then a bitter chancery suit that wouldn't be resolved until after her death (here again she'd prove to be a trailblazer, becoming the first woman in Ohio to win protection of the assets with which she entered marriage against the predations of an ex). She spent a couple winters at Nashoba, attended by a hired carpenter and subsisting on crackers, eggs, scraps of potato, and the great old stories. In the winter of 1852, she slipped on icy steps outside her daughter's house in Cincinnati, and after a long, anguished convalescence during which Sylva refused to visit her, she died on December 13, 1852. Her obituary would say little about the career that had won her such renown and such animosity.

Wright's grave at Spring Grove bears the epitaph she wrote: "I have wedded the cause of human improvement, staked on it my fortune, my reputation and my life." A bit surprisingly, it mentions, too, the lesser cause to whom she was wedded—though her married name is inscribed in a smaller font below. But the biggest surprise involves Sylva. She would remain embittered enough that a quarter-century later she would testify in Congress against women's suffrage—and in doing so would pointedly invoke her mother's name. She moved to Nashoba, transformed it into a private estate, raised her children there, died there. But Sylva too is here in Spring Grove, buried not with her father or with her husband but—together at last—with her mother. The side of Fanny Wright's monument reads "Erected to her memory by her daughter Frances Sylva Phiquepal D'Arusmont/ Born April 14, 1832/ Thirty-two years/ the widow of/ Dr. William Eugene Guthrie/ Died July 26, 1902/ and now lies beside her mother."

There's one more memorial to glance at before we go—the plaque erected at the site of Nashoba (or, actually, not *quite* at the site) by the Tennessee Historical Commission. Mrs. Winner's Chicken & Biscuits is visible in the background. The marker includes one of the most artfully vague descriptions you'll ever see. Nashoba is described, first of all, as a "plantation"—a word familiar to aficionados of Dixie historical markers, and one that here isn't precisely *wrong*, but that seems spectacularly inapt. Wright is dubbed a "spinster heiress."

Why mention Wright's marital status, and make her—a woman who would in fact (if not in an orthodox way) be married and with child just five years later, and who was barely thirty—a permanently sexless maiden aunt? Is it an attempt to account, to the chicken-craving passerby or history-seeking

4E 10
NASHOBA

To the south lay this plantation. Here, in 1827, a Scottish spinster heiress named Frances Wright set up a colony whose aims were the enforcement of cooperative living and other advanced sociological experiments. It failed in 1830.

Tennessee's historical marker for Nashoba

pilgrim, for the confluence of bored, alone, and affluent that can result, if you don't watch out, in "sociological experiments"? The phrase has the tone of Catharine Beecher, who granted that people like Fanny Wright were intelligent, to be sure, skilled, talented . . . but they lacked "that fine mental balance called common sense" and were equipped, instead, with dangerous excesses of "enthusiasm." How different, in effect, is that sentiment from the one enshrined on this marker in "and other advanced sociological experiments"? The tendentious vagueness of that sentence is a marvel.

I haven't been able to pinpoint the year the Nashoba marker was erected, but it seems to have been between 1949 and 1954. This was the height of Cold War paranoia about Soviet "enforcement of cooperative living," so one may hear a whisper of opprobrium in that phrase. And is one wrong to see passive aggressiveness—even sarcasm—in the needless adjective "advanced"? "Why listen, lady!" says Flannery O'Connor's Mr. Shiftlet in "The Life You Save May Be Your Own," of 1955,[7] letting it be known that he doesn't "mind sleeping in that car yonder" and so will accept the farm-handyman gig he's been offered. "The monks of old slept in their coffins." Replies the smug old lady, "They wasn't as advanced as we are."

But most shocking of all—shocking but not in the least *surprising*, a bit of rhetorical jujitsu the Jim Crow South excelled in—is the elision from the marker's legend of slavery, indeed of race altogether, this on a marker put up between the Dixiecrat ticket and *Brown v. Board*. What kind of "advanced sociological experiments," exactly? One won't learn *that* here.

Sure, the white sheets rehearse the corpse they will cover. Our times, stubborn to the end, never change, and the world sucks, we too come to think, and the grounds for pride, and likewise the grounds for optimism, are soft enough to bog a buzzard's shadow. But tomorrow morning *someone's* going to have to get up and believe enough in the cause of human improvement to stake her life on it. For a time that genius, that Great Red Harlot, that hero and spinster heiress and great glorious bunglehood of woman, was Fanny Wright.

INTERLUDE
THE BANK-SHOT UNMEMOIR

—————

I WAS SLOW ON THE UPTAKE. Only at this point in the year (mid-autumn) and in the project (having been sucked into Fanny Wright's orbit for a few weeks, yet another puny satellite buffeted and held in place by her powers of will) did it occur to me that rather than the brief diversion I'd been imagining, I might be working on a *book*. But if so, what kind? And why?

The first question *should* have had an easy answer. Obituaries revisited. An extended illustration of John Barth's point about story's oceanic ubiquity. An ambler's teensy-scale travelogue. But I realized that underneath all this lay a humiliating substrate of self. A decade or so ago, my friend Brock Clarke had great fun ridiculing a certain navel-gazing cult in his novel *The Arsonist's Guide to Writers' Homes in New England*.[1] The protagonist, Sam Pulsifer, who has accidentally torched Emily Dickinson's house (and two people with it), takes solace wherever he can find it. "There were people in the world," he reassures himself, even "more desperate, more self-absorbed, more boring than I was." Those people belong to the category of narcissistic untouchables called *memoirists*.

Please God, let me not be *that*, I thought.

So why was I tramping around a graveyard every day? If asked, I might have opted for the mountaineer's glib, evasive "Because it's there," which would at least contain some literal truth: I couldn't get an oil change or go to the grocery store or even sneak a drive-thru sausage biscuit without passing Spring Grove. But to reply like that would be to crawfish away from a darker, more personal *why*. What *else* was always there, and as my age advanced, and my parents' and my in-laws' and my friends', ever less ignorably so? Oh yeah, right, *that*.

The Las Vegas country music concert that turned shooting gallery, then killing field; joggers and tourists mowed down by a rental truck in Manhattan; the envied athlete from high school who was wasting away with cancer back home; the shaken-looking officers standing in strobing lights between a mangled sedan and an unhurrying ambulance as my daughter and I inched past in traffic. The nineteenth-century deaths I'd been writing about were of course no less real or permanent and tragic than these, but they were more remote in time, easier to translate into narrative.

And I wasn't encountering Spring Grove deaths on the car radio as my daughter and I left the gymnastics-center lot, which would yield a pause in her bright stream of anecdote and the question "Papa, are you crying again?" Yes, Papa was crying again, taken unawares for the umpteenth time, like a baby slow to pick up on the trick behind peekaboo.

So thanks be for cemeteries. What kind of fool is surprised to discover deaths in a place divvied into plots and designed for such contemplation? They'd made death a *garden* you could *visit*, a joyful place.

There was pleasure to be had—á la David Haskell's *The Forest Unseen*,[2] in which for a year the author minutely observes a single square meter of forest—in watching Spring Grove change with the seasons. November's palette was darker, the light spookier. Underfoot, a damp gray squish of biology that had spent itself. Everything exposed, sightlines opened wide; almost no one around but me and a few workers pruning trees, the occasional person alone in a closed-up car I would sidle past with my head down, hoping—I'd been infected by the mood—not to hear a single gunshot or discover one's aftermath. Spring Grove in November was grim, and I found that I loved it in a way that I couldn't love the ordinary drear of that season, outside the gates. Here was gloom in its proper habitat, death confined to its ghetto. To get in and out, you crossed a border—a sharp metal frame that jostled your tires, frightened your shoes.

Was I giving in, then, to that cliché of middle age—"facing up to mortality," and trying to do it on my own terms, in the abstract, before death made it personal? I can offer no defense. About memoir I shared Sam Pulsifer's prejudice, and I had no desire to excavate my own supernally boring navel lint. But I also recognized that whether I liked it or not, there would be a filament of *auto* running through the biographies I chose to write. For which, Mr. Pulsifer, sorry.

If this were a proper memoir, major plot points might enter here. During this book's composition my parents turned eighty, my wife fifty. I hit fifty-three. There were weeks during which my wanderings in the cemetery were halting and limpy, the result of a pulled calf muscle, which—as with every little injury now—occasioned a panic that this was it, and unpained movement at its end. Thankfully, plot kept its grubby paws off. But what was I *doing* here every day, devoting myself to strenuous distraction from the obvious fact of such a place? Was I a real-estate looky-lou trolling the neighborhood to get comfortable before the time came to get down to brass tacks and make my own offer on eternity?

That story in the introduction of being driven from my attic room by the Great Tom Fogarty? I'd meant it to be a joke, in part, but how could I not be rattled by his example? Sometimes in my low-ceilinged study—now, for example—I envision Fogarty sixty years ago, working through his confusions up here by bashing that support beam with his baseball bat. From my chair I can see the dented beam, just twelve feet to my left. *That's* how one takes on big, important, life-saving questions. Meanwhile I go at my toy-scale conundrums by wiggling fingers and ticking keys, by dithering and walking. He took some lumber to the lumber; meanwhile I poke almost silently through the lumber room between my ears. On many occasions during the writing of this book I've imagined—or fantasized about?—striding through that low doorway to take a big cut, make a noise to rival his.

Now I had to grapple with the possibility that I had more ego invested than I wanted to admit. Who gets obituaries, and why? Were my walks and researches an extended pep talk to myself to *Stop fucking around and do something* New York Times–*worthy*? Where was *my Star Trek* theme? Had *I* done anything to transform the oven from a Schrödinger's black box into—if you just clicked the little button by the window—a bright-lit stage? What slaughterhouse fence had I jumped, what city inspired? Fanny Wright's idealism was a train that couldn't be stopped; what had decoupled mine and sent it down irony's dead siding?

Far better under the circumstances to stick to biography, and the present. One day I was hunting for a stone—I had the section but couldn't find the plot, so I was circling slowly, gazing hard—when a group of older women in exercise gear passed by. One of them peeled off the back and took a couple steps toward me. She held up a hand, I think consolingly, but she could also, if needed, have brained me with the five-pound lilac barbell she was carrying.

"Are you OK?" she asked. "Are you looking for your people?"

"DEATH'S TAXICAB"
WILLARD HESS AND MARTIN HALE CRANE

ON NOVEMBER 25, 1963, A DAY seared into American collective memory by the image of John-John Kennedy saluting his father's passing coffin, the car JFK died in arrived home to Cincinnati.

The photo of the dead president's namesake, a bare-legged toddler standing alongside his mother and his identically dressed sister, the two children all the more striking for wearing red, white, and blue against a sea of grievous black, can be instantly conjured up even by many Americans—myself included—who weren't alive then. So far as I know, no snapshots exist of the procession that delivered the broken and bloodied X-100 home to Willard Hess of the Hess & Eisenhardt Armoring Company. Nor do we have snapshots of the Cincinnati mourners gazing forlornly at their copy of the Plexiglas bubble top—a safety feature designed and manufactured, but not used that day in Dallas—which sat under a tarp behind the company's offices.

But the limousine would not—could not—be interred or scrapped. Instead, over the next six months, it would be Hess & Eisenhardt's task to redesign and refurbish the car, which would go on to convey and to protect Presidents Johnson, Nixon, and Ford before being retired in 1977. The story of how and why all this came to be stretches all the way back to a Cincinnati precursor of Hess & Reinhardt, the Crane & Breed casket company, and the small but crucial role it played, a century earlier, in the aftermath of the *first* American presidential assassination.

Near the end of 1848, a New Yorker named Almond Fisk (born Fiske) patented the first metal coffin, a slender, filigreed case that looked like a cross between a sarcophagus and a diving bell. These new boxes, custom-fitted to the departed's proportions, were a bizarre hybrid of ancient Egyptian form with Industrial Revolution materials. They featured sculpted arms and shroud (the latter designed to look like a furrowed burial cloth), a choice of molded decorations (angels, acorns, berries, thistles), and a sealed and bolted-in pane of window-glass through which to view the face of the deceased. Two of the new caskets' selling points were impregnability (in this age of grave-robbing, coffin makers were resorting to ever more extreme measures, all the way up to the booby-trapped "coffin torpedo" designed by an Ohio inventor named Phillip K. Clover) and airtightness, which Fisk promised would have the "property of preventing putrefaction" (another contention built on a mix of marketer's hoopla—note the alliteration!—and flawed science, if one credits an 1858 Chicago news story about a Fisk coffin that exploded because of the buildup of gases from decomposition inside).

Fisk's *objet d'art funèbre* was, at up to twenty-five times the cost of a simple wooden coffin, prohibitively expensive, but it took hold quickly as the properly august choice for public figures. The boost the new technology needed came in 1850, with the death of Senator (and former vice president) John C. Calhoun—the most celebrated and most reviled person ever to hail from my home state of South Carolina, where his name and image are ubiquitous even now. (Late in life, as in the photo taken by Mathew Brady in 1848 and reproduced here, Calhoun was shockingly severe and ghoulish, with a terrifying turkey wattle pinched up by his collar—so much so that as a child I thought him the prototype for all kinds of bogeymen: Mr. Hyde, Scooby Doo villains, and so on.)

Calhoun was conveyed home to the Sandlapper State in a Fisk case, which was subsequently endorsed by the surviving two of the "Great Triumvirate," Senators Henry Clay of Kentucky and Daniel Webster of Massachusetts, and Calhoun's protégé Jefferson Davis. The Fisk Metallic Burial Case, they testified, was "the best article known to us for transporting the dead to their final resting place."[1]

Alas, Fisk would not live to reap the benefits of his revolutionary design. His New York State foundry burned to the ground in 1849, and in the aftermath of that fire he sold manufacturing licenses to firms in Providence and Cincinnati (and to his investors in New York City). Fisk had contracted a severe cold while helping fight the flames, and his health failed; he was bedridden for much of 1850, and died that October at age thirty-two. In his final days of invalidism he had no choice but to surrender his patent to his New York investors—chiefly the Forbes family.

One indirect beneficiary of Fisk's misfortune was Martin Hale Crane. Fisk's licensee in Cincinnati was W. C. Davis & Co., a manufacturer of stoves, pans, firedogs, kettles, hobs, and nails, among other items. In 1853, Davis sold off the casket portion of his business, including the license to produce the Fisk case, to Martin Crane and a partner, who began what would come to be known as the Crane & Breed Casket Company. Crane's brilliant idea—forerunner of Henry Ford's in another metalware field sixty years later—was to devise a way to make Fisk's cases affordable for the wider public. In 1855 he patented a revised design that dispensed with the mummyish shape and featured an octagonal glass window, a nameplate, and molded ornamental surrounds. Crane's was recognizably a sibling of the Fisk case, but less rococo, less costly, and, crucially, mass-producible. This had the effect of opening up new markets for the firm—including the southern states. The result was that over the next few years the Crane name surpassed even Fisk's. And so in 1865, after Ruination Day and its aftermath, after the tumultuous two-week train trip west to Illinois that included stops and processions or lyings-in-state in 180 cities and towns (and eventually required chalk to be daubed onto the deceased's face to decrease public alarm after his skin began to blacken), Abraham Lincoln was interred in a Crane-patented metal coffin.

Crane & Breed (after Abel Breed, who joined just months after the company's founding) diversified, extending their product line to all kinds of death-adjacent fields. They produced caissons, hearses, and nameplates; fancy handles and finials and other hardware; plumes. The firm innovated as well in steam heat—a business that came about as a byproduct of Martin Crane's successful push, through the 1860s, to produce the industry's first sheet-metal casket. The company flourished in part because of the railroad system they helped to expand southward (another metal business from which to reap profits). The investment was doubly remunerative, since trains made shipping massive wares like coffins feasible. Crane & Breed were pioneers, too, in the use of marketing brochures and catalogs, including a twenty-four-pager as early as 1865—the last, thankfully, of an awful five-year boom-time for deaths.

But the biggest boon for the firm may have been the peculiar economics of the funeral trade. As Mark Twain put it in 1883, in *Life on the Mississippi*:

> There's one thing in this world which isn't ever cheap. That's a coffin.... There's one thing in this world which a person don't say—'I'll look around a little, and if I find I can't do better I'll come back and take it.' That's a coffin. There's one thing in this world which a person won't take in pine if he can go walnut; and won't take in walnut if he can go mahogany; and won't take in mahogany if he can go an iron casket with silver door-plate and bronze handles. That's a coffin. And there's one thing in this world which you don't have to worry around after a person to get him to pay for. And that's a coffin. Undertaking?—why it's the dead-surest business in Christendom, and the nobbiest.[2]

"Nobby" usually denotes "chic" or "smart," but here Twain extends the meaning to "status-conscious." The "dead-surest business in Christendom" merits that superlative, and not only among the well-to-do. Even the poorest weren't inclined to stint on funerals. Among African Americans in particular, an elegant "homegoing" became not just a custom but almost a requirement of theology. This stemmed in part from older African traditions and in part from the fact that in the antebellum South slaves had often been forbidden to participate in such rites—which deprivation, after the war, helped make funerals expressions of two kinds of joyful deliverance: from the evil of the "peculiar institution" *and* from this fallen, unfair, exploitative world to the tender mercies of God.

That funerary tradition provided an opportunity for further exploitation, as in *Blessed Assurance*, Allan Gurganus's novella of white guilt and tangled ethics, in which an elderly North Carolinian reflects on his job in youth collecting funerary-insurance premiums.[3] His clientele, mostly elderly blacks scraping by, the oldest of them born into bondage, had to pony up a small amount each week to keep policies current, with the dangled promise in the end of a grand sendoff to their Reward. For many policyholders, the bejeweled bon voyage would be the only luxury in—or, poignantly, *just out of*—a long life of injustice . . . but the business model called for pitilessly cutting off anyone who missed even a single week. Jerry's boss implored him never to take pity. "Once they smell heart on you," he warned, "you're finished."

I'm reminded, too, of Evelyn Waugh's great 1948 satire of American funerary customs and our florid, absurd way of talking about death, *The Loved One*.[4] And of the dark, hilarious mid-1960s movie version, directed by Tony Richardson from a script by Terry Southern and Christopher Isherwood, with Liberace (!) as the smooth Mr. Starker. Starker upsells and upsells and upsells: from the merely waterproof coffin in the contemptible middle range to the "moisture-proof" (better) to, ah, yes, the "dampness-proof"; from a skimpy synthetic lining—"Rayon chafes," Starker drily remarks—to one of silk; and finally to the bereaved's choice of graveside flame for his Loved One, a contest pitting "standard eternal" (turned off outside visiting hours) versus "perpetual eternal." Thus does death debase, or break, the very language. *You loved the departed? HOW MUCH?*

Over the next decades, Crane & Breed grew into the world's largest manufacturer of what the professional euphemists at Waugh's "Whispering Glades" (and the novel's pet cemetery, "The Happier Hunting Ground") might call necropolitan accoutrements. With this success came social cachet for the business's principals, especially the suave Crane, "in handsome black satin and

Spanish lace, with Breton lace fichu," as an *Enquirer* account of a soirée late in his life put it. But it also brought susceptibility to scandal, which touched Crane most publicly in August 1880.

On that occasion, per the *Enquirer*, "[T]he green-eyed monster is again portrayed in all its hideous proportions, and a gentleman well known in both business and social circles is dragged into a most disagreeable prominence." A local whiskey dealer, married thirteen years, had grown suspicious of the behavior of his wife, Lou Ransom Schnell. Shortly after the couple moved to a new house, John Schnell received at his office an accidentally redirected note for Lou, proposing a meeting. It was signed, in what may have seemed to Crane a delicious subterfuge but from this distance looks like a pretty clumsy blunder, "Your Uncle." (That signature must have felt to Schnell like a taunt, an ill-concealed laugh behind his back.)

The livid Schnell quickly faked a response, outfitting his messenger with a ready lie in case his forgery of his wife's penmanship wasn't persuasive. He also mimicked Crane's hand in a note to Lou. Then he enlisted the aid of a detective/second, and the two of them hired a carriage and followed Lou to her rendezvous. The observant Mrs. Schnell made her tail, however, and by the detective's account, spun on him in the street and offered $25 if he revealed who's "dogging me up." Eventually she passed close to the carriage where her enraged husband was waiting, and he leapt out with a pistol he'd concealed and began firing, hitting his wife in the shoulder before he could be tackled by the detective. When taken down, according to the *Enquirer*'s sober account, Schnell's finger was on the trigger of the "still-smoking weapon."

Lou Schnell, convalescing in the hospital, indignantly backed up Crane's claim that he—at fifty-nine nearly twice her age—was merely a family friend from her youth who intended to lend her a spot of cash. But the combination of the clandestine meet-up (punched up by the report of Mrs. Schnell's mastery of streetwise tactics and patois) and what seems to have been Crane's reputation as a roué sparked skepticism of the Tale of the Avuncular Loan.

The paper is quiet on what became of the hotheaded Herr Schnell and his *Ehegattin*, and any other extramarital aunts or uncles. Crane, insulated by money and status, seems to have suffered no lasting harm to his reputation. He died at the end of November 1886, and was buried (son "to furnish stone and let it down," says the paperwork) at Spring Grove.

Two years after Crane's death, the company, now led by the next generation of Breeds—Abel's son William and subsequently his three sons—would supply the heating system for Cincinnati's City Hall. But caskets remained their core business. William James Breed (1835–1908) was not only president and chairman of the firm but also an ingenious tinkerer, and one of the funerary conundrums to which he turned his attention—a problem it's hard even to imagine today, thanks to Breed—resulted in what is surely his cleverest and most lasting invention: the casket-lowerer. As late as the turn of the twentieth century, burials were almost always conducted above open holes. Today the "yawning grave" has declined to mere metaphor, but then there was scarcely a person who hadn't seen them yawn in person. Lowering the casket by way of "the crude and unsympathetic present method," as a journalist put it, required stout pallbearers, ropes, and pulleys, and mishaps were frequent and inevitable—a problem exacerbated by the popularity of heavy metal coffins like those sold by Crane & Breed. Who could abide the last sound heard from a beloved spouse or child being her or his corpse clumping against metal as the casket lurched into the pit?

Breed devoted years to solving this and a related issue: might one spare mourners from the anguishing noises that came as the grave was filled in? The scritch of digging, the muffled fall of soil or sharper report of pebbles, the occasional ringing of spade against burial case? Breed's solution, revealed to fanfare at the 1904 World's Fair in St. Louis, was the "Floral Mantle." The mantle is a miracle of artifice, and one wonders what Waugh would have made of this bit of American ingenuity, designed to deny what any fool can see, not to *defeat* death but to hide its dominion behind a screen of blooms and can-do spirit. It consists of a framework that, at its height, stretches sixteen inches aboveground, and fully encloses the grave. This frame is covered with green broadcloth and velvet, to conceal the machinery and harmonize with the color of grass (if it's spring or summer). Evergreen boughs might also be heaped onto the cloth, another unnatural gesture at naturalness—and one that must have registered as false in just the way the chipper color of Astroturf does nowadays. Below the sturdy frame—made in part of aluminum, for lightness—were suspended four bands of webbing, and the casket was set atop these. As a crank was turned, the casket descended slowly. Meanwhile, on the principle of the rolltop desk, two half-screens, decorated with greenery and flowers, rose from the sides to meet at the middle. The funeral would end, the bereaved disperse, and then the contraption was removed, the straps rolled up, the grave filled.

By the time William Breed died in summer 1908, the company had commenced work on the industry's Next Big Thing. Just nine months later, Crane & Breed introduced their automobile hearse. It boasted a top speed of thirty miles per hour—double the pace, the promotional material cautioned funeral-home

"Full fathom five thy pharaoh lies . . ."

"If it hadn't been for you meddling kids . . ."
John C. Calhoun, circa 1849

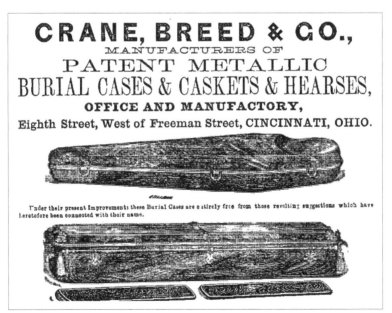

"Under their present Improvements these Burial Cases are entirely free from
those revolting suggestions which have been heretofore connected with their name."
Ad for Crane, Breed & Co. in the *Williams Cincinnati City Directory*, 1865

Liberace hawking a coffin. Still from the film *The Loved One* (1965)

Martin Crane's hillside monument in Spring Grove

Barnhorn's "Angel of Memory" hearse. Those elaborately ruffled curtains at center freaked me out on first glance; they resemble bony, reaching hands

Bianca Canales Torresola, leader of the Jayuya Uprising, 1950

Blair House circa 1950. The guard house Griselio Torresola attacked is at left. Collazo collapsed at the foot of the steps to the right, directly below the second-floor window from which the groggy president peered mid-firefight

hot-rodders, that any such phaeton "should have to go." For the next two decades, Crane & Breed would concentrate its advertising on high-end motor vehicles: hearses, ambulances, and the corpse-delivery vans popularly known as Black Marias. Only after the firm was rocked in 1924 by the mysterious suicide of Austin Breed, who had succeeded his father, would they retreat from that business and recommit their resources to the old, steady, less glamorous work of coffin-making.

In the meantime, though, the firm was a marketing juggernaut. To the extent that the Crane & Breed name has survived into the twenty-first century, it has done so largely because the company produced, throughout this period, indestructible promotional keepsakes. The bronze paperweights they distributed to funeral homes and their employees included ghosts, sailboats, Buddhas, a whole bestiary (camels, hippos, lions, frogs, Scotties, the see-no-evil-hear-no-evil monkeys), and a sarcophagus-shaped ingot that today fetches hundreds of dollars. The paperweights spawned, and still support, a lively collectibles marketplace. (I've noticed there's a special glamour attached, in some collecting circles, to *weight*; in a culture now necessarily wary about carbon footprints and fuel costs and thus obsessed with shipping weights, nothing could seem more exotic and anachronistic than the dense freebies of yore. That's all the more the case if, as with paperweights, avoirdupois is the thing's very reason for being. By *God* no paper will blow away if it's pinned to the desktop with three pounds of dead pharaoh.)

My favorite bit of Crane-&-Breediana, though, is their 1914 "Quality Talks" brochure, which includes what must be the one and only Great American Poem from the Point of View of a Funeral Car, F. F. Woodall's "Behold Me—The Hearse." "In the world I stand aloof from other transportation," brags our eponymous hero, sounding vaguely Ozymandias-like—and also echoing Twain on the funeral industry, in a weird, taunting key. "None hire me for pleasure; none choose me for a ride; yet ne'er a one objects to take his outing." The poem closes rousingly—or, rather, the opposite of rousingly, lay-to-restingly: "I am the Hearse — Death's taxicab; the carriage of the dead!/ None ride with me but once./ Thereafter upon earth—Their riding days are over."

Perhaps Crane & Breed's most formidable rival in the hearse business was Sayers & Scovill, founded in 1876 by William Sayers and A. R. Scovill. S&S concentrated from the beginning on vehicles: delivery wagons, a popular "young man's coach" (the red T-bird of its day), buggies, horse-drawn hearses, and invalid wagons. But when the new century dawned, and with it the automotive age, Sayers

& Scovill innovated and thrived; they are the only American hearse company to survive the transition to combustion engines and continue through to today. The firm produced the first gas-powered ambulance, which they introduced at the 1907 Chicago Automobile Show, and by 1912 they'd begun making gas-run funeral wagons, too. By 1914 they began making Sayers passenger cars as well.

The first three decades of the twentieth century saw a frantic pace of change in funeral vehicles, thanks to the confluence of rapid technological advances; the nascent American love affair with the car; and the prosperity of the 1920s, which created a hearse-designing arms race (the kind of arms race that comes with heavy froufrou, leaded windows, Art Deco gilding, and more). Sayers & Scovill at first hesitated to change its conservative twelve-column hearse . . . but by just after World War I, evolving public tastes—plus what turned out to be the opportunity presented by a 1919 fire that required S&S to retool and build new manufacturing facilities—had spurred them again to lead. S&S introduced two-tone gray vehicles, and they experimented with beveled windows; leaded glass in Gothic ogival shapes; nickel plating; trimmings made of ivory, or rosewood with mahogany inlays; even landau-style tops covered with artificial leathers and lacquers like Fabrikoid and Zapon. The workhorse of their line was the "Masterpiece" funeral coach they introduced in the early 1920s. It would be Death's Taxicab of choice for years to come, and would remain in the catalog for a half-century.

In 1929, as designs grew more and more like Tim Burton fever visions, S&S teamed up with Cincinnati artist Clement Barnhorn, a Rookwood Pottery luminary,[5] on a "Signed Sculpture Hearse." Barnhorn produced the "Angel of Memory," two cast bronze-relief sculptures mounted on either side of an elegant hearse. The Angel of Memory model sold for $8,500—roughly $125,000 today. The onset of the Depression hampered sales, and the Barnhorn hearse was off the market within two years.[6]

Emil Hess and Charles Eisenhardt, both of whom came to work for Sayers & Scovill in 1891, played important roles in the company's success. Emil's grandson Willard Hess joined the firm in 1930 after graduating from GM's Institute of Technology, and eight years later he and Eisenhardt's son Charles Jr., with the backing of their fathers, purchased an interest in the firm. Soon after, at the beginning of World War II, the Sayers and Scovill heirs decided to shutter the business, and young Hess and Eisenhardt seized the opportunity. They renamed the company after themselves, but also purchased the S&S trademark and continued producing the renowned Sayers & Scovill ambulances.

During World War II, Hess and Eisenhardt earned multiple military con-tracts—especially for the design and manufacture of trailers for laying railroad track and retrieving bogged or disabled tanks—and developed a reputation for efficiency, meticulousness, and discretion. Those contacts and that reputation would pay off in an unexpected way in 1950. Early that year the United States had granted Puerto Rico new status as an "Associated Free State," which to the island's nationalists read as a pat-on-the-head Newspeak insult rather than the substantive change they'd sought. On October 30, amid a police crackdown and chafing against what they viewed as American colonial domination, Puerto Ricans mounted what became known as the Jayuya Uprising. By the end of the fray in Jayuya, one police officer had been killed, three wounded, the U.S. Post Office burned, telephone lines cut . . . and the Puerto Rican flag flew over a town square that the revolutionaries declared the origin point of a new republic. Nationalist forces would manage to hold the city for three days.

The U.S.-backed government responded with immediate and overwhelm-ing force. Nationalist headquarters in San Juan were overrun; incipient revolts in other cities were crushed. But Jayuya took the brunt. American P-47 Thun-derbolts strafed the city, and the Puerto Rican National Guard pounded it with artillery fire, destroying 70 percent of structures. The government declared martial law and, knowing how the news of large-scale military devastation in Jayuya and elsewhere would play in the court of world opinion, imposed a news blackout. In Washington, meanwhile, President Harry Truman down-played the events in the Associated Free State as merely "an incident between Puerto Ricans."

This incensed expatriate nationalists, who'd heard a very different version from relatives on the ground in Puerto Rico and who wanted the revolution to catch fire and grow. In New York, Griselio Torresola, cousin of the insurgency's leader, Bianca Canales, and brother of another major figure in the uprising, decided to make a dramatic, immediate strike against the superpower and its false narrative: He and a countryman, Oscar Collazo, would assassinate the American president, thus demonstrating to all the world that this was not the intramural squabble to which Truman had tried to diminish it, but a hot war between sovereign nations. Truman was staying in Blair House while the White House was being refurbished, and Torresola and Collazo decided to exploit what might be either reduced protection details, unpracticed new security arrangements, or both. On November 1, the two took a train to Wash-ington and approached Blair House separately. Given the timeline, Torresola could only hastily prepare Collazo, who had no weapons expertise, and when

Collazo went to fire on a Secret Service officer, it turned out that he'd failed to chamber a bullet beforehand. A firefight broke out. Meanwhile Torresola attacked. He shot an officer in his security booth, then wounded another, Joseph Downs, in the hip; Downs took additional bullets in the back and neck as he scurried to a basement door, slipped in, and secured it. At this point Torresola went to join his partner Collazo. But first he stood aside and reloaded, during which pause Truman—who'd been taking a nap on the second floor—ventured to the window, just thirty feet away, to see what was happening. He was shouted back by Secret Service officers.

The first officer Torresola ambushed, Leslie Coffelt, was, it would turn out, fatally injured; he would die hours later at the hospital. But now he managed to brace himself against the booth's door and get off a long-distance pistol shot, killing Torresola. Meanwhile Collazo, who'd made it as far as the steps of Blair House, was felled by a shot to the chest.[7]

The shootout had spanned some forty seconds—it remains the longest gunfight in Secret Service history—and not surprisingly, it spooked those tasked with preserving the president's safety. They approached General Motors for advice about the feasibility of limousines that could hold up to small-arms fire. GM sought advice from Hess & Eisenhardt, which thus entered the presidential-car-armoring business. Truman had already ordered a new set of limousines to replace the aging fleet, and he'd chosen Lincoln over Cadillac—and therefore rival firm Henney over Hess & Eisenhardt. He'd made the choice in part out of vengeance, rumor had it: the president was lingeringly irked that GM had disdained to provide cars for his 1948 campaign, which the automaker (followed in this, infamously, by the headline-writers at the *Chicago Tribune*) figured the unpopular incumbent would lose to Thomas Dewey. Now the limousine order was amended, it seems, to stipulate that Hess & Eisenhardt would handle the armoring.

Through the next decade, Hess & Eisenhardt would fulfill specialty orders and design expensive one-offs for heads of state (Queen Elizabeth II, King Hussein), the potentates of other realms (J. Edgar Hoover), the international rich (for instance the Saudi sheik for whom they produced a series of "harem cars," outfitted with one-way glass that allowed his wives to see out without being glimpsed themselves), and captains of industry (in 1961 they adapted a Ford Thunderbird for a Coca-Cola exec who suffered a rare eye ailment that made it impossible for him to see through a traditional curved windshield; H&E's solution was a windscreen custom-ground to match his eyeglass prescription—which must have made a pretty trippy ride for anyone else). Hess

& Eisenhardt also contributed to 1950s Cadillac innovations like the power sunroof and the padded vinyl top.[8]

But the work they would be renowned for in the early 1960s, for all the wrong reasons, would be for the government. JFK's X-100 began as an off-the-assembly-line 1961 Lincoln Continental convertible. Either Hess & Eisenhardt, Ford, or Hess & Eisenhardt and Ford in concert—stories conflict—cut the car in half, extended it by three and a half feet between the front and rear axles, made transmission and engine alterations, raised the roof by several inches (in service of what was called "top hat dignity"), and reinforced it with sheet steel.

Then Hess & Eisenhardt made further refinements they had worked out in hush-hush consultation with the Secret Service and an unwieldy committee of thirty, including military brass and national security officials. They installed retractable handles and steps for the protection detail. They divided the passenger compartment in two by setting a retractable glass divider behind the front seat. They added reverse-flow fans in case tickertape debris clogged the vents and caused overheating, and they snaked five thousand feet of wiring throughout—for communications equipment (including links to escort cars), warning lights, and more. A hydraulic control could raise the president's rear seat by 10.5 inches for better public visibility, and a stainless-steel roll bar was put in behind the front seat, too; this would give Kennedy a sort of mobile balustrade to steady himself against if he wanted to stand in a parade.

Ignore, for a moment, the X-100's Cold War–spycraft code name, the *Strangelove*-ian megacommittee, and so on. As the list above suggests, many of the refinements Hess & Eisenhardt were contracted to make had nothing whatever to do with safety—in fact, they were about making the president *more* accessible and visible. The tragedy in Dealey Plaza is often said to have ended a certain kind of American innocence, and items like the railing and the hydraulic seat-lift—a mechanical contrivance that reminds me, uncomfortably, of Crane & Breed's Floral Mantle—underscore the truth in that argument. Neither of these ideas would have been conceivable after November 22, 1963, and in today's jaded, gun-mad, conspiracy-minded America, they would read as features *designed* for ease of targeting.

In retrospect, one of the most surprising decisions was not to install bulletproof glass—not even in the special canopies Hess & Eisenhardt fabricated. Indeed, if the bubble top left off the car on November 22 were to save Kennedy, as some speculated it might have (Hess, late in life, would claim this, too), it would have had to do so not by stopping Oswald's shots cold, but by either slightly deflecting the bullets or—more likely—deterring the attempt in the first place. The X-100's windshield was standard two-ply safety glass, the kind you could switch out at any dealership. Part of the reason for eschewing bullet-proof glass may have owed to concerns about the trade-off between armoring and maneuverability: The finished limousine, with the additional sheet metal and reinforced undercarriage, weighed a staggering 7,822 pounds.

Willard Hess took great pride in his company's contributions to the X-100, and—a bit of gamesmanship directed at Ford/Lincoln—he sought permission to attach commemorative nameplates: "Custom Built for the President of the United States by Hess & Eisenhardt Company, Rossmoyne, Cincinnati, Ohio." The rules forbade their installation anywhere on the exterior, so Hess ordered them attached to the rear doorjambs, just above the locks, so that anyone who climbed in or out could see them. When they got wind of it, livid Lincoln executives balked, but the work was done already.

And so we return to suburban Cincinnati, November 25, 1963. Consider for a moment how strange the scene at Rossmoyne that day must have been. The nation was draped in black crape, grief-stricken, frightened. Kennedy was being interred at Arlington, his eternal (or perpetual eternal) flame being lit.[9] Jack Ruby had killed Lee Harvey Oswald on live television just twenty-four hours earlier, and outlandish and intricate theories of a plot—involving Cuba, the Soviets, the Mafia, LBJ; the Israelis, the New Orleanians, the Trilateralists; Umbrella Man, Badge Man, Dark Complected Man, The Man from the Grassy Knoll—were already being skeined out. Some accused the Secret Service itself of complicity. And yet, just three days after what would become the most controversy-clouded murder in American history, the *crime scene* was delivered to a distant city for cleanup, disposal, and rebuilding. It's a decision that has stoked conspiracy theories for more than fifty years.[10]

Think, too, of what Hess and his fellow engineers must have felt as they watched the flatbed bump into the lot with its somber cargo. The car that arrived in Cincinnati had been processed for evidence, to the extent that was done in those pre-*CSI* days. The FBI had dismantled the rear seats, ripped out much of the leather in a search for bullet fragments. But the armrests and upholstery and jump seats these men had spec'd out and labored over were still bloodstained, and the carpet they'd brushed and napped and glued may still have harbored smudges of brain matter or tiny shards of skull. What did Hess and company see when they threw open those rear doors and saw the nameplate they'd ratcheted in with such pride a couple years before? Their initial reencounter with the car they knew so well, on that day of mourning, must have seemed ghoulish and

The X-100 on delivery day, June 15, 1961

horrible and solemn and sorrowful and guilt-inducing; the moment when the tarp came off must have been awful for them, like identifying a loved one on the coroner's slab. And what second thoughts were provoked that morning about the kinds of modifications they had made, the kinds they hadn't?

Contemplate, too, the oddity, in this immediate aftermath, of not preserving the X-100 for evidence, or crushing it into a cube, or sinking it in a quarry to give it a grave safe forever from prying eyes. (Bizarrely, there was talk, once the limo returned to Andrews Air Force Base, of possibly cleaning it up in case President Johnson needed it for his predecessor's funeral . . . but one look inside sufficed to end that.) In the moment, though, the government made—perhaps had to make—a practical decision. The truth was that *they needed the car.* Having a new one designed, manufactured, armored, and fitted might take several years. And, too, crass though it might seem at such a time, there was the expense. They'd sunk $200,000 (in today's dollars around $1.7 million) into modifications to the X-100, and starting from scratch wasn't a viable option.

For Hess & Eisenhardt, the work on this second go-round—Operation "Quick Fix"—may have provided the succor of busyness in a time when they needed it. Second thoughts didn't tease and nag and tug at them, as they would have otherwise; given the task at hand, such thoughts were a practical necessity, were their job. Just as funeral arrangements and closet-scouring and account-settling—however painful—can provide the bereaved a distraction from raw grief and an alternative to it that feels productive, I imagine that plunging into the engineering of Quick Fix may have spared those at H&E, and those who'd devised the plans they were to execute, some uncomfortable stock-taking.

This time, decisions were made by a more streamlined committee of six (including representatives of Hess & Eisenhardt, the Secret Service, the Army Materials Research Center, and the Pittsburgh Plate Glass Company), and safety was the paramount concern. The timeline was urgent. Work on the new X-100 began on December 12, less than three weeks after the assassination. They affixed a permanent bulletproof top; installed shatterproof glass everywhere; rearmored the passenger compartment. All in all, the revamp would add two thousand pounds of steel and titanium bulletproofing, which necessitated a new and more powerful engine. Solid aluminum rims were set inside the tires to make them flat-proof. H&E also stripped the old car down to its shell and thoroughgoingly—oh, poignant euphemism—"retrimmed the rear compartment." The cost—absorbed primarily by Ford and its subcontractors—was half a million dollars (roughly four million today).

Hess & Eisenhardt delivered the car—now painted black, as the original midnight blue with micalike glitter was, Johnson feared, forever tainted by association—on May 1, 1964. In 1977, after thirteen more years of happily uneventful service, it was retired and returned to its owner, Ford—which, per longstanding custom for presidential automobiles, had been leasing it to the United States for the pittance of $500 a year.

Willard Hess was appointed as a consultant to the Warren Commission. He would sell his company, which still exists as O'Gara-Hess & Eisenhardt and still armors vehicles, in 1974. When Hess died in 2000, at ninety-four, he was conveyed to his grave at Spring Grove in one of death's most elegant taxicabs, a 1938 Sayers & Scovill LaSalle Damascus hearse.

Willard C. Hess's stone, Spring Grove

ACCIDENTAL CHARON
JACOB STRADER, DRED SCOTT, AND BODY-SNATCHING

JACOB STRADER (1795–1860) WAS A BOATMAN, then a captain, and eventually a shipping magnate who owned a fleet of twenty-three steamers that plied the Ohio, among them the eponymous side-wheeler *Jacob Strader*, called by one journalist "the finest boat, all things considered, that I ever saw on the American waters." By the time of his death, Strader's fortune extended to railroads, banking, and insurance as well.

But despite his contributions to the history of river shipping, Strader is best known these days—who knows what will land face-up in the muck of memory?—for two "crimes," one tragic and one macabre, neither of which he committed. The former he wasn't present for (and the crime wasn't his but his country's), and the latter took place two decades after his death.

The first of these culminated in the Supreme Court case *Strader v. Graham* of 1851. Three slaves who lived in Harrodsburg, Kentucky—it's important to give these men their names: George, Henry, and Reuben—were allowed by their "owner," Christopher Graham, to make forays into Indiana and Ohio, both free states, to perform music at fêtes and weddings. On one such trip, the three took passage on a Strader steamboat, the *Pike*, up to Cincinnati, then headed north to Canada and freedom. When he realized the band wouldn't be returning this time, Graham sued Strader, Strader's partner, and the vessel's captain to get remuneration for his loss, and the Kentucky chancery courts agreed, placing a lien on the boat and demanding $3,000. On appeal, Strader and his lawyers countered with the argument, derived from British law, that because Graham had voluntarily allowed the men to go north before, the specific written permission from Graham that Kentucky law required did not apply. George, Henry, and Reuben had long before this become free men, they argued, on the basis of their travels to and residency in states that in their constitutions outlawed and invalidated slavery. Once a free man, always one.

When the case reached the Supreme Court, Chief Justice Roger Taney and his colleagues declined to enter the fray on jurisdictional grounds, upholding Kentucky's ruling. But Taney then went well beyond, saying that even if the

Court hadn't upheld the judgment against Strader on technical grounds, it would have rejected his argument that the men had, by Ohio law, been free at the time when they booked passage to Cincinnati. The Court's decision established the right of southern states to determine who was a slave or not, and to ignore or flout the laws of free states where those came into conflict with local statutes. *Strader v. Graham* became the legal basis, five years later, of the infamous Dred Scott decision, in which Taney—pressured by the southern justices on the Court not merely to decide on the basis of the Strader precedent but to go further—ruled, sweepingly and outrageously, that slavery was specially protected under the Constitution and that free blacks were not U.S. citizens and could not claim any of the rights attached to citizenship. (The *Strader* decision was also cited in the case of Margaret Garner, who fled to Cincinnati with her family across the frozen Ohio River in January 1856, and then—hunted down by slavecatchers—slit her infant daughter's throat rather than see her returned to bondage. Garner's story became the basis of Toni Morrison's *Beloved*.)

The second crime is bizarre. A bit of background: through the nineteenth century, medical schools had a rapidly growing need for cadavers for dissection, but in many places religious stricture or social stigma made it difficult to obtain them. Schools started dealing on the sly with so-called ghouls or resurrection men, who provided bodies reliably enough as to blunt the schools' curiosity about the corpses' provenance—those were questions best not asked.

The most notorious case occurred in Edinburgh in the late 1820s. Scottish law dictated that corpses for medical research must come only from prisoners, suicides, and foundlings or orphans, which restricted supply considerably. Because cemeteries were now being vigorously patrolled, spot-lit, even booby-trapped, grave-robbing had grown increasingly difficult, and cadavers had become an expensive commodity. When one of Edinburgh landlord William Hare's tenants died in 1828, he consulted with his friend William Burke, who came up with a scheme to sell the dead lodger to an anatomist for ready cash. Pleased with the proceeds from that transaction, Burke and Hare seized the entrepreneurial initiative and started making corpses of their own. Eventually they murdered sixteen people, and Burke honed his almost untraceable method so well that even now, "burking" remains a synonym for smothering.

The key to the scheme, and the reason it didn't unravel for almost a full year, was that Burke and Hare (with the aid of their spouses, it seems) took care to

Portrait of Captain Jacob Strader, attributed to Joseph Oriel Eaton

choose victims whose disappearances wouldn't attract attention—the infirm, the poor, the isolated, the anonymous, those living close to the bone. If they had stuck with their initial stratagem and simply, ghoulishly, identified the imminently-to-die, perched nearby until they expired, and delivered them for a profit, they might never have been caught, much less reviled for centuries. Medical science was paying dividends, and the wider society wasn't inclined to linger overlong on distasteful questions about how faculties acquired fodder for research and training, so long as that "fodder" consisted of the already dead—and so long as it wasn't "decent people's" loved ones.[1] So specimens tended to come—as the Scottish law implied, even demanded—from those at the fringes of society: suicides, drunks, orphans, addicts, immigrants, minorities, the poor.

Which is what made the case of John Scott Harrison so unusual and so splashy. In late May 1878, Harrison—the only man in American history to be both son of a president (William Henry, #9) and father to one (Benjamin, #23)—died at his farm north of Cincinnati. During his funeral, gathered friends and relatives noticed that a nearby grave—that of twenty-three-year-old Augustus Devin, who'd died a couple weeks before of tuberculosis—had been violated, the corpse pilfered. Harrison's relatives, determined not to have the same fate befall their dear departed, took precautions: They dug an unusually deep hole, lined it with bricks, and got sixteen men to wrestle an immense stone over the metal vault container. They even tried a version of the trick that noir movie detectives would employ sixty years later to tell if their rooms were searched: they inserted into the tumulus two wooden pegs or dowels, easily displaced, so that they'd be able to spot tampering immediately. Finally, as a failsafe, they hired a man to guard the tomb for several days.

And then they went hunting for the unfortunate Devin. The next morning, Harrison's son John—outraged by the desecration of the young consumptive's grave—had his suspicions piqued by a squib in the *Cincinnati Enquirer* that reported on a buggy seen proceeding at 3 A.M. through the alley just north of the opera house. Curious neighbors reported seeing something swathed in white removed rapidly and furtively before the buggy trundled away. The brief item concluded: "The general impression was that a 'stiff' was being smuggled into the Ohio Medical College." Harrison and a friend, figuring the "stiff" might be Devin, obtained a warrant, and, accompanied by a detective and constables, entered the school. No faculty were present, so they were shown around by a janitor. On the top floor they entered the dissecting room, and in it a student "chipping away" at the head and breast of a black woman's corpse, but no sign of Devin's remains. The janitor asked to be dismissed so that he could alert the faculty to the visitors, and the detective gave permission—but, cagily, had the man followed. The investigators trailed him to a bare "injecting room" with a windlass and a rope that disappeared into a covered square hole in the floor—a pulley contraption used, it became clear, to lift heavy bundles from the basement.

The rope, they discovered, was stretched taut. They hauled up the weight on the other end, revealing eventually a body, secured at the neck by the rope and with the head covered. It clearly wasn't Devin—this was not a youngster ravaged by tuberculosis but a robust-seeming older man—and when they removed the cloth shroud over the head, Harrison gasped, "It's Father!"

The case sparked a conflagration, as might be expected. The hubbub included a call to remove the body of William Henry Harrison—dead four decades, and thus presumably well beyond the body-snatchers' powers to "resurrect"—from ghoul-infested Ohio to the safety of Indiana. The investigation widened, and Devin's body was eventually discovered in a pickling vat at the University of Michigan's medical school. Amid public revulsion, several midwestern states passed Anatomy Acts like the one that had been enacted in Great Britain in 1832, in the aftermath of the Burke-Hare murders.

Oh, and the role of Captain Strader? The liberated corpse of John Scott Harrison was restored to his family and temporarily interred in Strader's crypt, where the two old friends could keep company while the family worked out a more permanent, less violable final resting place.

"DUE ALLOWANCE FOR FOAM"
MARTHA MCCLELLAN BROWN AND
THE OHIO WOMEN'S CRUSADE

IN THE SUMMER OF 1879, the *New York Times* published what could have been an exposé of Cincinnatians' prodigious beer-drinking habits. The article, occasioned by a campaign to unionize breweries, began with the anecdote of a firefighter in the city's Mohawk Company who boasted that he could consume twelve glasses of beer while the station's bells were striking noon—and who backed up/gulped down his boast. But the fireman felt he could do better; all that glass-lifting and wrist-tilting wasted time and cost chugging efficiency. So he consolidated his beers into a punch bowl, reared back just once, lingeringly, and upped his record to seventeen: "A gallon and a half," wrote the reporter, agog, "after making due allowance for foam."

That last phrase doesn't belong to the genre of exposé, you may have noticed. It sounds instead like something the frat's official recordkeeper would say as he extols a taproom legend. It's the language of sports writing, in which fandom takes cover behind a mask of objectivity.

From there the article shifts focus to the policies of Cincinnati's beer barons concerning on-the-job tippling. Kauffmann's brewery employees, the *Times* reported, averaged thirty-five small glasses of ale per day; J. G. Sohn permitted workers one and a third gallons. The abstemious (or frugal, or safety-conscious) owners at another outfit used a strict hole-punch system, allowing brewery men six to fourteen glasses per shift, depending on age, weight, and the quality of their work. The reporter chronicles all this in a tone of lightly stunned admiration, adding that many of these men—though perhaps a bit torpid or glazed-eyed (and carrying extra pounds)—never seemed to get inebriated.

The article ends with an expression of sympathy for the subset of zythepsary workers who, by unbreakable custom, had *no choice* but to toss back mind-bending, liver-swelling amounts of beer: the breweries' money collectors, who went all day from tavern to tavern—1880s Cincinnati, with a population of just 225,000, had more than 1,800 bars, a ratio of one for every thirty-seven adult men—and who upon entering any pub were compelled to buy a round for the assemblage and bolt one down themselves. These men sometimes downed a hundred short glasses of lager (Cincinnati's dominant style then) per day, and their salary included a bump for hazard pay.

But perhaps there's presentism in that account of it. Cincinnati's water was notoriously unhealthy, after all, and much of what workers consumed would have been "small beer," with a lower alcohol-by-volume percentage than would be typical of a lager or ale today. To some extent, then, the numbers are skewed. Nevertheless—one and a third gallons? I feel confident that the twenty-first-century employer that offers free water or diet soda in the breakroom doesn't need to allot anything like that volume per employee. Beer is a special category, and Cincinnati was a special place for beer.

The two decades after the Civil War were marked—especially in the Northeast and the German-influenced Midwest—by a dramatic increase in the number and capacity of American breweries, and in the number and capacity of American beer drinkers. In 1880, Cincinnati produced thirty-six million gallons (over a quarter-billion pints), and half or more of that amount was locally consumed. The per-capita figure for adult men would have been over one hundred gallons—more than a thousand twelve-ounce beers per man per annum. These numbers made Cincinnati the third-biggest producer of beer in the country, the number-one most besotted.

Brewing was not permitted within the original city limits, which created— as happened elsewhere—a vice district just beyond, in Cincinnati known (because the city limit was Liberty Street) as the "Northern Liberties." Initially, a law required production and sales to be separated by a public thoroughfare, and many of the city's breweries were designed with subterranean passages from the brewing side of the street to the distribution side. Today there are tours of the mysterious old lagering tunnels underneath breweries carved into the hillsides just north of the city center. One story often told on those tours—and beloved by dipsomaniac Cincinnatians like me—derives from the *WPA Guide* to the city, from the early 1940s.[1] When the legendary temperance advocate Carrie Nation—who described herself as "a bulldog running along at the feet of Jesus, barking at what He doesn't like"—came to town in 1902, the story goes, she "did not lift her hatchet arm as she moved up Vine Street; she seemed awed by the formidable array of saloons, beer gardens, and concert halls. Asked why she had not broken any windows, she replied, 'I would have dropped from exhaustion before I had gone a block.'"

The passage bears obvious signs of embroidery. "Seemed awed," for example, has the hoppy bouquet of myth. The reporter's having-his-ears-scratched tone is conflated with, or wishfully substituted for, that of the barking reformer.

Sure enough, contemporary accounts of the visit omit any mention of Ms. Nation's having confided grudging respect—one pro to another—for the city's championship-level dissipation. My suspicion is that the Lord's Bulldog would not be silenced, no matter how "formidable" the "array," and the Vine Street of the time, a hellscape of filth through which sots wobbled, would have been to the L.'s B. like a mail carrier and a fire hydrant rolled into one. Instead of awe, the newspapers reported Carrie Nation's frequent expressions of regret at being unable, because of pending charges in Kansas, to unscabbard her avenging hatchet.

But it's no wonder the city's natives like to tout that quote. For one thing, they have to contend again and again with the yet more prominent statement (equally apocryphal, it seems), attributed to Mark Twain, that when the world ends he'd like to be in Cincinnati, as it's always ten (or twenty) years behind.[2] For another, there's a grubby glamor attached to Cincinnati's status as the most schnockered place in nineteenth-century America. It goes against the prevailing vision of the city as the capital—worse, as a backwater subcapital—of boring Middle America. If you're from Cincinnati, you take your edge where you can get it.

I'm not arguing that Cincinnati was unique in its taste for demon rum (or demon malt). Every town—especially every town of the Midwest—had its feats of alcoholism, has its tales of how engrained drinking culture was. My grandfather grew up in tiny Grafton, Wisconsin, and often told the story of bartending as a young teen, soon after World War I, in his family's hotel. At day's end, the dairy farmhands would haul their milk cans or buckets into town, pour them into the tanks, collect their pay, and then, having washed out one five-gallon bucket, bring that oaken super-tankard to the bar so my grandfather could fill it with ale. My grandfather would then hoist the bucket, sloshing to its rim, onto the bar, and the men would ladle it out. All evening, every evening. Cincinnati wasn't *sot generis*, but it was extreme.

But why? One factor may have been that for many immigrants, beer-drinking excess provided not only an escape from daily cares but also a nostalgic link to home and heritage. I was never more southern than in my first year out of South Carolina, in school up north, when suddenly my accent and oddities of phrase weren't incidental and invisible but everywhere and always conspicuous, to be grappled with every day: rejected, embraced, or apologized for. I imagine that first- and second-generation German Americans must have felt something similar. The local tavern would have provided company and familiarity—*Gesellschaft und Gemütlichkeit*—as well as a retreat . . . but draining beer after beer must have felt like it might count, too, as an expression of ethnic pride. Slake your thirst, forget your troubles, *and* connect to your past? Bartender, keep 'em coming. In such a situation, how to figure out where authenticity ends and parody starts—how to tell where to stop? I was never more anguished by the South's racial past (and present) than I was my freshman year of college, but to compensate for having turned my back on home, I became a partisan of regional food and music and folkways I'd always disdained, and after a beer or two, my accent broadened into a brassy Foghorn Leghorn thing.

My first couple of years in Cincinnati, 2002–04, local beer culture was at what turned out to be its low ebb. Almost all the city's old brands—Hudepohl, Schoenling, Moerlein, Little Kings, and others—had suspended production or died out altogether, leaving a cheap, watery swill called Bürger as virtually the only local beer standing . . . and even it wasn't brewed here, having been contracted out to a factory in Maryland. What Cincinnati did still have in profusion was dusty last-leg taverns, many of them shot-and-a-beer joints that used to cater to blue-collar drinkers post-shift. As the factories closed, many of these bars stayed stubbornly open for years, even decades. Often the proprietors lived upstairs, and their places hung on as clubhouses, hangouts, swap meets, time capsules. There's an early Vladimir Nabokov novella, *The Eye*,[3] in which the protagonist shoots himself and then discovers that the border between life and death is murkier than he'd thought: "Some time later," the narrator says, "if one can speak here of time at all, it became clear that after death human thought lives on by momentum." So, apparently, does the Cincinnati barroom. For twenty years or more, like headless chickens shocked to discover that there's no imperative to *stop* doing laps of the yard, these pubs had been preserved in amber lager, aided by airlessness, dim aqueous light, and the city's persistent urban nonrenewal. They lived on by momentum.

Those first years in Cincinnati, several friends and I developed a rigorous, academically legitimate research technique that we called the Bender. Every few months we'd set aside an afternoon, walk or take the bus to a neighborhood we'd chosen, eat a filling diner breakfast, and then—beginning at noon—spend the afternoon drinking one beer at each of four or five nearby pubs. We quickly discovered that at noon on weekdays, these establishments were reliably near-empty, with at most a few grizzled habitués and a bartender, who was invariably—would you *pay* someone to open your tavern for two people?—the owner.

In that circumstance, both the bartenders and their everyday drinkers—
many of them decades-long regulars, leftovers from the exodus to the suburbs
and Sunbelt—tended to be loquacious. Talk was what they had left, that and
their appointed barstools. Usually our group consisted of a couple of fiction
writers, a feminist historian of medicine, an urban environmental historian
(a Cincinnati native), and an urban sociologist. And oh, the things we saw.
One bar had a shelf stacked with sample-sized detergent for sale; it turned
out that there had years before been a coin laundromat next door, and the
bar had stocked cleaning powder to court customers who ran out of change,
hoping to entice them back for a nip while they waited on the tumble-dry.
When the laundromat closed, no one bought the detergent anymore, but the
stock stayed on its display shelf, evolving from surplus to joke to Museum
of Jurassic Technology exhibit. (Today's white elephant is tomorrow's legacy
brand—a strategy of patience that turned out, in the case of Cincinnati bars
and beers, to be shockingly prescient, given the brewing renaissance of the
last decade, which has brought crowds back to the places that managed to
keep their doors open and their premises unruined.)

In a sketchy bar downtown I was asked—pointedly, with the suggestion
that my life might depend on the answer—whether I was a Serb. Um, ah, no,
I wasn't? Was I *sure* I wasn't? Yes? I got a bloodshot doubting look and a curt
"OK, then," and the guy stalked down the bar to cleanse other ethnic enemies.
Another bar had been outfitted with furniture from a defunct casino in Indiana, and to get to the bathroom you had to pass through a room piled high
with skateboards and phonebooks. Beyond the restroom was a courtyard
paved with maybe a thousand discarded tires; here was where the two-dollar
environmental disposal fee was landing them. Across the street—and just
outside Spring Grove's gates—in a bar that specialized in "fish logs," burrito-
sized loaves of battered cod, the young woman behind the counter seemed
overwhelmed by what she called the "lunch rush" and warned us that it might
take a while. Her sincerity made us peek around behind us to find the hordes
we hadn't noticed . . . but there were only four people there, sipping beer from
the dirty juice glasses they handed out to class the joint up to Lunch Spot from
Day-Drinkers' Dive. The sense the server gave of being buffeted from all sides
was enhanced by the homemade necklace she was wearing, a cord with a
whirring plastic fan that, trained upward, kept her bangs always lightly aloft.

In the bar closest to my house, I saw the proprietor hurl himself into a
wingback to belt out Elvis Presley's "Kentucky Rain" on a karaoke machine
while waiting for the late-arriving hipsters who made Karaoke Night sing.

With his head about halfway up the chair's back, rear end straining off the cushion's front edge, and feet stretched before him, his torso was closer to horizontal than vertical; he looked like someone pinned by some combination of gale and despair. The microphone rested on his sternum, and he sported a maroon bathrobe, loosely tied. It's hard to imagine someone arguing more persuasively that he knew whereof he spoke, "seven lonely days and a dozen towns ago"–wise.

One chilly night a friend, walking past a tiny local bar that we'd never seen open, found the lights on and a few people sitting inside, looking cozy. Thrilled to have found a new watering hole so close to home, he tried to shoulder open the door, only to find it locked. The bartender ambled over to tell him that it wasn't a pub anymore, just an extension of the woman's living room; she and a couple of friends had unlocked the space, fired up a couple of the old barlights, and were now sharing a bottle, reminiscing. "But you're welcome to join us," she said.[4]

But of all the bars we visited, perhaps the most memorable was near campus—and has since been plowed under, a casualty of Uptown's revitalization as the university grew and prospered. The bartender told us that he'd been here over fifty years, since his parents moved from Pittsburgh to run this tavern and live overhead. He showed us around and gave a lively gloss on the wall poster we found that depicted faded Cincinnati brands and breweries. Then he escorted us to the courtyard out back. It was dominated by a wheelless and windowless Studebaker that had a surprisingly stout elderberry tree growing from a crack in the upholstered backseat. The courtyard was hemmed in by stone walls, chain-link, and hillside, and there would be no moving that car until the bar itself was bulldozed and a path opened up to the street. It wasn't an inviting space: litter-strewn, weeds poking through crumbling pavement, with trash saplings springing up at its verges but no mature trees. Discolored toilets clustered at either end of a cement runway to one side, and there were vestiges of a bowling lane open to the air, suggesting a roof gone missing. "I've been planning to fix it up," the owner reported listlessly, "maybe draw more college kids." We nodded. Then he brightened, for the first and only time in our conversation. "What I'm about to show you," he confided, "is *proprietary*. Strictly. I don't want anyone stealing my idea." Once we'd murmured promises, he led us over to the rust-stained johns, reached into one bowl, and plucked out three roughly hockey-puck-sized blobs, made of soft rubber, that were shaped and colored to look like turds. His eyes gleamed. "Crapper cornhole," he said. "It'll be my moneymaker. Now remember—it's *proprietary*!"

Carrie Nation, brandishing hatchet, Bible, and moue of disapproval

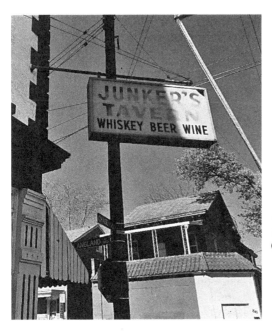

Junker's Tavern, former home to the trial-size detergent cache. I've never been clear on whether it bears the name of its (unfortunate) owner, or whether the reference is to trashed cars, or to a 1970s term for addicts. Or perhaps—this is Cincinnati—the bar was named, proudly, after its proprietor's claim to ancestry among the Prussian nobility, the Junkers?

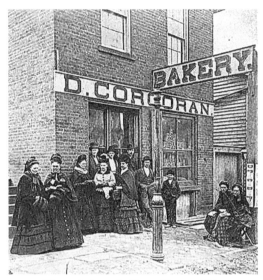

Women's Crusade, Mount Vernon, Ohio

I've kept my eyes open, honestly hoping and rooting for this bit of silk-purse entrepreneurship, but I've seen no signs of the game catching on. I'm hoping that the fifteen intervening years put me past the statute of limitations created by his invocation—and repetition—of the word "proprietary." But if anyone who reads this goes on to create a turd-cornhole empire, I'm going to have to insist that you pay that man the royalty he deserves.

In 1873–74, all across southern and central Ohio, there arose a mass movement that in some ways resembled the #MeToo groundswell of 2017. It was the winter of the Women's Crusade, during which, over just three months, female protestors are said to have chased alcohol out of 250 towns and forced the abandonment or shutdown of 17,000 drinking establishments. Those numbers may be overblown, the closures temporary, but the political power discovered and unleashed by the crusade would play a big role not only in the ultimate victory of prohibition forces (which turned out to be both ephemeral and pyrrhic) but also, more important, in the entwined fight for women's suffrage.

The man who stoked the blaze that winter was an intriguing figure whose *Wikipedia* entry begins with this humdinger of a sentence: "Diocletian Lewis (March 3, 1823–May 21, 1886), commonly known as Dr. Dio Lewis, was a prominent temperance leader and physical culture advocate who practiced homeopathy and was the inventor of the beanbag." Alas, that last tidbit strays into hyperbole, since the beanbag has been around since ancient Egypt, and in what's now the Midwest, before white America and its notions of intellectual property existed, Native American tribes were already playing a precursor of cornhole using pig bladders filled with dried beans. But the beanbag claim is in a limited way true: Lewis, as part of his decades-long push for girls' fitness and physical education (centered on Dr. Dio Lewis's School for Young Ladies in Massachusetts), devised a workout that employed large beanbags; he can be said to have "invented" them as an exercise tool. (His "new gymnastics" also involved hoops, poles, "Indian clubs," and even a heavy cast-iron crown intended to build neck muscles.)

But I want to zero in on one of Lewis's less contested contributions, his championing of temperance, a subject about which he lectured tirelessly for much of his life.

Exercise and abstention from intoxicating drink were related subjects for Lewis and his auditors—and not only because both fell under the rubric of health but also because both contributed to the cause of women's rights. Freeing women from corsets (another of Lewis's causes) and freeing them from the scourge of male alcoholism were both tenets of a kind of feminist theology that would never have called itself that. In 1873, Lewis was traveling through Ohio, delivering a lecture called "Our Girls" and advocating— his contribution here was pivotal and has lasted—for organized physical education programs in every school, for playgrounds and a gymnasium to be part of every campus, and for such education not to be limited to boys. On Sundays, though, he would take a kind of busman's holiday and turn from secular preaching to the pulpity kind. In Hillsboro, on December 23, 1873, Lewis gave a sermon called "The Duty of Christian Women in the Cause of Temperance."

Lewis had been delivering a similar oration for twenty years, and I can't say what it was about this particular speech that so galvanized his listeners. But that won't stop me from speculating. This was a fierce and primed audience of women who despised alcohol, "mother's ruin." The country was just plunging into an economic slough, and such threats tend to accentuate anxiety. Some accounts suggest, too, that the speech had changed subtly in its rhetoric and in its aim. Earlier versions were titled "The Influence of Christian Women in the Cause of Temperance," but by now Lewis had swapped out that first noun for "Duty," which may imply an evolution away from abstract encouragement and toward agitation. What precipitated immediate action, it seems, was that in Hillsboro he ventured into the personal, telling the story of his own mother—dismayed by her spouse's uncontrollable drinking—going to a publican (a grave breach of decorum, since bars catered only to men, a segregation rigorously enforced) and pleading with him to stop selling to her husband. When the barkeep refused, Lewis reported, his mother gathered her friends, and they returned to the sinful dispensary, sat down, and began praying. The publican's opposition melted.

Ostensibly the tavernkeeper relented because he was moved by the wife's anguish and her sincere Christian faith . . . but the canny Lewis seemed to realize now that it didn't much *matter* whether a change of heart precipitated the change of policy. For the parable's theology to work, the pubman's reversal had to be a Saul-on-the-road-to-Damascus conversion . . . but for the political cause of temperance to be advanced, it was fine if the barkeep acceded out of exhaustion or embarrassment or just to get her and her friends by God *out*. In the Hillsboro speech Dr. Dio suggested that women—and *only* women, en masse and unaccompanied, a status that would magnify the protests' effect and thwart any aggressive defense—go to tavernkeepers, ask for a signed pledge not to sell liquor, and if rebuffed or denied, stand on their thresholds to conduct prayers for the souls of the sinners inside, sing songs, and generally raise an uproar.

Among the women at Lewis's sermon that Sunday was Eliza Daniel "Mother" Stewart. A longtime temperance activist, she had the previous year traveled the region to give a speech called "The Liquor Traffic and How to Avoid It." But in recent months her emphasis had been moving away from avoidance and toward confrontation. Two months before, Stewart had helped a woman bring suit against a saloonkeeper in Springfield under the "Adair law," which provided that the wife, child, guardian, or employer of an intoxicated person could collect damages. Stewart took a prominent role in the argument, and the woman was awarded $300. Lewis's story gave her the tool she'd been wanting to inspire mass action.

It's hard now to imagine the shock that men in small-town 1870s Ohio would have felt at seeing women invade what were then two uncontested male spaces: the barroom and the political realm. In a terrific 2009 *Yale Journal of Law & Feminism* essay, "Courts and Temperance 'Ladies,'" Richard Chused quotes a rather florid account of one of the Mother Stewart raids on a Hillsboro tavern. The story reads like a frontier ambush narrative: see the men at leisure in their shirtsleeves, in their "familiar half-circle" around the hearth, guard down, enjoying their camaraderie. All at once the "rustle of women's garments" violates the sacral hush, and they are surrounded by dour killjoys who have the drop on them. The men are terrified to see, among what seem to be the "thousand" women crowding in, the familiar faces of friends, family members, even a prospective mother-in-law.

The account Chused quotes tries to mitigate the threat by playing it in a comic key:

> Had the invisible prince of the pantomime touched them with his magic wand, converting all to statues, the tableau could not have been more impressive. For one full minute they stood as if turned to stone; then a slight motion was evident, and lager beer and brandysmash descended slowly to the counter, while cigars dropped unlighted from nerveless fingers. The women began singing, "O, do not be discouraged, for Jesus is your friend."[5]

But the crusaders were in deadly earnest, and over the next three months, all across the state, these crowds of formidable women—dressed in black, either Sunday finery or widows' weeds—terrified tavern owners and their clientele with their petitions, their hovering moral suasion, and (if those failed) their boisterous public prayers and hymns. As the winter wore on, many men felt "hectored and goaded," and, perhaps inevitably, the contest moved into the courts.

The legal arguments against the crusade began with fulsome praise of the these upright, often socially prominent women (the crusade had an element of class war, pitting Anglo-Saxon elites against hardscrabble, hard-drinking immigrants from elsewhere in Europe), but then proceeded quickly to the idea either that they were being manipulated by men behind the scenes—Dio Lewis, the "Yankee peddler" of poisonous ideas, for one—or that these poor, benighted crusaders knew not what they did. But as the movement grew and the pressure ratcheted up, men shed their condescension and their restraint. Now, it was implied, the women had become power-mad, and the tone of the arguments against them turned uglier, the metaphors more martial. In Hillsboro, a lawyer seeking an injunction against the protests argued, "The spirit of conquest was aroused; and they fired prayers at his front door like hail." The judge in that case, William Safford, granted the injunction—and promptly left the bench to serve as a lawyer for the man he'd granted it to. Safford claimed that these good but misled women didn't understand the moral peril they put themselves in by entering "the purlieus of vice and immorality" and making themselves subject to the remarks of the "rabble."

Perhaps Safford's most remarkable line of argument was that the crusaders were misusing prayer, which ought to be private, quiet, ladylike, and apolitical: discreet murmurs and snuffles from a place curled up at their Master's feet, not growling and snarling in the streets á la Carrie Nation. Instead of the "ridiculous attitude of prayer" they were striking in public, they should be "soliciting help against the liquor trade from on high." How dare they use God to encroach upon male choice, male space, rather than sincerely "to supplicate the throne of the Deity"? In other words—words Safford wouldn't have approved, but which he was in his way echoing: the opium of the masses must stay in its dens. In a subsequent trial in which Safford took part, concerning the Palace Drug Store in Hillsboro, his co-counsel pushed this line of thought even further, implying—in a way distressingly familiar to students of present American politics—that the crusaders had left Christianity behind and were pushing for something like sharia law; the women had morphed into "Mahomedan . . . dervishes" who howled at the doors of taverns to "extort" their desired result.

That lawyer, Ulrich Sloane, veered—in his arguments before a packed and appreciative courtroom—between sneering humor and an assertion of male privilege he made no bones about: "It is a well-known fact that ladies have no idea of their legal abilities, and most of them probably do not know the component parts of a promissory note, and *I am inclined to keep them from knowing anything about man's province*, because when they forget their woman's sphere they lose that respect which should be paid to them." Sloane then turns to literature for backup, citing "poor Jerry Cruncher," a graverobber in Charles Dickens's *A Tale of Two Cities* who is beset by an ultra-pious wife who puts constant prayer above his livelihood and thus above her "own wittles and drink." Cruncher excoriates the missus in exactly Sloane's terms of duty and motherly "sphere": "Look at your boy. . . . Do you call yourself a mother, and not know that a mother's first duty is to blow her boy out?"[6] Nor did Safford himself hold back. In his five-hour summation, he charged that the women had, by turning prayer toward this secular and political aim, "prostituted the holy services of the church"(!)—thus introducing a surprising new phylum for the taxonomists of harlotry. When the women stormed the aptly named Palace, Safford and his co-counsel implied, they didn't just constrain its owner's right to trade in innocent and helpful pharmaceuticals ("jalap" and "paregorio" were mentioned); they were waging, by nonsexual yet still obscurely whorish means, the same gender war Aristophanes had described two millennia earlier in *Lysistrata*.

"Lips That Touch Liquor Shall Not Touch Ours"

Above is a famous image—or infamous, given that it became an excuse for sexists to play a tiresome game of "Hot or Not"—and one with a bizarre history. The 1874 Women's Crusade spawned a song with the risqué title "Lips That Touch Liquor Shall Never Touch Mine," a tune not surprisingly written by two men. The lyricist, Sam Booth, made the chorus a kind of ode to mansplaining: "With this for your motto, and succor divine, 'The lips that touch liquor shall never touch mine.'" The photo has sometimes been treated as a parody—note the extravagant frowns, plus the woman at center, her eyes wide as if she's even now being goosed. (The woman at bottom right appears to have pioneered the cheeks-sucked-in "fish face" that became a feature of glamour selfies a hundred years later.) Others have claimed that the photo is exactly what it appears to be, a documentary image, undated, of temperance crusaders, and in that guise it has sometimes appeared in legit histories (and elsewhere, for instance the men's room of a Carrie Nation–themed pub I visited recently in downtown Cincinnati—a pub whose exterior door-handle has been fashioned from a hatchet). But the truth—which explains the hammy expressions—seems to be that the photo is a still from the world's first film studio, Thomas Edison's tarpaper-shrouded Black Maria, which operated from 1893 to 1901.

The tone of male hysteria (to overturn an old slur) one can detect both in Safford's courtroom speech and in sneering responses to the image makes clear that what grated most about the Women's Crusade wasn't the cause embodied in the noun, but that noun's preceding possessive. If it's religious, ladies, then talk to God (quietly, please); if it's worldly, stop agitating and seek aid from the *secular* authorities on high. Respect authority! Often, in this period, political meetings were held in taverns precisely so as to keep politics a preserve of men. By attacking male redoubts, women were—and knew they were—mounting a broader assault on masculine privilege.

That "assault" made many women uncomfortable, too—those who, in following Mother Stewart's lead, favored restraint and abstemiousness in all its forms, political as well as alcoholic. The shift to the courtroom was controversial within the Women's Crusade, and may ultimately have been what ended it. Many participants in the movement were radical only on this one issue, and they were startled and discomfited by the success of their tactic—and by the response it elicited—even as they may have been exhilarated by its boldness. But they had social status to maintain. When the contest moved to the courts, the movement became explicitly about challenging male power, rather than being about pressing the bounds of passivity by praying aloud, in public, among throngs of like-minded others. The taverns were an away game, but the courts were a long-term invasion—and here the women were again sidelined and subordinated, made spectators to male performance rather than, as in the streets, acting on their own behalf. Safford and Sloane had hit upon an argument that, bankrupt though it seems now, struck home with many of the more timid crusaders.

Even radical women, whom one might expect to rally to the cause, voiced ambivalence. To suffragists like Miriam Cole, the ballot was "the only ax to lay at the root of the tree" of alcohol. If the movement was to be political, *that's* where it should aim. On one side, then, were "proper" women made nervous by the incursion into public policy; on the other, women not at all nervous about the politics, but wanting to keep the ammunition dry for the real and central cause: the equality of women, the first big step toward which was the vote. All this led to Cole writing an editorial, during the midst of the Crusade, that struck this in retrospect peculiar-sounding note:

> Their singing, though charged with a moral purpose, and their prayers, though directed to a specific end, do not make their warfare a whit more feminine, nor their situation more attractive. A woman knocking out

the head of a whiskey barrel with an ax, to the tune of the Old Hundred ["Praise God from Whom All Blessings Flow," derived from Psalm 100], is not the ideal woman sitting on a sofa, dining on strawberries and cream, and sweetly warbling "The Rose That All Are Praising." She is as far from it as Susan B. Anthony was when pushing her ballot into the box.

Cole's message, conveyed by an invocation of the sexist myth she wanted to overturn, to me reads as, "If you're not serious, go home to your chaises and your proprieties. But if you are radicals, here is the *real* cause to support!"

Martha McClellan Brown did not adhere to the sofa-sitting ideal, either. Born in 1838, she was orphaned at eight and brought up by a neighbor. In 1858 she married the Reverend W. K. Brown, and by 1861 she'd joined the Independent Order of Good Templars, a group devoted to temperance. The next year she was the top graduate of her class at the Pittsburgh Female College, where she had been the first married-woman boarding student in America. Then "Mattie" Brown embarked on a five-decade career as an advocate for temperance, female suffrage, and racial equality—meanwhile bearing and raising six children. By the time she was thirty-five, Brown had become the Grand Chief Templar in Ohio; then the editor of a newspaper she and her husband purchased, the *Alliance Monitor*, from which position she railed against the German brewers' lobby and the "rum oligarchy." In 1869 she was a pivotal figure in the founding of the Prohibition Party, now—entering its sesquicentennial year—the oldest still-existing minor party in American politics.[7]

By the time of the Women's Crusade, Mattie Brown had established herself as one of the most eloquent and implacable foes of alcohol in Ohio. True believers like her must have felt a dual amazement as events unfolded: that the long-awaited revelation was finally occurring, and that it had taken so long. (When the scales fall from one's fellow citizens' eyes, is one more flabbergasted by the shedding of them, or by the fact that, hey, up until this moment you people had *scales* on your eyes?) Brown's friendly rival Frances Willard would describe the Women's Crusade that winter with this joyous hash of metaphors: "[A] match and a wisp of grass were all that was needed, and behold the spectacle of a prairie on fire sweeping across the landscape, swift as a thousand untrained steeds and no more to be captured than a hurricane."

Brown recognized that equine cyclone-infernos come along only so often, and that this was an opportunity that must not be squandered. She wanted to ensure that the Crusade created lasting political infrastructure, so in February 1874, as the protests crested, she helped establish the first statewide women's temperance society. That summer, at a conclave of like-minded friends in Chautauqua, New York, she proposed that there be a fall meeting in Cleveland to establish a national organization. Her allies agreed, and Brown drafted the call for the convention, held in November, that culminated in the founding of the Women's Christian Temperance Union.

Martha McClellan Brown, 1893

Mattie Brown wanted the presidency of the fledgling organization, but she was balked in that ambition by her radical politics, and especially by the plank in the Prohibition Party platform that called for female access to the ballot. When her name was put into nomination at the Cleveland convention, there was derisive laughter from more conservative delegates. Brown rose immediately, with what I imagine was a terrifying dignity, to remove her name, and thereafter broke ties with the organization she had helped to found. She would have little to do with the WCTU over the rest of her life.

Rock-ribbed adherence to principle would cost Brown other alliances over the years. In the 1870s she abandoned the Templars' movement she'd once led because lodges were rejecting black members, and in 1896, when it dropped its commitment to the cause of suffrage, she renounced the Prohibition Party—an institution to which she had devoted more than a quarter-century, including a difficult stint living away from her family, twenty years before, to fulfill the duties of party vice president.

Mattie Brown would devote her last decades to her work as a professor and vice president, alongside her husband, at the struggling Cincinnati Wesleyan College; to successful lecture tours at home and abroad; to local philanthropy around Cincinnati; and to family—including a rousing correspondence with her daughter Charmé's husband, Edward Shippen, an evangelist for the cause of spiritualism who claimed to conduct séances with Pythagoras, Mary Queen of Scots, Pontius Pilate, Cleopatra, and Stonewall Jackson, and who in one memorable instance revealed to his skeptical but intrigued mother-in-law, via trancelike "automatic writing," the hitherto unknown designs of the airships

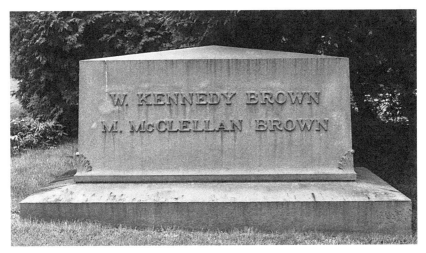

The Browns' memorial marker

of Atlantis. (Those crafts, as you may know, were gigantic, mathematically precise replicas of eagles, made from a magnetic light metal.)

Brown died of ptomaine poisoning in 1916, four years before the ratification of the Nineteenth Amendment. She is buried in Spring Grove alongside her husband, who preceded her by just a year. It's their unusual headstone that drew my attention in the first place. On it, they're granted equal billing, and listed in a way—true to their principles during nearly six decades of partnership—so as to obscure or elide gender. Theirs is a broad, blank stone, unadorned except for two names in stark, simple caps: W. KENNEDY BROWN, and just below it, M. McCLELLAN BROWN.

One striking element of the story of the Ohio Women's Crusade that winter is how quickly and decisively the tone of male response shifted from amusement to pinch-faced sarcasm to grievance to all-out vitriol. Even after due allowance for foam, the rhetoric of Safford and his co-counsels in the Palace Drug Store case seems shocking. And would have to the protesters, too, I think. They'd poked a hornet's nest the size of an Atlantean airship. The patriarchy remained unsmashed, but the tools for its destruction were finally finding their way into women's hands.

I hope the formidable Ms. Brown will take it in the spirit intended if, when the spring thaw comes, I pour one out for her at graveside and hoist one of my own in tribute. I promise to make it one modest beer rather than a wassail bowl holding seventeen.

CHARLES A. MILLER, M.D.
AUG. 27, 1839. — NOV. 21, 1890.

LULU MILLER,
OCT. 23, 1874. — FEB. 16, 1894.

"ANOTHER
WELL-PICKED SKELETON"
HOMUNCULI, MAIL-ORDER TREE STUMPS,
PETRIFIED LOGS, AND THE MANY,
MANY CHARLES MILLERS

FOR MILLENNIA, GRAVEYARDS HAVE BEEN DESTINATIONS for the dead, but the notion of the cemetery as a recreation spot for the living was a nineteenth-century innovation. Spring Grove was in the forefront of the movement toward the grand, spacious, lake-dotted, manicured necropolis—a city of the dead meant to allure those still alive. These new garden cemeteries included a bewildering array of stones and memorials designed to compete for the eye's attention. For citizens of prosperous towns like Cincinnati, grave decoration became a bourgeois sport.

In the realm of funerary monuments, indeed in all the stations of death that took place before interment, Cincinnati grew into a hotbed of ingenuity (see "Death's Taxicab" essay). Artisans produced catafalques, carriages that resembled cathedrals or cakes and later motorized hearses of every description; intricate hardware; coffins with portholes, terra cotta sarcophagi shorn of the "revolting suggestions heretofore connected with their name," and self-sealing zinc caskets; in the early 1880s the Cincinnati School of Embalming became the country's first college of mortuary arts.[1]

Some of what drove the elaborate monument-making was venal earthly competition waged from belowground just as it had been from above. You can't take it with you, but you *can* leave the erectest monolith. But choices of gravesite and marker are trammeled in fascinating ways. There are first of all the practical questions: of what one has to spend, of who—the dead or the survivors, with more mundane expenses in mind—is dictating the spending, and of what is seemly. The powerful vie for real estate, too. Prime locations are limited. The most meretricious markers tend to cluster along Spring Grove's labyrinthine lanes; and high hillsides and southern exposures (Spring Grove runs, generally, uphill from south to north) command extra prestige and require extra cash. Materials have to last, which limits the choice to stone, concrete, or metal. One must depend for the most part on local minerals and the skill sets of local artisans. Family, cultural, and denominational tradition play a role as well. But the chief tension owes less to practicalities than to the fact that in cemeteries, the worldly and the eternal intersect in especially poignant and messy ways.

Extravagant nineteenth-century grave markers were simultaneously modern expressions of self—this a newish idea in the realm of funerary arts—and ancient professions of faith. But the paradox of humbling oneself before God by way of earthly peacocking creates strains. The choices of stone and shape and font and verbiage call for an expression of individuality (or family identity), yes, but that expression must fall within the narrow confines of custom and taste, of What's Done. Here of all places, one must avoid seeming eccentric or self-vaunting or Ozymandias-like. How shall the King of Kings subordinate himself to the Prince of Peace?

More than any other places I know, cemeteries like Spring Grove provide an opportunity to *witness* the drama of the rich trying to thread their camel through the eye of the needle and enter the kingdom of heaven. What they're trying to do is tricky, as Jesus warned. I recall the minister in my childhood church—a congregation of relatively well-off white Presbyterians—going through all kinds of contortions to wriggle clear from the import of those words in Matthew 19: "And again I say unto you, It is easier for a camel to go through the eye of a needle, than for a rich man to enter into the kingdom of God." Jerusalem, the preacher explained, had a low and narrow gate, shaped like an offset keyhole, which would require the cooperation of a patient driver and a limber camel; *that* was what the blood-red letters in our Bibles meant. Even when I was eight or nine, this felt like an attempt at *post hoc* haggling, at a renegotiation of terms. Jesus often spoke in riddling parables, but here he made plain sense: Why was the minister ignoring it? I was unsurprised, years later, to read that so far as is known, Jerusalem had no such gate . . . and to read, too, the argument that even if it did have one, wouldn't the camel-driver—or the savvy plutocrat—simply opt for the larger, easier portals? In fact, wasn't this Jesus' point? Not *Learn contortionism*, but *Choose a wider gate*.

In the cemetery, then, standing out constitutes both chief aim and moral peril. The stock of symbols and materials is scanty. Think of color, for instance: Spring Grove's beveled columns and neoclassical crypts are shows of plumage, but with a palette squinched down to black, gray, brown, and white. Custom, religious doctrine, and social pressure all narrow the choices further. A simple iconographic vocabulary emerged, featuring angels and crosses, willows and flowers, draped urns and upturned lanterns and ankhs and birds and anchors.

All of which is why, I think, departures from expectation—signs of spontaneity or oddity or naked grief—tend to hit the cemetery walker hard. So little eccentricity gets through the filters of sobriety and dignity and custom. Sometimes these departures take the form of prolix in an epitaph: the unartful but touching poem incised by a stonecutter husband for his wife; uptilted tablets inscribed with side-by-side biographies that end abruptly, in one wife's poignant case, with a pointing finger and the legend "I'm with him."[2] A monument for married couples who can't stand to be parted that links two columns with a concrete "rope." Leon Van Loo's artist's palette.

But there are whole genres of monument, once popular, that have long since disappeared, and that have the poignancy of relics, especially for someone, like me, who had never seen them before I came to Spring Grove.

On my walks I've been struck by how many stones feature dogs curled up on rugs to provide company—sometimes with their paws resting on chains they've been unleashed from, almost always with their muzzles resting on the ground, in the posture of grief's eternal torpor.

Not surprisingly, lambs feature prominently in iconography for the graves of children. There's something touching in seeing tininess depicted in a massive medium like stone, in seeing the vocabulary of permanence applied to a state, babyhood, that's supposed to be fleeting. Another thing the cemetery walker can't help noticing is that stones that face upward deteriorate much more quickly than those that face out, and this, too, contributes to the terrible sadness of infants' graves: the lettering has often been worn away or mossed over, and the delicately carved animals or cherubs have faded to indistinctness, have had their limbs whittled and their faces blanked.

To me, though, the most heartbreaking infant stones are the ones that—as if the hurt is too raw for metaphor, and God must be shown what he has done—depict not animal familiars but the children themselves. The most wrenching of these that I know is a small monument pictured here, which I assume depicts twins who died either in childbirth or soon thereafter.

The stone is badly eroded, and in ways that only make it more harrowing to look at. One assumes and hopes that these side-by-side siblings didn't always look quite so fetal, or so homuncular (the weather- or disease-emaciated arms of the one on the left, the knobs of their knees above vanished feet). The irregularity of the surface may once have represented the folds and furrows of swaddling clothes. I've been unable to figure out who the departed are. Their marker is by itself, several feet away from any other, pinched between the plots of two families they might belong to or might not. The closest thing is a stone marker with writing long since worn away to indiscernibility—no help there. The style of the stone and the age of the graves in proximity to it would suggest that these two infants died in the second half of the nineteenth century; the condition of the stone might imply the early end of that spectrum.

Tree-stump stones appealed to consumers (the prospective dead, a category that includes us all) in part because of their versatility, because of the options for personalization—type of tree, texture of trunk, details of branching, plus the possibility of a medallion at every chink or limb. In the United States, this iconography peaked in popularity from the 1880s to the 1920s, by which point tastes had changed and production costs had become prohibitive.

Such stones are common in Victorian cemeteries, especially in the South and Midwest, and they're most often identified with the Woodmen of the World, a fraternal organization that was founded in 1882, flourished through World War I, and limps along even today. The W.O.W. was founded by Joseph Cullen Root, who was inspired by a sermon about frontier woodsmen clearing the land to make way for prosperity—and by the implied metaphor of his own surname, which contributed to the development of the organization's symbology. (The W.O.W. consisted of local "Groves" that together made up a "Supreme Forest" ruled over by a "Sovereign Camp.")

Fraternal organizations ranged from the ecumenical, racially progressive, and immigrant-friendly all the way to the Ku Klux Klan (which required members to be white, Protestant, and native-born), and they were near-ubiquitous in the late nineteenth century. There were dozens or even hundreds, of every aim and description. These clubs often restricted membership to men, but had a female auxiliary or separate sororal group (the WKKK would be one grim example); one women's Freemasonry offshoot—organizations did love their pomp and their preposition trains—was known as the Cauldrons of the Mystic Order of Veiled Prophets of the Enchanted Realm. Around the turn of the twentieth century, it was estimated that just the three biggest such groups, the Oddfellows, the Freemasons, and the Knights of Pythias, could boast membership of around five million—more than 5 percent of the total American population.

Early on, Root and his offshoots, tendrils, sprigs, and boughs embraced the emerging trend of the tree-trunk gravestone. Such markers, often featuring the W.O.W. logo and the inscription "Dum Tacet Clamat" ("Though Silent, He Speaks"), became so identified with the Woodmen that from 1890 to 1900, the group offered a rider to every life insurance policy—like other fraternal organizations, it offered a nonprofit insurance pool—that would provide a

A faithful mourner, resting on chains

Twins

Memorial for Jacob Fritz and family

Andrew Ernst's marker

The family Wheeler, with petrified log behind

tree-trunk monument for the deceased, should he die in a state of paid-up grace. The striking markers (an upright stump for grownups, with additional height and additional lopped branches available for a fee, and three stacked logs for children) grew popular enough that the Sears Roebuck catalog began to offer similar markers to the public: "The Sturdy, Grand Trunk of a Tree for $28.75 (and upwards)." The masonry monuments Sears offered might even be seen, I suppose, as the company's gateway to the famous kit houses they would begin offering in 1908.

The Woodmen of the World still exist as an insurance nonprofit, recently reorganized under the awkward moniker WoodmenLife, but if they're known widely these days, it's mainly to taphophiles (as graveyard enthusiasts, another sorority with a taste for sonority, sometimes style themselves), Nebraskans (company headquarters are in Omaha), and fans of that state's unofficial film-maker laureate Alexander Payne, in whose *About Schmidt* (2002) the curmud-geonly title character, played by Jack Nicholson, is a retiring W.O.W. actuary.

And—full disclosure—the Woodmen of the World haunted my early adolescence. When I was in sixth grade, my parents forced me to take a ballroom-dancing class. This was by far the most calamitous moment in their campaign to sivilize me, and if I'd had anything like Huck's moxie and ability to fend for himself, and if there had been territories handy, here is where I would have lit out for them. Instead, I sobbed in the way-back of our station wagon—featuring a stripe of fake-woodgrain all the way around, another of destiny's cruel and petty ironies that I couldn't see then—and afterward dutifully clipped on a tie and went to learn the waltz and the cha-cha and the Virginia reel. Classes were held behind the defunct whites-only high school, which had closed less than a decade before, in a tiny building on a side street that looked from the front like a 1950s ranch-style house. The W.O.W. Hall was designed, it occurs to me now, like a passage to the after-life. Outside was the first handicapped ramp I ever saw, a serpentine path with rails. Once you wound your way across the Lethe, you'd pause at the door, look back, and—the ferrywoman having been paid by the vision of her child in formalwear, tugging on a door too big for him—Mom's station wagon would creep away from the curb. You entered a combination vestibule/cloak-room that was religious in the queasy-quasi way of funeral homes. Beyond it was the main hall, an open room lined down each side wall, in military-cemetery uniformity, with gravestones—or in this case, with yellow-pine folding chairs printed with the clumsily stenciled names of the Woodmen dead. As in Spring Grove, most but not all of the names in my South Carolina hometown were German: Fersner, Shuler, Wannamaker, Inabinet, Gressette, Fogle.

Boys were told to sit on one side, girls on the other. Some kids from old Orangeburg families took care to choose their ancestors' chairs, rousting interlopers who'd accidentally plopped down on Uncle Shug or Grandpa Felkel. I've never felt more hapless and forlorn (though to be honest, I didn't often in adolescence feel *less* hapless and forlorn, either) than I did among those wooden grave markers. They were apt to squeal or to collapse with a crash if vacated too quickly, as always happened when the teacher gave permission for the boys (or, on exactly one occasion per night, the girls) to proceed "at a polite and restrained, a *gentlemanly*, clip" across the floor to ask for a dance. Ten or fifteen seconds after the first, confident wave left, I'd look down the row and see that there were just two or three of us now clinging to our flotsam, hoping in vain to have been swallowed by a swell. But still the traitorous chairs held us up. "Chop, chop!" our teacher would say, her little woodman joke.

Spring Grove contains many tree-trunk stones, as one might expect. Unusually, though, many of them precede both the fashion and the Woodmen of the World. The oldest I've found is for Andrew Ernst, born in the winter of 1796 and died just after his sixty-fourth birthday, in 1860. In Ernst's case, the tree trunk—mounted on a rock and decorated with a scroll that gives (in his native German) birth and death dates—was a personal tribute: Ernst was a horticulturist, the author of *Catalogue of Fruit and Forest Trees, Ornamental Shrubs, Plants, Cultivated and for Sale at the Spring Garden Nursery* (1843), and, as a director of Spring Grove, among the shapers of the cemetery's landscape. Near the bottom of his tree-trunk, a flower, still lovely after 160 years, is incised into the stone.

My favorite subgenre of Spring Grove gravestone, though, is the petrified log. In cross-section, with their ends planed and polished, they're gorgeous: a rich marble with tones of russet, black, pink, yellow, and cream that indicate the presence of iron oxides and manganese. The bark is craggy and dark, but the ends look neatly lumberjacked, an effect of the fact that quartz—like chalk—tends to break in straight planes. One such log, unadorned except for its smoothed ends, sits on the ground; two others are displayed on high plinths. (There may be more such stones in the cemetery, but I know of only three.)[3] The petrified logs bear some resemblance, physical and metaphorical, to tree-trunk stones, only in this case with the artisan middleman or middlewoman cut out; this is not stone playacting as wood, but stone naturally transmuted from it over millions of years.

As I understand it, most of the massive petrified logs one sees scattered around the country—the biggest here I'd estimate at four feet in diameter and five feet long—were plundered from petrified forests, especially out West, during the first decades of the twentieth century. In the 1920s in Texas, petrified wood was so plentiful and was considered so unremarkable that it sold for $5 a truckload. By the 1930s, the depredations had grown bad enough that something had to be done, and large-scale removal was forbidden. Whether coincidentally or by preservationists' clever design, a myth emerged about a mummy-style curse on those who took souvenirs from the Petrified Forest National Park in northeastern Arizona, and people started returning their ill-gotten gains, often accompanied by letters of apology. Once removed from their scientific context, though, the logs could not be returned to their original places, so at entrances to the park there accumulated towering piles of "Conscience Wood" given back by people bedeviled, post-visit and post-"theft," by romantic disappointments, medical woes, sour luck, or the kind of general blahs that we'd all like to attribute to hexes rather than thinking of them as our lives' ground state.

As a concept, Conscience Wood appeals because it helps whisk away guilt, yes, but the decluttering achieved by returning one's ill-got gain is not only moral but physical. Easy to understand the desire to take home a piece of such a lovely place, one whose time-scale inspires awe and gives a glimpse of the sublime. We feel the urge even at truck stops, amusement parks, and roadside attractions. How many shot glasses or postcards or baseball caps do we accumulate over a life? And where do we store them? This problem becomes more acute if our vacation pelf is staggeringly, chassis-loweringly heavy, and if it's been moved hundreds or thousands of miles. Once you drag your white elephant home, what do you *do* with it?

Twenty-five years ago, I began a novel about barbershops that I could never quite get traction in, though I accumulated pages of notes, snippets of conversation (asked "How you doin'?" by a Baton Rouge scissorman, one of my fellow customers answered, cheerfully, "Everything's chicken but the gravy"), and the Louisiana barbering license, including rules for cuspidor cleaning and placement, that a friend somehow scammed for me from the state board. Soon after my wife and I bought our first house, a friend who was moving away offered to sell me, for $25, a vintage barber chair. I jumped at the chance.

I loved that thing, a finned beauty from the golden age of Populuxe, maybe the 1950s? It was greenish aqua, hailed from St. Louis, and was streamlined like a Cadillac, with sleek lines and a lacquered-leather cushioned footrest for comfort. If it was wet outside and shoes were dirty, the cushion could be flipped to become a grille to catch mud.

The buyer's remorse began immediately, when my friend and I struggled mightily to get the chair—bleeding hydraulic fluid whenever it tilted too steeply—into the bed of his pickup. This turned out to be prelude to an even direr struggle to get the chair out and down at my end. What was I to do with my prize? No floor in our house could hold it up, we couldn't afford to reinforce the joists, and I could scarcely ask my spouse to sacrifice one of our few rooms to accommodate my ridiculous trophy. The chair became a secret fetish, to be visited occasionally in the garage, unveiled, slap-dusted with a rag the way the barber would do it, and then sat in, briefly, before I moved on to whatever task had called me out there in the first place: finding a post-hole digger or extricating the lawnmower from its straitjacket of junk. Soon the thing started shaming me—My Moral Hazard, a reminder of the perils of acquisitiveness. Life is short, and heavy shit is immovable, and what the hell were you *thinking*? We sold the house and moved away fifteen years ago, and it's been through at least two owners since, but my guess is that the chair still sits dead center in its garage crypt, under its bedsheet shroud; it's an ancestor I should pack a picnic and go pay homage to.

The story with petrified wood might be similar, I'd think. Most logs I've seen in the Midwest have been donated to museums or park systems, churches or fire stations. What else can one do with them? Touchstone becomes millstone becomes . . . yes, right—life turns to death, wood to rock, and permanent transitions need to be marked with incalculably heavy things.

Two of the petrified-log stones I know of in Spring Grove mark the resting places of lumber magnates and their families; the other is more mysterious.

The log placed modestly on the ground seems to belong to a family from San Mateo, California: Margaret Culbertson Wheeler (1878–1960), her husband John Egbert Wheeler (1879–1943), and their son William, who died before them, in 1938, at twenty-nine, and was the first buried here. The plot belonged to Margaret's father; she had grown up in Cincinnati. But attributing the stone to the Wheelers requires a little guesswork, since the log is unadorned and unlabeled. Its connection to the family has to be surmised from proximity and the orientation of their graves. The stones are aimed toward the petrified log but not centered on it . . . an asymmetry that owes, I think, to room being left for a second son, John Pogue Wheeler, who died in Ithaca, New York, in 1979 and was buried there with his wife.

There's also the circumstantial evidence that John Egbert Wheeler was by trade a timberman, part owner or director in some fourteen lumber companies, as well as the one-time publisher of the Portland (OR) *Telegram* and a high muckety-muck in the Associated Press. I have no idea how the petrified log came to Spring Grove, or when, but it seems reasonable to infer that it was placed at the time of William Wheeler's untimely death, perhaps as a wayfinder for visitors from afar, since all three Wheeler stones are small, discreet, flush-to-the-ground markers in a crowded part of the cemetery.

All three Wheelers died in California and were cremated, perhaps for ease of shipping—an option not available for the stone.

The Robertson family plot is well-populated; I count more than a dozen inhabitants, beginning with Charlie and Grace, six- and four-year-old siblings who died of scarlet fever just three weeks apart in 1878. Among the others buried here are the Reuben Buck Robertsons, Senior and Junior. The elder Reuben was born in Cincinnati in 1879 and graduated from Yale in 1900. Among his classmates in New Haven was John Egbert Wheeler.

Reuben Buck Robertson Sr. began his career as a lawyer, but in late 1907 his father-in-law, Peter Thomson, owner of Champion Coated Paper, pressed him into service—for a planned fifty-day stint—to oversee the opening of a pulp mill near Asheville. Robertson would die at ninety-three in 1972, having spent the last sixty-five years of his life in western North Carolina, for much of that time as president or chairman of the board of Champion.

In my childhood, as environmental awareness took shallow, tentative root in the chemically leached soils of the filthy early 1970s, paper-mill owners were the South's ecological villains-in-chief. This was after the infamous Cuyahoga River fire of 1969,[4] the beginnings of Earth Day and of the Environmental Protection Agency (1970), and also that year's revised Clean Air Act, which for the first time allowed for the development of ambient-air standards around factories. Part of the bad reputation of pulp mills (among those who didn't have jobs reliant upon them, I should say) may have had to do with their being especially egregious offenders—paper is resource-intensive and contributes significantly to water and to air pollution—but much of the public odium was due to literal odium, those tall stacks spewing plumes of stench. Paper mills were the most conspicuous heavy industry in the region thanks in part to the use of the bleaching agent sulfur dioxide, a chemical required in prodigious amounts to transform yellow southern pine into white paper.

As in almost every region of the United States at the time, there were towns one held one's nose while traveling through. Jesup, Georgia, in the early 1970s home to the largest pulp mill on Earth, was a pungent example—as was Georgetown, South Carolina. (A side note: for over fifty years, the response from locals to outlanders' held or wrinkled noses, choking sounds, or impertinent questions has been word for word the same in every milltown in the country, I think: "That's the smell of money." Its corollary in towns near military airfields, and often indignant: "That's the sound of freedom.")

No doubt we can, if inclined, charge Reuben Buck Robertson with his share in the defoliation and despoliation of old-growth forests, the fouling of the air, the rise of acid rain, and the rest of the dire symptoms of an environment under siege that we now have no choice but to recognize.[5] But by all accounts Robertson was an unusual lumber czar. Under his leadership, Champion was scientifically innovative; it was the first major paper company to create an in-house lab and to give some deference to its researchers' findings. Champion achieved two breakthroughs that made large-scale paper production in the South possible. The first involved marrying a commercial interest with an environmental one. Since the introduction to North America of a fungal blight from Japan in 1904, both the American chestnut and, in the upland South, the chinquapin (also known as dwarf chestnut) had been dying out. By 1940, those tree stocks would essentially disappear from the East. Champion scientists discovered a way to extract tannins from dead and dying trees and make satisfactory pulp from them, thus becoming the first to manufacture paper from so-called "spent wood." The second? In the 1920s, the company devised a way to make high-quality paper pulp from plentiful southern pine, which led to the explosive growth of the region's timber industry.

Robertson was also an innovator in worker safety, profit-sharing, and pension benefits. It should be noted that the principle underlying these grants was not negotiation (Champion wasn't unionized) but noblesse oblige. Robertson's style was often called—not decried as: the term seemed meant often as a compliment—paternalistic. Champion was at the time a private company, run by Robertson's father-in-law as a hereditary monarchy. Thomson even had a rule of primogeniture, which stipulated that the power structure should include one member—preferably the first-born male child—from each branch of the family. But rank-and-file workers had steady jobs at better than prevailing wages, and by the standards of his time, if Reuben Buck Robertson was a despot, he was a benevolent one.

Unlike many peers, Robertson pursued an interest in sustainability—or, as it would then have been called, in stewardship. One lasting contribution, only partly intentional, was his role in selling the government almost a hundred thousand acres of North Carolina timberland in the early days of the Depression. The acquisition of that acreage finally assured that the long-planned Smoky Mountains National Park, just the second or third such park east of the Mississippi, would become a reality. But the sale was made under some duress, and the infusion of cash it provided was hugely useful to the company in a lean season; Robertson excelled in aligning his commercial and environmental aims.

Perhaps his greatest ecological contribution, again born from that intersection of profit motive and ethics, was that he pioneered the replanting of logged forests and the creation of flood prevention programs. Robertson Sr. is thought to have introduced the concept of the renewable "tree farm," and he proposed a long fifty-year cycle for harvesting. This strategy led, too, to be fair, to the predomination of loblolly and slash pines and the near-disappearance of slower-growing natives like the longleaf, which requires fire to germinate—but Robertson did far more than might be expected of a midcentury pulpwood titan.

After World War II, during which he served on FDR's National War Labor Board, Robertson proved to be an ardent Cold War anticommunist and, in late life at least, a devoted Republican. His archives at North Carolina State contain at least one box relating to a series of talks about "Our Imperiled Free Enterprise System," and there's also a copy of Richard Nixon's nomination acceptance speech at the 1968 Republican National Convention in Miami Beach. (My guess is that Robertson, nearly ninety, probably didn't venture to Miami and wade through the chaos of the convention and its surrounding moat of protests; a copy of the acceptance speech sounds like a perk extended to whale donors who couldn't attend in person.)

The sad story of Reuben Buck Robertson Jr. offers another indicator of the family's Republican bona fides. A Yale graduate like his father, Reuben Jr.—as first son—was expected to enter the family business, and did. His career at Champion was interrupted twice by national service, first in World War II and then by a stint as deputy secretary of defense under Dwight Eisenhower. Reuben Jr. was energetic and forthright, it seems: as one Champion executive put it, after meetings with the boss, he left "with the feeling that I've had a missile up my rear end." (But in a *good* way—this is not the *other* kind of ICBM suppository.)

Reuben Buck Robertson Sr.

Longview State Hospital

In March 1960, Robertson Jr. and his wife, Peggy, were returning home from a social event in Cincinnati when he sideswiped a stalled vehicle in the darkness. When Robertson got out to help the stranded motorist, he was struck and killed by another car. After his death, it was reported that he had been high on Republicans' short list of vice presidential nominees. Nixon eventually chose Henry Cabot Lodge, and America chose JFK.

I intend, here, neither hagiography nor demonography, and even if I were inclined to judgment, I don't know enough to make one stick about the Reuben Buck Robertsons; I'll leave that to historians or to gods. I mainly want to note in their lives a set of tensions that remain anguishingly familiar to us, and that are exemplified, too, by the petrified log that became the family's graveyard trademark (if you read the choice of the log as a declaration of pride) or talisman (if you see it as a mark of submission to God/nature). Again, petrified logs were often removed from their eons-long resting places singly, by tourists, not for profit but out of awe and admiration—as a way, perhaps, of keeping close to hand and to mind a little shard of the sublime, with its reminder of our puny scale and its injunction to humility. In the end people mean well, or want to. In some sense this is the message that graveyards are meant to convey, too. We may have sucked, but we *aspired* not to, and cemeteries are records not of our deeds so much as of what we meant to do, and to be.

These same tensions are visible in Reuben Buck Robertson Sr.'s business practices, in the combination of environmental ruin with stewardship and concern—just as they can be seen in our own struggles with carbon footprints and ethical vegetarianism and so forth. We're temporary, yet we flit and fret and fail within the flow of something like permanence. How to balance our needs and our values, the now and the later, the imperatives of biology and of morality?

There's a terrific short story by Joan Connor about a mid-nineteenth-century showman, a wannabe rival to Barnum, who buys a whale, has it thoroughly embalmed, and travels with it from city to city to extol the miracles of the sea, to give landlubbers an idea of cetacean scale and wonder. The problem, inevitably, is that over the months that he barnstorms, or pier-storms, the carcass steadily deteriorates, bloats, putresces. The crowds thin, then disappear; the dream sours with the corpse. At the end, the impresario sinks into despair:

> When he surfaces in my nightmares now, I stave his rubbery hide with the pointed toe of my blacked boot. Maggots squirm from the hole I gore there, and this fetid wisdom effuses: We are all swallowed up. We drop like forgotten carcasses back into an immense sea where we bloat, leucous and flabby, and rock in a cradle of decay.

While the hucksters scream, and the carnies play their shell games, and the hawkers hand out flybills with frenetic futility, the whole of us, from birth, goes on and on, putrefying from within from this primitive knowledge: memorize it; we are meat.[6]

We are meat. In my experience, the person who purveys this truth almost always wants to lay claim to being more a realist than the rest of us—even if, in this impresario's case, as his dais day by day sank lower into the carcass, the fact required no great feat to figure out. But not all wisdom needs to be fetid. There's wisdom, too, in Reuben Buck Robertson Sr.'s replanted seedlings; in the attempt at Good Samaritanship that left his son, the certificate coldly reports, "D.O.A." at the hospital; and even in the petrified log set atop a plinth in a cemetery, offered as an object of veneration. *We* can't last, but some things can.

If we don't fuck them up.

Which leads to the mystery of the third petrified-log stone. It's a gorgeous specimen, and unmissably placed at the confluence of two cemetery roads. Four family members' names are raised in low relief in its sides. The first of these to die was Charles A. Miller, at age fifty-nine in 1890. His daughter Lulu is buried alongside him. Miller's elder brother Isaac (1833–1910) and his wife, Martha (1838–1913), occupy the other two spaces.

A book like the present one, centered on a grand mid-nineteenth-century cemetery in a midwestern American city, will almost inevitably suffer from what my social-scientist friends call self-selection bias. For reasons of geography, ethnicity, racial and gender politics, religion, economics, cultural mores of the time, and research materials left behind, the available subjects in Spring Grove skew white, male, Christian, German or English, wealthy, and prominent. But I have succumbed to another, perhaps less obvious kind of selection bias, too: peculiarity of name. First of all, I'm more likely to look up a name that's unfamiliar or dimly familiar; second, I'm less likely to get enmeshed in a Googly canebrake while researching Phoebe Zepenrick or Temperance Keckeler than while pursuing, say, Charles Miller.

By my count, no fewer than sixty Charles Millers reside in Spring Grove. And when I poked my head down the rabbit hole of the *Cincinnati Enquirer* archives for 1872–1922, it quickly got stuck.

Was this Charles Miller . . .

- the man who suicided twice in the same day, failing the first time because he knocked over his boardinghouse chifforobe while making the rope tight, thus drawing a crowd, and then regathered his energies and several hours later fulfilled his aim, resulting in the poignant head-line "Charles Miller Hangs Himself Because His Heart Is Oppressed"?

- the drunken stabbing victim of 1874? Or perhaps the drunken stabber ("he certainly cut to kill") of 1878?

- the one whose death notice was accidentally mixed up with an ad for "Tropic-Fruit Laxative" (1883)?

- the early-voting-machine advocate?

- the one bitten by a mad dog on the shoulder near an incline railway, then rescued by a "well-known wrestler [who] killed the brute"?

- the one who fell to his death down a narrow hatchway at a furniture maker's, with the result described in photorealistic detail: "His fea-tures were mashed beyond recognition, and a wide fracture of the skull exposing the brain substance"?

- the milkman who clobbered a colleague with a bell in 1887?

- the one arrested in 1888 for stealing a horse and carriage who, denied permission to change into prison stripes behind a privacy curtain, was forced to acknowledge being a woman in long-term drag?

- the train brakeman who offed himself with morphine, motive unknown?

- the old man who nearly killed one of his coevals with a gridiron after a merciless bit of "kidding"?

- the one who fell under the wheels of a freight train while rushing to a baseball game?

- the bartender who poisoned himself with carbolic acid after his wife died young?

- the barber who eloped with another man's spouse in 1886 (the news-paper describing the scandalous couple this way: "one the wife of an ice-cream man, and the other a Knight of the Razor")?

- the local politician who gave a tub-thumping speech at the Soldiers' and Sailors' Memorial Association in 1881?

- or the one, formerly an Indianapolis cigar-maker, who died soon after moving to Cincinnati, had no relatives findable by telegram or other conventional mode of inquiry, couldn't be buried by the cigar-maker's union because his dues were delinquent, and thus had his corpse claimed for research by the Indiana Medical College ("and it was not long until another well-picked skeleton graced the laboratory of that institution")—and only then did the Aetna Company and his relatives arrive to reclaim the skeleton and establish that this was indeed the Charles Miller who had taken out a hefty life insurance policy?

None of those possibilities panned out. Nor did this turn out to be the Charles A. Miller (glimpsed above as the golden-tongued Soldiers' and Sailors' orator) who was for decades the dean of Cincinnati undertakers . . . and who, it happens, appears in that professional capacity on the death certificate of his namesake, *our* Charles A. Miller.

This Charles turns out to be the one who was, for twelve tempestuous years late in the century, superintendent of the county's insane asylum, Longview. Early in his tenure, scandal erupted when attendants were found to be abusing patients—or perhaps we should say were abusing them in unprescribed ways, as opposed to the brutal treatment that was then standard. Mental hospitals in those days were warehouses for the weird and damaged (or rather the "weird" and "damaged," categories that at the time would have included such "afflictions" as promiscuity, uppitiness, poverty, and a wide variety of physical disabilities cruelly transposed into mental ones). Loud, fetid, chronically overcrowded, understaffed and underfunded, depressing, dangerous, and with medical science lagging far behind the ability of modern life to produce new and befuddling forms of "madness," these institutions were chaotic in the extreme. (No accident, of course, that the word *bedlam* derives from the name of London's most notorious madhouse—which in turn derived its name from Bethlehem, slurred and shortened. Nor that, in every place I've lived, whenever a child was acting "crazy," parents warned that such unruliness would land you in the state asylum: South Carolina kids were threatened with internment at "Bull Street," Georgia kids with a one-way ticket to "Milledgeville," Louisianans with "Pineville," and so on.)

It was during Miller's tenure at Longview that, to write an exposé for the *New York World*, journalist Nellie Bly famously feigned madness and was remanded to that city's Bellevue Hospital. Her stay resulted in the muckraking classic *Ten Days in a Mad-House*, in which Bly documented deplorable conditions (gruel, wormy bread, and unpotable water served amid piles of human waste and teeming rats), abuse (patients roped together, beatings, viciously administered ice baths), and the constant looming threat of rape. In 1879, Longview was engulfed by an abuse scandal of its own, and the new superintendent, who professed perfect ignorance of the punishments being doled out by his staff, was castigated in the press and suspended from his duties. The ugly scene played out in the papers over many months.

Miller showed himself to be pugnacious (and grammatically plural). Asked what he would do about what he saw as a political ploy to scapegoat him and relieve him of his keys, Miller told the *Enquirer*, prophetically, "Do about it? . . . We will show you what we will do about it. I hope you may live long enough to see the end. I come of a stock that doesn't give up, you know." He added that to get the institution into its present apple-pie order, he'd "had to fight a lot of g-d d—d set of rum-gullions," a phrase notable not only for its pungency and its fearless obscenity, but for the sputtering pleonastic rage of "a lot of . . . set of" and the glorious neologism "rum-gullion." A "gullion" is an old dialectal word for sewer, and a "slumgullion" is a foul, thin stew; one guesses that perhaps rum-gullions are the swillers of rotgut liquor? Dr. Miller was indignant, and not averse to saying so.

Because Longview was a public institution, Miller had been appointed by the governor, and the inquiry would be conducted by his partisan allies. Even so, the investigators' report dispensed harsh criticism. Among the accusations were that attendants routinely "took down" female prisoners, then held them in place with a knee to the chest while the patient was gagged, and that they "spread-eagled" men (a punishment that involved stripping patients, pinioning all four limbs, and administering a beating with wet towels, the weapon chosen to leave minimal marks); that force-feeding and the like were common; and in general that attendants ruled like petty tyrants. The committee found that the evidence "seems to destroy entirely the suggestion that the various hideous things were done without [Superintendent Miller's] knowledge and consent."

The *Enquirer* piled on with a story called "How Dr. Miller Does His Own Body-Snatching." It provided a grisly account of Miller's autopsy lab: "The pipe spoken of is for the purpose of carrying off the flesh and offal of the corpses cut up in the interests of science (?) by the enterprising Superintendent." (That parenthetical question mark!)

But once public outrage ebbed, the defiant Miller was restored to his post. That's no surprise. I'd bet that the defense he mounted behind closed doors— this phenomenon remains common today—boiled down to the assertion that he was exercising lordly disregard of the minute-by-minute details; Miller had *by design* not known what was going on. He was a doctor, hired to administer limited funds and minister to not-nearly-limited-enough patients. If order reigned, if deaths by "marasmus" (essentially starvation) dropped, and if no one was out-and-out murdered by an attendant, then he was doing his job. The old "It's an ugly business, and you and I know it, and let's let the public hoo-ha die down, introduce minor reforms, make sure we plug any leaks, and proceed" prescription.

Accusations of corruption or malfeasance continued throughout the decade, as did Miller's salty pushback, and he remained a punching bag for the *Enquirer*. In 1881, a previously docile board member, a retired minister named Chalfant, objected to the way the asylum's meat-supply contracts worked. The *Enquirer's* account of the furor included a damning subtitle that it set in quotes—"Bulls and Dairy Cows' Beef Good Enough for Lunatics." But the subtitle turns out to capture not what anyone said, but rather the sentiment the reporter *imputes* to the butchers and the asylum's powers-that-be. (By the way, an implicated supplier, Jacob Fritz, who at one time provided the hospital with 500 pounds of meat per day, would die a couple years later and be buried under perhaps Spring Grove's most rococo tree-trunk stone, this one topped with a classical female figure. A photo of it appears earlier in this essay.)

The *Enquirer* article about the set-to ends with an ode of praise to the crusading Chalfant: The "doughty superintendent" will rue the day he "had the temerity to throw down the glove" at the feet of his "new-made enemy." The minister boasts, "Oh, I've only begun. The meat business disposed of, I'll then be ready to take up the heavy whiskey bills." Pa-dum-*pum*.

Over the coming years, Chalfant would prove to be an unappeasable enemy, and he was aided by the paper, which provided a steady backing drumbeat of criticism in articles like "Miller's Mischief" and "The Way Superintendent Miller Cures 'Em," an 1881 one-off that accuses the superintendent of releasing incurable or intractable patients to fend for themselves so that they don't count against his statistics. On a few occasions there are pieces predicting Miller's departure or reporting the rumor that he "would make a virtue of necessity" and resign. There's even a weird bit of Tinseltown-type myth-making, an article in which the heroic Chalfant calls a meeting of the narrowly divided (but Miller-supporting) Board of Directors, then tears up the road to the asylum behind his "magnificent span of grays," only to be thwarted by the others, cowards who've manufactured excuses to stay away and deprive him of a quorum.

The Rum-Gullion Slumgullion finally boiled over in 1883, when the time came to reappoint or replace Dr. Miller at the end of his five-year term. The *Enquirer* account of the climactic meeting is one of the most gleefully mischievous articles I've ever seen, an evisceration in a comic key. Bearing the title "Hot Directors" and the glorious subtitle "It Proves to Be a Regular Parrot and Monkey Time," the article begins with an account of the tensions among the board before the meeting convenes: "It was plainly seen that the Directors were not true followers of Damon & Pythias, as the greetings between them partook slightly of the nature of icebergness." From there the scene deteriorates quickly. Portly men are said to swell with indignation, thighs get clouted for emphasis, and the seething pot is set to "boiling most fiercely." Stains upon character, trickery, disgrace, and dishonor are invoked.

The reporter clearly delights in the pure juvenile scrap and yawp of this. I'm reminded of the time, twenty years ago in Baton Rouge, when I was playing in a basketball rec league and a teammate, an engineer named Sean, was tossed from a game—and when he kept screaming, thrown out of the gym—for abusing a referee. Ten minutes later, the game long since resumed, the door along the baseline flew open, bringing with it a whoosh of winter chill, and there was Sean again, resuming his monologue as if it had never been interrupted: "And another thing . . ." After about ten seconds, the startled official found his voice and said, "I kicked you out!" At this point, Sean flashed a triumphant grin. Then he squatted, pointed at his shoes, which were one inch outside the doorway's metal threshold, and crowed, "I *am* out!" It was infantile in a way that was utterly exhilarating to watch—and all the more so because Sean pointed to his feet, from about six inches away, with *both hands*, and because his shoes were, as always, aged low-tops wrapped heavily but inexplicably with duct tape. He looked like a Halloween spaceman showing off his tinfoil boots. Oh, the joy of parrot and monkey time for those who get to look on, unimplicated.

Back in 1883 Cincinnati, the Board of Directors meeting ended, as it was destined to, with a 3–2 vote to renew Dr. Miller. Afterward, the *Enquirer* cast out its vanquished knight, even allowing Miller a measure of revenge in "Plain Talk: Dr. Miller, of Longview, Tells Something He Knows about Dr. Chalfant" (1884). Miller suggests that his rival is a skinflint, a busybody, a liar, and a speaker from both sides of his mouth who publicly objects but privately praises the superintendent's methods; he says that Chalfant wanted special privileges, and demanded whenever he was at Longview that someone from the asylum dance attendance on his horse and carriage—that "magnificent span of grays" we heard about. But all the asylum's employees are *busy*, Miller avers; everyone has crucial duties to perform, and "Does he expect we will get down on our knees and bow to the great Mogul?"

Miller's boldest cut? Echoing the minister's earlier jab at him, he tut-tuts Chalfant's "looking at wine too long when it is red" and laments the ex-churchman's "sickness in consequence." This is the one accusation that the paper tries, in passing, to rebut, noting that it's hard to believe given Chalfant's "well-known abstemious habits."

Miller's relationship with the newspaper never grew cuddly, and intermittent criticism continued, most harshly after a patient was scalded to death in 1885. But Miller mostly kept out of the limelight—so much so that the *Enquirer* seemed almost to miss its old adversary. In 1886, a squib details the paper's prank call to the asylum to ask, "Who Is Superintendent of Longview?" An accusation lay under the question: The superintendent was said to have been on leave in Florida for a month, tending his "private schemes," but there was no hint as to what those schemes were or how often and lastingly they kept him away. Once Miller consolidated power in 1883, there seems to have been no renewed threat to his position until his death from complications of diabetes in 1890. By the end, Miller had so faded from public attention that no pomp attended his death. The funeral was conducted discreetly out of Longview, and the *Enquirer* seems to have eschewed any obituary notice. There's an unusual note on his death certificate, ostensibly to spare him the stigma of madness; Miller's place of death is given, overexplanatorily, as "Longview where he was supt."

One imagines, in those final years, a somewhat lonely, isolated life for Miller and his family. The superintendent's quarters and the grounds of Longview—sloping down to the fouled and nasty waters of the canal, with the cries and moans and chitterings of the poor patients as constant backdrop—must have seemed both a gilded cage and a nagging reminder of the tragedy that had befallen them there. Sometime toward the beginning of Miller's time at Longview, the daughter buried alongside him, Lulu, her parents' only child, sustained grievous injuries in a fall from a window while playing. She was permanently paralyzed. Lulu would outlive her father by just fifteen months, dying at age nineteen of an abscess. Afterward her mother remarried, and Matilda Oberdieck Miller Kiechler lived on for nearly three decades. She is buried alongside her second husband, not far away from the family that predeceased her.

But why and whence the Millers' petrified log? I find not a clue in the public record. Perhaps it was acquired by Charles's older brother Isaac, a lawyer and politician? Perhaps it was kicked up by Dr. Miller's "private schemes"? A gift from a grateful family on behalf of a "mooncalf" or "loony" whose suffering the doctor alleviated . . . or just removed from everyday sight? There's no way to know.

We know, of course, that we won't last, can't last. Nor can we control what scraps of our lives will survive us. How will we be remembered, and for how long, and by whom? Which stories or details will catch in the sieve of memory? Years ago, when I was at the *Southern Review*, we published a black comedy by Stephen Dobyns called "A Happy Vacancy."[7] The story begins with an austere formalist poet, Jason W. Plover, a man who for decades has cultivated a reputation for high seriousness and devotion to his art, walking one morning through Boston. Meanwhile a helicopter, hauling a pig to a film shoot in a heavy-duty sling, zips overhead. But the truss fails, the hog plummets, and the poet gets crushed to death in a crosswalk.

This reads, fleetingly, as just a mean joke on Dobyns's part, a revenge against stuffed shirts in the literary world, perhaps—the piping Plover was doomed by the time he was named. But Dobyns digs in, takes his silly premise with perfect seriousness, and the story turns out, touchingly, to be about the grieving widow's plight: How, after such an exit, to reclaim her husband's prestige and his work's? How to return some semblance of the dignity he spent his life cultivating when in the public imagination he's been cast forevermore as the highbrow laughably lowered, crushed into a "splop of jelly" by a flying pig? In his surprising way, Dobyns poses a question well worth asking: What vanity is more pitiful—or more poignant and inevitable—than the one that moves us to try, and fail, to dictate the terms we're remembered by?

Gravestones, and this is true a fortiori of markers made of living-things-turned-over-eons-to-rock, represent an attempt—conscious or not, self-ironizing or not—to claim for ourselves a limited permanence. We mark our fleetingness with something durable; it's a gesture of defiance and surrender at the same time. But we cannot control what the relict of our time on earth will be. What of us will land in newspaper archives, obituaries, anecdotes, the fading or unreliable memories of friends and spouses, the long, whispered game of telephone that is posterity? Who will be left to mourn us, or to celebrate us, or to defend the tatters of our (the very word seems absurd) *honor*?

Flesh decomposes, memory fails, archives burn or molder. We are gradually reduced to the stories about us that seem most sordid or entertaining or quirky (poor Sean! poor Plover!), and then to unnamed shades and after-echoes. But a petrified log will hold up. And maybe, just maybe, it will move some passerby to dig further into our pasts before every vestige fades.

OUTLOOK HAZY

LAURA PRUDEN, HARRY HOUDINI, AND ARTHUR CONAN DOYLE INTERROGATE THE SPIRITS

ON A JUNE SUNDAY IN 1922, Harry Houdini, Arthur Conan Doyle, and the latter's spouse Jean Leckie Conan Doyle gathered in an Atlantic City hotel suite for a séance to summon the spirit of Houdini's mother. Houdini was a skeptic of spiritualism, and one with both the professional know-how and the ardent desire to expose frauds—but he was also a man who very much *wanted* to believe in the possibility of reaching across the Greater-Yet Divide. He'd been trying to contact his beloved mother, Cecelia, ever since her death in 1913, and later he would ask his wife, if she survived him, to convene a séance every year on his birthday. Houdini promised his widow-to-be that if crossing that barrier was possible, she could count on him to accomplish it.[1] He left a series of secret words and phrases she could use to verify that the contact was authentic.

For now, though, his death was more than four years in the future. The world-renowned escape artist and the world-renowned creator of Sherlock Holmes had become friendly two years earlier, bonding over their mutual interest in spiritual phenomena. But they were on distinctly different sides of the question. Where Houdini was an adamantine skeptic, Doyle, the Bard of Ruthless Logic, was a crusading naïf, one whose gullibility was legendary. As the debunker Harry Price put it: "Poor, dear, lovable, credulous Doyle! He was a giant in stature with the heart of a child." Doyle was coming off a humiliation, his role in the Cottingley fairies hoax of 1920. In that instance he'd made a double mistake: deferring to experts who lacked expertise (they were able to declare the photos unretouched, but failed to recognize that the fairies were cardboard cutouts), and trusting that innocent young girls would never participate in such a deception. Alas, it turned out that though he might possess the heart of a child, children might not.

The Atlantic City conclave was a respite for both from the rigors of the road. Doyle was on a stateside lecture tour, trying to convince Americans that there was life after death and that glimpses of it were readily available if only they'd open their minds. His performance in a press conference preceding his talks had been panned, even ridiculed, by some of New York's cultural elites, but

Doyle's eloquence and the force of his conviction carried sway with ordinary Americans, who came in throngs to hear him. As the *New York World* put it, "His audience was profoundly attentive. Evidently it was a crowd which had its dead." Doyle's trustworthiness and his oratory skill were part of the problem, his detractors said; he represented a clear and present danger to tractable minds, as evidenced by a rash of suicides in the wake of his performances. His rhetoric about life after death was so persuasive that it moved several people to hasten their way to the other side. And not only their own way: one man killed his roommate and then himself, and left a note explaining that in the afterlife there would be no gas bills.

Doyle, now in his sixties, had been interested in spiritualism for four decades. The modern phenomenon began in 1848 in Wayne County, upstate New York, with another set of mischievous girls, the sisters Kate and Maggie Fox. They claimed communication with the ghost of a murdered peddler who'd been buried in their basement (and later they would invoke a demon they called "Mr. Splitfoot"). First the pair convinced their elder sister, then their parents, then the community. From there the circle widened to Rochester, to New York City, and then—thanks to a barnstorming tour—to almost every major city in the United States.

The allure of communication with specters—a belief, in an era of bloodbath wars and massive pandemics, that the border between death and life might be permeable—can scarcely surprise us: in America of the late nineteenth century, *every* crowd would have its dead. Spiritualism attracted millions of adherents, and though the movement's influence and the ever-increasing variety of manifestations waned a bit toward the end of the century, no setback or exposé could dissuade believers. By the time the Fox sisters came clean, four decades later, not even their public confession could make a dent. There was too much edifice stacked atop the false foundation. Initially, the sisters would divulge, they were just bored girls, fifteen and twelve, who amused themselves with a prank involving nothing more sophisticated than an apple strung to a stick, which they would drop to the wooden floor, raise, and thunk down again. Later, pressed to greater inventiveness by the rising tide of belief and the pressure to sustain it, the sisters would develop a bodily symphony of joint cracks, finger and (especially) toe snaps, thumps, creaks, and rumblings, a musical form in which they both proved to have virtuoso talents. In 1904, children playing in the cellar of the girls' old house would discover human remains, which some—Doyle among them—took as proof that their 1880s confession had been false, and that the dead peddler existed. Later investigation would suggest that the remains were a miscellany of ribs and phalanges and chicken bones, and would have made up a very strange-looking victim.

Houdini found it easy to handle hoaxers, grifters, and mountebanks. His interactions with abusers of public credulity were adversarial in a simple, predictable, rule-bound way. They were opposing teams playing the same game, and he was unbeatable. His job was simply to lay bare their falsehoods by explaining and sometimes replicating their methods and then to move on, a little sadly, to the next possibility of *real* paranormal contact. Sincere believers, among them the Doyles, would have been more sympathetic figures for him, but also more confounding.

Jean Conan Doyle was noted for her ability to convey messages from the spirits by way of trancelike "automatic writing," and so far as I know, her faith in this power was genuine. For Houdini, behind shuddering blinds on a breezy New Jersey Sunday, she produced a fevered burst of communiqués from beyond: fifteen pages from the voluble Cecelia Weisz, Houdini's mother, in the course of an hour. Houdini had vowed to approach the séance in as "religious" a spirit as possible, and not under any circumstance to "scoff." Arthur thought him to be deeply moved.

I would imagine he was. Who has a heart hard enough not to be awed by and grateful for the Doyles' combination of zeal and utter untrickiness? They had no commercial interest here, and therefore employed none of greed's shortcuts for him to expose. As Jean took furious scrawled dictation from beyond, shedding a sheet of paper every few minutes, Houdini had no bell boxes or wires to find, no accomplices to unmask, no oozing "ectoplasm" to identify the source of. He had seen plenty of the vaudeville effects that sharps employed; this was something far weirder and more profound, an attempt to *help* him in his heart's dearest desire: "I excluded all earthly thoughts and gave my whole soul to the séance. I was willing to believe, even wanted to believe.... [W]ith a beating heart I waited, hoping that I might feel once again the presence of my beloved Mother."

But he wasn't moved because he *believed*, and Doyle was bitterly disappointed when, after holding his tongue for more than a year, Houdini in late 1923 repudiated Doyle's account of the day. For one thing, Houdini said, Jean Doyle's transcribed message from beyond had begun with the drawing of a cross—not a likely choice of symbols for the Jewish Cecelia. And how to explain Jean's production of sentence after sentence of perfect grammatical English, a language Houdini's mother couldn't write and spoke only haltingly? (Arthur Conan Doyle would attribute this, later, to a mystical translating effect—Death putting its bony finger on the scale to help.)

Afterward, Houdini and Doyle remained friendly correspondents, even mutual admirers—as Doyle had written in another context, "Mediocrity knows nothing higher than itself; but talent instantly recognizes genius"—but their relationship took on an edge of distrust and rivalry. They became proto-frenemies.

This was the context as Houdini arrived in Cincinnati in 1925. He'd visited on several occasions since 1899, when—"Harry Houdini Mystifies Police at Headquarters"—he talked his way into a stationhouse and escaped three sets of manacles and a pair of leg irons in less than three minutes. Now, he wrote a friend, he was back, not only to do another round of performances but also to visit—to assess and presumably to debunk—a medium Doyle had certified as genuine and whom the Englishman counted "among the world's greatest."

That medium was Laura Pruden. But I came to her stone indirectly, by way of the husband she survived, Judge Andrew Pruden, a jurist valued by all, it seems, for his sobriety and sound judgment—a man whose name fell just two letters shy of his cardinal virt-. Pruden was born in 1818, and alongside a political career as councilman, city prosecutor, state legislator, judge, and attorney, he amassed a fortune in railroads and real estate. His wife of close to half a century, Mary Powell Pruden, died in 1890, and in May 1894, at seventy-six, he shocked his friends and the city by eloping, in essence, with Laura Carter, who at thirty-nine was already regarded as one of the country's most prominent practitioners of spiritualism. The *Enquirer*'s article on the marriage is a wince-inducing exercise in wink-wink-nudge-nudge-say-no-more. Its title seems now near parodic: "Oh, Judge! How Sly You Are, to Be Sure!" After making a point of giving the couple's ages (inaccurately—if I'm reading the blurred microfilm right, the paper overstated the difference by almost ten years), the writer goes on to detail the couple's surreptitious preparations (there was no witness to their nuptials except the minister) and even subterfuge (they gave false addresses on their license application so as not to excite attention). It is reported that the newlyweds immediately decamped for a honeymoon in Washington, DC; the next day there would be a follow-up article, ostensibly to report on the surprising vote by the judge, a staunch Democrat, for a reformist candidate in city politics, but mostly just a chance to simultaneously chortle at and celebrate the sly dog's virility and to call him "one of the most spry and happy bridegrooms" roaming the nation's capital that spring day.

The wedding article began, "No one would ever have thought it," and by the end made apparent who the most outraged member of that *no one* might be: the judge's surviving child from his first marriage, Thomas, who was his partner and rent collector in several real-estate ventures.

The frenemies Doyle and Houdini
at truce.

The Fox sisters. Maggie is at left, Kate center,
and their elder sister Leah is at right

Jean Doyle, circa 1910
(with lapel and bodice phantasms?)

Judge Pruden's monument at Spring Grove

A séance (still from the 1922 Fritz Lang film *Dr. Mabuse, the Gambler*)

Thomas, born in the same year as his stepmother, must have found the tone of the article unendurable. For many years, he would battle and thwart and frustrate his father's widow, contesting every testamentary provision he could. In that he was aided by one of his father's idiosyncrasies. Shortly after Andrew Pruden's death, the *New York Times* published an item called "Man of Many Wills." It reported that the judge had cultivated the unusual habit of writing a new will virtually once a month. These he would hand-deliver to the probate court, so often that eventually the presiding judge ceased to collect the usual costs. "Each time he appeared with a new will," the article's penultimate sentence asserted, "Pruden would laugh hard, as though he was playing a good joke on somebody." There's a paragraph break before the coda and payoff: "The Estate is large."

Over the decades of legal tussles after Judge Pruden's death, both Laura and Thomas may have felt like that good joke's butt from time to time. It's important to emphasize, though, that there's no evidence of a mercenary motive for Laura Carter Pruden. The unseemliness of the *Enquirer's* wedding article is squarely focused on the idea of the sly-dog septuagenarian and his prospect of slap-and-tickle; the new Mrs. Pruden, meanwhile, garners praise for her handsomeness and intelligence, and the paper reports on her thriving business as a medium, estimating an annual income for her that's in the thousands of dollars.

From the beginning, women occupied the center of spiritualist practice. Much of that preeminence may derive, not surprisingly, from sexist assumptions on the part of men: thus Doyle's susceptibility to the guile of those who seemed guileless, for instance, whether they be girls or (as he would describe

One of Laura Pruden's slates, post-visitation

the Laura Pruden he met in the 1920s) "an elderly, kindly woman with a moth-erly manner." Surely, too, there was at least a submerged erotic element in male "entrancement" at séances, where they would sit hand in hand with their spirit guides, some of whom would swoon or bark or even exude ectoplasm from beneath their garments. Men's deference to and preference for female mediums surely owed, too, to the old canard that would keep logic as a male preserve and fetishize "feminine mystery."

But the point is not to sneer at benighted oldsters; we are of course little dif-ferent, and will be sneered at in our turn. Whatever one makes of the psycho-logical drama behind Doyle's attachment to spiritualism, whatever shadings one may give his motives, it bears acknowledgment that he spent much of his adult life deferring to and celebrating female power. But my main interest here is from the other side, to speculate about the allure of spiritualism for women. Here was that rarity, a business begun and sustained by women, one in which clever, enterprising females could thrive, achieving wealth, prominence, even a measure of respect from the press, professional men, and captains of industry who in other contexts would grant them none. Furthermore, it was an enterprise in which—this a special bonus for practitioners who were cyn-ics or profit-seekers—women could prove to themselves what frail, gullible, foolish vessels men were, and get paid for the privilege. Surely it's no accident that the history of American spiritualism and that of American feminism are tightly entangled—in fact the Seneca Falls Convention, that milestone of the women's movement in the United States, took place mere months after and just twenty miles away from the birth of American spiritualism, if we view the Fox sisters' deception as the starting point.

There's an early book review in which (noted feminist?!) John Updike laments the fate of women in nineteenth-century fiction, "denied all rights but the right to be adored, [. . .] assigned an exclusively sexual value and given only a black market to trade it on."[2] It's possible to view the rise of spiritualism as a Horatio Alger (or ghost of Horatio Alger) story in which women, exemplifying the entrepreneurial spirit, seize the right of self-determination, create new values and markets for themselves, and throw off the passive role ("denied," "assigned") that's implicit in Updike's formulation. Eve was no longer the only model available. Women were dropping apples all over now, and demanding that attention be paid. Strings were firmly attached.

Laura Pruden's special subfield was slate-writing, and Doyle, who had never seen this particular kind of inter-realm communication, was impressed enough not only to sit with her several times, but also to invite her to London to demonstrate her powers—an unusual honor, since most mediums' abilities didn't travel well; they required the comforts (and perhaps the secret contrivances) of home.

Pruden and her clients would sit (she often in a low rocking chair) around a small table over which she would place a drape. The petitioners to the spirit realm would be asked to write two questions on slips of paper, then to place one on the floor and one in a chair, where it would remain visible throughout. Laura Pruden would bring out two slates and ask her clients to examine them. She'd give the client a stub of pencil to tuck between the slates and a black cloth in which to wrap them—this last being necessary to create a "cabinet for the manifestation." The medium would then use one hand to insert the slates through a slit in the drape; her other hand rested in her lap. (Later in her career, it seems, she dispensed with the table; she'd merely place the slates under her foot, where they would stay.) After reciting the Lord's Prayer, she would engage her clients in chat while they waited. After a few minutes, the sound of the pencil scratching could be heard, and Laura Pruden would smile and say, "They are here." This element of the show had special appeal for Doyle the littérateur, who exulted at "the thrill and vibration of the pencil as it whisked away inside the cabinet." After several minutes, three sharp raps would come from the vicinity of the slates, and Pruden would interrupt the bright stream of palaver she and her clients had been engaging in—about mutual friends, issues of the day, et cetera—to announce that the spirits had finished. She would extract the slates, which now bore elaborate messages, often in the familiar script of the departed, that answered the questions posed on paper scraps. Sometimes, too, there would be vividly colored drawings—a spirit-realm lagniappe.

Pruden was a pretty agile thaumaturge, in sum, and no wonder Doyle was impressed.

I can't determine whether the missed connection resulted from evasive action by the medium (perhaps the likeliest surmise: Laura Pruden was nobody's fool) or because Houdini was otherwise occupied, but it seems that Houdini never actually managed to sit down for a slate-writing session during his 1925 visit to Cincinnati. In Doyle's 1927 essay "The Riddle of Houdini," published in the *Strand Magazine*,[3] he alternately lauds and snipes at his rival as he states his case that Houdini not only believed in spiritualism, but that he was one of its most ingenious practitioners . . . or unwilling vessels: "Who was the greatest medium-baiter of modern times? Undoubtedly Houdini. Who was the greatest physical medium of modern times? There are some who would be inclined to give the same answer. I do not see how it can ever now be finally and definitely proved, but circumstantial evidence may be very strong, as Thoreau said when he found a trout in the milk jug." Belief in spiritualism, Doyle asserted, was just another (double-chained, underwater) milk jug that the slippery trout Erich Weisz was trying to wriggle free from. Doyle's essay could scarcely provide more compelling proof that history is written by the survivors, and that—this perhaps the core principle of spiritualism (and of this book, too, to be fair)—the living get to speak for the dead.

Laura Pruden lived on until 1939, continuing to ply her trade nearly to the end. But after her death she had one more contribution to make to the practice of clairvoyance, perhaps her most lasting one. The medium for this posthumous contribution was Albert Carter (1888–1948), her younger son. Soon after his mother's death, Albert invented a fortunetelling device to carry on her legacy. It was a tube containing a murky liquid and two dice that, when the tube was upturned, would float to the top, revealing the spirits' answer to any question. Carter took his idea to Max Levinson, who brought in his brother-in-law, Abe Bookman, to tinker with the design. In the mid-1940s the three, partners now, marketed the toy as the Syco-Seer—and later (in tribute to Albert's mother) as the Syco-Slate.

Carter would die in 1948, shortly before his patent for the "liquid-filled dice agitator" came through and two years before the toy, with an assist from the Brunswick Billiard Company, would take on its enduringly popular form: the Magic 8 Ball. Carter is buried next to his mother and her other son, but without a stone to mark his place.

GHOSTS OF THE WALLDOGS
GUS HOLTHAUS

THESE DAYS, WHEN ADVERTISERS TALK ABOUT competing for eyeballs in "the public square," that last phrase is figurative. But in the nineteenth century and on into the twentieth, until radio and its electronic descendants took the square indoors and eventually compressed it into people's palms, the public square could be a riotous free-for-all for those with businesses, events, or ideas to publicize. Outdoor advertising dominated, especially for small enterprises—and in the first half of the twentieth century, in red-brick cities like Cincinnati, its most prominent mode was the giant sign painted straight onto the exterior walls of buildings by the artists known as walldogs.

Advertising was professionalized in the 1800s, with some of the impetus for that development coming from the lucrative bunkum surrounding patent medicines—which tended to be inert concoctions containing pungent herbs like fenugreek in a solution of 35 or 40 proof alcohol; they were held in especially high esteem in teetotaling households.[1] ("When the going gets weird," as Hunter S. Thompson would write in another context a century later, "the weird turn pro.") But by the time the ad biz made its bid for respectability, the battle had already been waged by other means for centuries.

Advertising may have been beaten out for the status of oldest profession, but even in *that* field it has for centuries played a role. By the early Renaissance, many European cities codified special costumes for prostitutes: high-heeled slippers and a bell on one's head in some Italian municipalities, striped hoods in London, and so on. These getups were intended, by churches and states that viewed whoredom as a necessary evil, in part to create a stigma and provide a warning to the unwary, but the collateral effect was often to help these women find their customers. (The same effect was achieved later by bedizenment with makeup, red lanterns left in windows, a flash of garter, and so on.)

There's a useful analogy to be made here, I think: like profession 1A, profession 1B has almost always been stigmatized, and the stigma almost always ignored—or used to advantage. In the end, moral disapprobation may turn out to be just another brand of empty ballyhoo that commerce uses to consummate itself. Disfavor can have its high ground, so long as the traffic flows below.

If we think of advertising as simply the public competition for attention, it is of course ubiquitous, and ever more densely and dispiritingly so, it seems. One question that recent social media seem implicitly to pose, and then explicitly to answer and answer and answer, is this: In a hype-driven culture, who's going to lug your banner if you don't do it yourself? Right. Hence our world of humblebrag and vaguebook, EgoTweet and selfie stick—of near-constant advertisements for ourselves. But the phenomenon didn't spontaneously generate itself in Mark Zuckerberg's dorm room; putting oneself forward along with one's art or ideas or moral convictions has as long a history as humans do. We are the products we sell. Our clothes are ads, our manners, even our names—and also the shingles or signs we hang out to trumpet them.

By this broader definition, one may consider the ninety-five theses Martin Luther tacked onto the cathedral door at Wittenberg in 1517 a kind of guerrilla advertising, an incursion into a public space "owned" by the Catholic Church to bring attention to a scrappy alternative.

But back to the literal public square. By the early nineteenth century, Western urban centers teemed with handbills and posters. This was perhaps most dizzyingly the case in London, where by the 1830s taxes and restrictions on newspaper advertising—together with merchants' desire to tap a broader market than just the elite and the literate—created a pandemoniac playground for the rough-hewn men who posted flybills. These freelancers, hired by merchants, battled for space on every available wall, pulling bills from their satchels and affixing them to any available surface with a paste-soaked roller, then coming back to repost them when, inevitably and often immediately, they were pulled down or blotted out. (Fisticuffs—or worse—were not unheard of.) By the 1830s, most available walls were thickly impastoed with bills, with layers accreting until the chaos became three-dimensional. Now the public square didn't just teem; it *bristled*. (For a present-day analog, think of the staples one finds layered by the hundreds on telephone poles in commercial districts, looking like scale-model city skylines; you can read in their braille the history of the band gigs they've plugged, the lost cats sought, the stained sofas offered for sale.) In 1839, London's Metropolitan Police Act outlawed posting bills on private property . . . but the ordinance defied enforcement: how to prosecute a single drop of water from a spigot turned full on?

For Londoners, these "billboards" constituted a useful nuisance. Authorities could rail about them, property owners lament their profusion, but there was no stopping the practice. Part of this had to do with fear of commerce's low, messy democracy, of the "mass" in the mass market. One may see that anxiety reflected in the British term for the walls on which bills were posted—"hoardings," a term taken from medieval castle defense: a projection to keep out insurgents who might mass and try to climb the battlements. The word came to be applied, especially, to temporary barriers around construction sites or private property—the kind of blank surface most alluring to flybill posters. (In the United States, the term "wheatpaste posters," derived from the kind of cheap, weak glue employed, was more common.)

In 1835, the painter John Orlando Parry produced the most famous image of flybill advertising, a painting popularly known as *The Poster Man*. One thing to note in this remarkable image is how *high* the upper echelons of posters reach. In a chaotic, seize-your-own-turf system like this, having the technology or the patience to post way up would help your message endure; meanwhile the lower tiers were papered over again and again.[2]

I remember a similar phenomenon in Louisiana when I lived there. In 1991, Holocaust denier and neo-Nazi David Duke made the runoff for governor by exploiting racist sentiment and the state's unusual electoral system, which places all candidates into a so-called jungle primary, then moves the top two vote-getters forward. Worse, once Duke made the runoff it seemed that he might win. His opponent was the flamboyantly corrupt ex-governor Edwin Edwards, a man who, in a previous "comeback" campaign, asked by reporters what it would take to squander his late lead, answered, "I'd have to be caught in bed with a dead girl or a live boy." The bumper sticker (another humble form of ad) one saw all over a panicked Baton Rouge that fall was *Vote for the Crook. It's Important.*

Edwards would go on to win, before finally encountering a charge he couldn't wriggle free from and spending nine years in prison, then—giving new meaning to the term "supervised release"—several more in the purgatory of reality TV, where he played the role of the doddering possessive in *The Governor's Wife*.

My most vivid memory from that campaign, though, was the fact that David Duke's signs—instantly ripped down when they appeared in accessible locations—migrated higher and higher up power poles and buildings and trees. Liberals, his people correctly calculated, didn't have access to cherry-pickers. For fully a decade afterward, driving through the bayous of south Louisiana, you could often spot a faded Duke sign twenty feet up a pole, curled next to an old glass-bell insulator.

In their 1972 book *Learning from Las Vegas*, the architects Robert Venturi, Denise Scott Brown, and Steven Izenour argued, among other things, that Las Vegas was the first cityscape *designed* to be encountered from a car window and at cruising speed—thus the huge, glitzy signage, the unwalkable chasms between casinos on the Strip, the vast sun-baked parking lots, et cetera.[3]

Some of their claims are still much debated, but what's stuck with me and seems incontestable is the basic underlying assertion: Las Vegas, historyless, conjured as if out of thin desert air in the late 1940s, was in its DNA a new kind of city, the postmodern city, and its scale and sightlines and glare represented a departure from what had come before.[4]

The transformation of American cities between, say, 1880 and 1929, driven by rapid technological advance, was similarly dramatic. And one marker of that change—the one that's our subject today—was the bold, enticing Carnival of Signs that cities became. Early-twentieth-century American metropolises can be seen as the slower-speed, pre-neon precursors of the Las Vegas that Venturi, Brown, and Izenour would write about . . . and equally well as the progeny of the visually chaotic London that Parry depicted.

In Cincinnati, by 1890, a few telephone numbers had trickled into the annual *Illustrated Business Directory*. Businesses could purchase a star next to their name. Bigger or deeper-pocketed enterprises might spring for boldface type or even, in a few instances, a display ad. But mostly the directory was just an unadorned list, with an enterprise's address serving as the primary attractant ("Hey, this one's just around the corner!"). Advertising beyond one's immediate environs was difficult and expensive . . . and what would be the purpose, in a city with only rudimentary transportation options? (The city's first electric streetcar system began operations just about the time that 1890 guide would have gone to press.)

Sign-painters abounded. Cincinnati's 1893 illustrated directory, for example, lists 165 under the housepainter/sign painter category and another 20 commercial sign painters. (Of those 185 total, only a dozen listed phone numbers.) In the hyperlocal city organized around small, discrete neighborhoods, signs played a critical advertising role. Signs had to indicate what kinds of businesses were transacted inside a building, where to enter, which stairwell to climb or elevator button to push, whom to ask for, and so on. Many signs were small and basic: first initial, last name, and profession, painted on glass or suspended from a lintel. But others made use of gilt, dramatic shading, extra colors; some businesses and tradespeople started including additional information about the services they performed, even a slogan or bit of hype or flashy trademark; still others opted for signs that either dwarfed or blocked others into irrelevance. These sign advertisements grew ever brighter and splashier, especially where there was intense local competition, and eventually some downtown blocks became forebears—all in paint—of the Glitter Gulches to come.

But the scale was about to go colossal, with signs that took up entire sides of buildings—sometimes with windows subsumed into the design, so that a person working inside might become a dot in the pattern, a cog in the wheel, or mote in the eye of advertising.

When ads got bigger than people, something changed. After the turn of the century, as telephones grew near-universal, streetcar suburbs developed, and automobiles became more prevalent, local businesses saw opportunities to broaden their customer base, and emerging national brands seized the initiative, too. By 1910, Coca-Cola was devoting 25 percent of its ad budget to signs painted on buildings, whether on brick in city centers or on wood-frame in small towns. They and other companies (most famously Mail Pouch Tobacco) adapted the strategy for rural landscapes, too, offering farmers near new highways cash in exchange for the right to paint their barn sides. In Cincinnati, many businesses used their own buildings as canvases for display ads, or raised cash by serving as a billboard for someone else.

The term *walldogs* originated, it's thought, from the fact that while doing the brushwork, the men who painted such signs usually had to dangle from harnesses, and they looked like dogs straining at their leashes. The job required skill and finesse, physical toughness, design and planning ability, plus a command of math for proportions, of color theory for contrast, of chemistry for paint-mixing. Many of the big advertisements painted in small towns were done by itinerant walldogs who moved with the work and the weather. But cities like Cincinnati had enough work to support an indigenous industry.

From our distance, a certain romance may attach to this labor. Walldogs had the chance to gaze upon the dynamic, growing city from a perspective not afforded many. I'm always amazed, in urban photos from the early twentieth century, by how few of the trappings of today's compulsive privacy had yet occluded the view: look at the salaryman gazing out from the third floor, his feet on the sill, as he peels an apple for lunch in a stripe of sun; halfway up the hillside beyond him a woman, pinning undergarments to a line, has paused to wave to a friend on the funicular that glides slowly past just thirty feet away. The early-twentieth-century city always seems to be in dishabille, and wariness of the camera hasn't yet blunted or averted people's gazes. Walldogs were on especially intimate terms with their environs.

Once, in an interview, John Updike was asked what animal he would like to be, and he chose the turtle; he'd always loved the sound of rain on the roof, he said, and he figured turtles must get a lot of that. I envy walldogs in a similarly fanciful way, for the point of view from which they could engage the city, for the benign voyeurism that was available to them.

But just as Updike understands the falseness in his choice, the sentimentality, I don't *really* want to have been a walldog. The work was dangerous and hard. Beyond the physical peril, exposure to harsh weather, and the enveloping haze of smog and stink, there was the paint itself. The painters had to concoct their own, using linseed oil, pigments, volatile driers like gasoline . . . and ultra-toxic white lead, in such copious amounts that they had to dip it out of buckets. Some walldogs counted bricks and then (astonishingly) free-handed their signs; others meticulously mapped their canvas in advance. The work, on rough surfaces often with impeding structural elements, could be tedious and technical—and the result had to look seamless, bold, unfussy.

Today, almost all of us have seen walldogs' work, in the form of so-called ghost signs still faintly visible on buildings that haven't fallen prey to urban renewal, and often alongside—but, you'll notice if you look, rarely marred by—the sprayed graffiti that reads as homage to it. Rust Belt cities and shabby towns, places that emptied out rather than being redeveloped, tend to be rich in such ghost signs. Cincinnati is a bonanza for the fan of them.

A ghost sign for Liberty Tire, in my neighborhood, was until recently visible (distantly) from several nearby highways and ramps. The iconography is mysterious: a Native American to embody "liberty"? Whose liberty is meant, then? And why invoke the choking black smoke of a tire fire by giving him a smoke-signal blanket? Is he running from the giant runaway tire about to round the building's corner? The ad is also unusual in being from its origin a concession to and acknowledgment of blight. It was painted after the building's abandonment (note that the letters on the blanket run directly over windows), and with the clear presumption—accurate, alas—that the structure wouldn't again be occupied anytime soon. The business, too, is now defunct.

Ghost signs have endured because of their poison. The clinging paint owes its tenacity to lead, which—this is why it's so hazardous—tends to bind hard, sink deep, and not leach away. Old-time walldogs often used unleaded or lightly leaded paints for contrast, which is why on many fading signs it's the letters themselves, and not the backdrops against which they were set, that have hung on.

The walldogs' fading but stubbornly visible art appeals to me for another, more personal reason—which can only be explained by way of a circuitous confession.

When I finished college in 1987, I planned to spend a couple years in Germany, studying literature and "mastering" the language, the related goals I had been working toward for four years. But senior year it suddenly dawned on me—I can only attribute the suddenness to a character flaw—that I was deluding myself.

I'd started language study late, discovered I had a knack for it, and the curve of my progress was steep enough that I fooled myself into believing that mastery was a milestone to pass rather than an asymptote to fall short of. I should have realized this when, after my sophomore year, I spent the summer working in a German bank, fetching foreign cash from the vault-keeper, counting and recounting it in a machine, wrapping it in banderoles, and then using a red signet and wax to seal it into the canvas bags we would dispatch to branches to be handed out to vacationers heading abroad.

On the one hand, my coworkers flattered me by complimenting my prissily constructed sentences, often thirty words long, with the verb suspended— as required, in written *Hochdeutsch*—until the very end. On the other hand, I could barely follow their short, sharp, colloquial German (or in the vault-keeper's case, the unintelligible dialect called Platt), and my ability to ferret out, say, phallogocentrism in Kafka did me no favors in the streets or the shops ("I am merely grazing," I told the bookstore clerk, proud to know a word for "browsing" but not quite understanding what the word literally meant in my own language).

I arrived back in the United States that summer with a poofy version of a British Invasion shag haircut, not as a statement—no one would have made this particular statement on purpose—but because I had both no idea how to negotiate a German barbershop and an aversion to looking or feeling stupid as I flailed for the words that might, or might not, mean "bangs" or "part." Every time I jogged during my final fortnight in Germany, the tips of my hair slapped me stingingly in the eyeball, a rebuke I ignored. By spring of senior year, though, the flattening learning curve had grown more apparent—how would I ever catch up to native speakers, or to those baptized in the language by childhood dunking rather than having it sprinkled over their foreheads in late adolescence?—and I decided to step back and try something else.

That August I moved to New York, squatting for a few weeks in a friend's apartment while hunting a job. Then I got lucky, landing a made-up position at what was then the only woman-owned and woman-run ad agency in New York, LMPM. My bosses were four partners in their early forties, all longtime veterans of Madison Avenue. They'd entered the profession during the sexist heyday of the Man in the Gray Flannel Suit (or of *Mad Men*'s Don Draper), and in 1986 they decided to go out on their own. They'd been in business less than a year when I came on.

They were wonderful to work for and with, and the setting was dazzling: our forty-fifth-floor office in the Chrysler Building faced south, and some evenings, as dusk gave way to city-sparkle, one of the partners would play the grand piano they'd installed, while the other eight or so of us sprawled on couches and drank the liqueur that was an early client, Péché Mignon. I initially imagined that the name meant "peach steak," but I had sense enough not to say so. (Fittingly, it turns out to mean "little weakness.")

My job was to be an apprentice jack-of-all-trades. I enjoyed my witty colleagues, especially my officemate, a soap-opera actor, playwright, and gardening writer. I enjoyed the weirdness of the job—hunkering for a whole morning in a conference room to sniff matchsticks of perfume-soaked paper as we searched for the scent to correspond to our concept for a cologne called "Cooler"; dining in Grand Central's Oyster Bar with a gossip-magazine media buyer who was at first annoyed to be passed off to the powerless newbie, but who after a glass of wine and some chat about rustic breakfast specialties, our unlikely point of overlap, relaxed and seemed to enjoy the meal his company was paying for; sitting in a darkened room watching reel after reel of music videos by directors seeking the agency's first TV commercial, a spot for Agree shampoo set to star ex-Go-Go's vocalist Belinda Carlisle. (We were gaga over the samples from a guy then in his mid-twenties, David Fincher, and I watched over and over his haunting video of Sting singing a medieval Basque carol called "Gabriel's Message." In the end, I think he was the director chosen.)

By this time I had, God help me, studied semiotics. New York was the frothing, roaring cataract of signs that Roland Barthes and others had told us about. Advertising required one always to see it as such: from our little redoubt of quiet, four hundred feet up, our job was to try to think up ways to add signs into the infinity that might, fleetingly, fix someone's gaze, grab someone's attention.

John Orlando Parry, *A London Street Scene*, 1835, watercolor

A Cincinnati street-scape—the corner of Race and Fifth, looking north—circa 1905. I stopped counting signs when I reached forty

Liberty Tire building

David Ogilvy, 1969

Chateau de Touffou

Walter Landor. The hat marks his captaincy of the *Klamath*, a ferryboat he bought at auction in 1964, moored in San Francisco, and made into his company's headquarters

Capital of a column in a Roman-esque church, the Collégiale St.-Pierre in Chauvigny, France

Paramount Vodka ad. Holthaus's signature, visible at this range only as a blur, begins beneath the gap between the 8 and 0

Spring Grove mausoleum. Holthaus's marker is at left

Ezzard Charles, the Cincinnati Cobra. Mural on Liberty Street downtown

Shepard Fairey's mural of Aung San Suu Kyi. The peace laureate's bloody fangs
are a late addition—the result of urban public art's, um, interactivity

I enjoyed, too, my forty-minute walking commute through the chaos every morning, time I spent trying to chart a course between clichés, Slack-Jawed Rustic Turning Awed Circles at the Center of the Universe and Dead-Eyed Cynic Trundling Along at High Speed. Long-time urbanites, I'd noticed, seemed to have developed a version of sidewalk echolocation, and could steer harmlessly away from all human need or contact without ever noticing it. I tried halfheartedly to duplicate the skill, but I sucked at it. I was avid for seeing and simultaneously afraid to look: every person I encountered might be Medusa. So I did all my observing through hooded reflections, cheating sidelong glances, and three-rail bank shots: rearview mirror to display window to . . . wait, did that guy really have tighty whities on his head, with pigtails poking through the leg holes and the fly at his forehead like a Cyclopean eye? The tone of these walks toggled between world-weariness and joy, resignation to the world's uglinesses and the young person's sense that things not only should be better but might be, any minute now. (It was a Kurt Vonnegut tone, and it happens that as I meandered south through Turtle Bay I'd often come up behind the writer himself, looking broad-backed and headless as he carried a child on his shoulders.)

My job occasionally allowed me to try my hand at writing. One client, *House Beautiful* magazine, wanted us to put together a city-bus campaign that would persuade media buyers that its readers were not dowdy old-timers but smart, dynamic—and, not incidentally, wealthy—women. The idea was to take clichés and set phrases and tweak them in a way that might read as unthreatening feminism lite. My officemate came up with "She's Heels on Wheels" for the ad that would focus on matters automotive, and his tagline for the objets d'art ad was "She's looking for prints charming." We had trouble coming up with a suitable phrase for an ad about high-end bathroom products: claw-foot tubs, faucets, marble, linens, lighting. I made a throwaway joke about "She Skips to Her Loo," we jotted it down, and to my shock, the client chose it.

For a couple of months that winter, I would occasionally see a bus flash by with my idiotic slogan on it, and I would cringe in shame. Or so I thought; I would have testified under oath that my emotion was 99.44 percent pure humiliation, and the .56 percent that wasn't *ought* to have been. Only later would it occur to me that there was pride even in the shame. Who would know or care that this ad—designed to get advertisers to flog their products in a magazine, and for the majority of Manhattanites and visitors just another irrelevant squiggle in the city's seething visual backdrop—had anything at all to do with me?

The slogan was stupid, yes. It was throwaway. But it was mine. And though I would never have acknowledged this at the time, I was laboring under another of the clichés of bumpkinhood, the ambition to *make my mark*. My response to those winter-grimy buses rumbling past seems now, after thirty years, wrong in multiple directions. On the one hand too harsh, because here—in whatever degraded, silly form, and detectable perhaps only to me—was a mark, and I might have felt lucky to make it. On the other hand too kind, because there is far more arrogance than I thought then in believing there's a hierarchy of marks, and to imagine that you can enforce your ranking, or decide what thing you do in your life will count, is not only arrogant but delusional. Only in a cemetery can we choose our memorials—and even there we can't choose what living memories will attach to them.

Which leads us, at length, back to Cincinnati and its walldogs. Or—well—almost.

I am a sucker for selflessness, real or fictive. I cry over books, kids' movies, newspaper articles, radio stories, pop songs (there's one, not to be named here, that has made me sob, alone in my car, at least fifty times in a row, its effect magically never diminishing). Fearing what I'll find, I've tried not to poke too deeply into the psychology behind this, but certainly my attraction to self-sacrifice has to do with knowing that in my case the only (limited) way it can happen, when it's called for, will be by conscious, long-cultivated moral decision. Like most of us, I have a troubled relationship with ego, which seems simultaneously the necessary precondition of and spur to doing the things that matter most to me . . . and a monster to be indulged only guiltily and fleetingly, and otherwise balked, throttled, suppressed.

One corollary to this has been a great admiration for professions in which one exerts serious skill invisibly, in service of someone else who will get the credit, if credit there be. I remember reading, twenty-five years ago, Marjorie Sandor's "The World Is Full of Virtuosos," about a gifted pianist who chooses to become an accompanist.[5] The story had the power of a revelation, not because the accompanist's art was selfless (he took immense but private pride in it, as I recall) but because he'd found a way to square the circle: to expend his ego in the service of something and someone else, but still to derive secret satisfaction from it.

I feel a similar draw to editors, translators, single parents, pit crews, defensive stoppers in basketball, vernacular architects, the designers of ordinary objects (zipper, grapefruit knife, lint trap, crisper drawer). The effect is heightened if the job pays poorly, as it often does (teacher, nurse), or if it involves creating what we might call surplus beauty, an artistry that might not be noticed or credited and that need not be there for the thing to work (furniture makers, metalsmiths, potters). This is, of course, nothing remotely like an exhaustive list . . . and almost any task, embraced in the right spirit, might qualify.

Even advertising. One thing that fascinated me, in my brief time in the field, was the apparent cleavage between the client's aim and the agency's. Often that tension gets oversimplified or burlesqued: the client wants sales, the creatives want flash, and the account executive negotiates between these incompatible values, the bottom-line stiffs on the one side and the me-me-me infants on the other. In reality, those who create campaigns know that the precondition of their getting to do imaginative work, of satisfying current clients and attracting future ones, is profit; all goes for naught if the consumer is moved but the product is not. And clients know that their brands may live or die based on whether their advertising can create a story, a "brand identity," that appeals. They are seeking an ad agency, too, in part for personal reasons—so as to be told (and to be able to tell their employees and friends and the public) a rejuvenating story about their product, and about the enterprise of their lives. In other words, the "creatives" attend closely to commerce, and the "suits" see the value of art.

But I took special interest in the elements of advertising that were least obviously inventive, and unlikely to win awards or plaudits: the crisp, plain paragraph about the nail-stiffening powers of clear gelatin, the font choice and tight layout of an ad for lotion. One of the cleverest examples I've ever seen of combining ambition, ego, and flair and then somehow reverse-engineering one's own near-invisibility is that of Walter Landor, one of the first people I met in the advertising world.

Another flashback, then. In 1984, after my freshman year, my girlfriend and I spent six weeks in Europe. The idea was that she—a student of French labor history set to begin her PhD in the fall—would lead us through France, and I would do the same (much less smoothly and ably) in Germany. She, far worldlier than I was, had grown up in suburban Chicago, where her father was an ad exec at Ogilvy & Mather. Because of this connection, we were invited to spend a few days at David Ogilvy's chateau in Touffou, France.

To prepare for the trip, I read our host's two influential books, *Confessions of an Advertising Man* (1963) and *Ogilvy on Advertising* (1983). Ogilvy (1911–1999) was a big personality and a fabulous salesman, not only of his clients' products but of the profession itself, and no less of his own self-curated myth. Even in 2004, five years after his death and more than three decades after his initial retirement from the agency he'd given his name, he finished first in an *Adweek* survey that asked what person, living or dead, had inspired the magazine's readers to take up their profession.

Ogilvy was an amazing raconteur and knew himself to be one, which would have ruined the effect except that his talent was so prodigious that it made you feel that the credit in some way redounded to you. It was as if, every time he told a story, he was newly rediscovering his gift, and you were the lucky soul who got to witness the discovery; or maybe you'd even caused it, by being such an excellent audience. He had begun his working life, the man himself told us in the kitchen at Touffou, as a door-to-door stove salesman in Scotland. After emigrating to the United States in 1938, Ogilvy took a job with George Gallup's innovative new polling company, where he developed his life-long devotion to understanding one's customer through data. He spent World War II applying those same research techniques and skills to matters of military intelligence. In 1949, he opened his agency in New York.

Among Ogilvy's many contributions to the field over the next quarter-century was his virtual invention of the Fictional Personage as Brand Identity, most famously the Man in the Hathaway Shirt. That character's hallmark was a rakish eyepatch, but the patch was never mentioned explicitly in the copy, so as to enhance its air of intrigue. It was the advertising equivalent of a McGuffin. Whence the underlying injury: War wound? Illness? Dueling society? Cufflink mishap? Pirate fetish? Or was it, as *Spinal Tap*'s manager cheerfully admits when the documentarian asks about the cricket bat he keeps rapping in his palm, just a . . . what is the word? *Affectation*? Yes, right.[6]

In today's adscape, perhaps the Man in the Hathaway Shirt's best-known lineal descendant is Dos Equis's "Most Interesting Man in the World," a character who seems born of mixing that campaign with another Ogilvy creation, this one also a precursor to those (by Chrysler, Coors, Martha Stewart Home, Papa John's, Bush Beans, Jimmy Dean, and many others) that involve making a corporate executive into a brand's spokesperson and image. In the 1950s, Ogilvy built his campaign for Schweppes tonic water around that company's Commander Edward Whitehead, with his signature Vandyke and adventurous twinkle, thus creating a more-or-less real-life character popularly known as Commander Schweppes, avatar of the brand's "Schweppervescence."

In 1973 Ogilvy and his wife, Herta, purchased Touffou, parts of which dated to the twelfth century, and moved to France. His retirement wouldn't quite take—David would emerge fifteen years later to head Ogilvy in India. Even in the interim, it was a retirement from the field but not the fray: Ogilvy's correspondence was so voluminous, he told us, that the nearby village's post office had to be reclassified and its postmaster given a bump in salary.

On our bewildering first night at the castle, we were led out across the old moat (not a landform met often in Orangeburg County, South Carolina) to an open-air meal, complete with wait staff, on a parapet. There I encountered for the first time both a food and a culinary concept: avocados (as exotic to me as yak steak or jackfruit would have been) and cold soup. The gourmet combination of these two novelties seemed, to a polite southerner obliged to eat a seemly amount of each dish, infinitely cruel. And so in a period of mere minutes that evening, I was introduced to at least six newnesses: moats, parapets, livery, avocado, cold soup, and (with every bite) my rising gorge.

The next morning, David and Herta graciously showed my girlfriend and me around, and he regaled us—here was the first person I ever encountered who earned and embodied that word, with its implication of a stiff wind encountered again and again—with more stories.

That night at dinner, as I recall, we were joined by another houseguest. Ogilvy was a force of nature, to be marveled at but not identified with—can one identify with a hurricane? Walter Landor was less a meteorological phenomenon, and so, though I'd been told he was a big deal, I at first underestimated him.

Landor and his host were not only well-matched as ad-world titans; they were also near coevals (in their early seventies, Ogilvy two years the elder), and both were Europeans who'd made their bones in America. Landor, originally Landauer, was born in Munich in 1913 and left (shortly before that verb would have had to be "fled") in 1931, first for England and then for the United States.

I have no idea what Walter Landor was like when he *wasn't* sitting next to David Ogilvy in the latter's dining room. It seems likely, given what I've learned since, that he was himself a magnetic personality. This was a man who in the 1960s made his corporate headquarters a refurbished ferryboat, the *Klamath*, docked in San Francisco Bay, and who sometimes sported an admiral's cap when he was aboard. But in this setting, at least by comparison, he seemed lower-key, softer-spoken.

Beyond a couple of basics about Landor—his mischievous wit and his white mustache—my memory of him that night is spotty. But I remember with perfect vividness my shock when he revealed his vocation and produced his sample book. This was nothing like an episode of the old game show *What's My Line*, in which a celebrity panel would conduct a yes-or-no interrogation in an effort to identify a guest's unusual job. There was no teasing reticence on Landor's part, no attempt to hold us in suspense. In fact, everybody else at the table already *knew*. So perhaps this was yet another in my string of Touffou-exposed Novelties That Shouldn't Have Been . . . but Landor's profession, once divulged, seemed as miraculous to me as if—*What's My Line*–style—he'd revealed himself to be the operator of a skirt-blowing machine in Rockaway Park.[7]

And in fact his job wasn't *exotic*. Landor was a graphic designer by trade, a brand-builder by profession. In retrospect, what surprises me most may be my own yokel-ish obliviousness. Because I'd never given commerce a thought, it had never occurred to me that logos—much less brand identities, a term that would have baffled me—were designed by anyone. Coca-Cola didn't *have* a logo; it *was* a logo. And indeed, to hear Landor talk about it, that conflation of brand and trademark was by design. He'd created—and showed us in his book—the famous symbols for Del Monte, Cotton, Frito-Lay, Levi Strauss, Delta Airlines, Miller Lite, Marlboro, Bank of America, Alitalia, and more.

But what impressed me most that night was the way Landor's work—and his mien, and his tone—combined two things I'd always thought incompatible: ego and humility. The man took obvious pride in his work. He didn't soft-pedal its importance, either, adopting as his credo "Products are made in the factory, but brands are created in the mind."

Nor did he balk at acknowledging the role of artistic ego in design. As he put it in a 1985 art-school commencement speech, "Some of us strive for self-expression—just like fine artists. And some of us strive to communicate—and that's a whole other fine art. I think we have matured as designers when we eventually realize that these need not be mutually exclusive goals." Landor's designs had what might be called the arrogance of art; they asserted the right to, as John Berryman put it, "not only express the matter in hand but add to the stock of available reality." But the art then neatly and quickly effaced itself, became not just work in the service of something else but *the something else*.

A few years later, when I read Marjorie Sandor's story about the self-abnegating musician, it was Landor—Sandor's cousin in rhyme, which probably helped—whom the accompanist put me in mind of. Here was the artist simultaneously unmissable and unseen.

Until then I'd ignored or glibly dismissed business. It was lower than and inimical to art; it was what you did when you gave up. My encounters with Ogilvy and Landor, and later with my LMPM colleagues, wrecked that fantasy. But it wasn't only my sense of the inferiority of commerce that had to go; the notion of art's superiority, too—an idea that had always made me queasy—could be jettisoned. As someone who aspired, vaguely and privately and embarrassedly, to do something that might someday be called art (not by me, Lord knows, but I hoped maybe someday by someone), I felt as if Landor had devised an ingenious way to simultaneously indulge in and mitigate the appalling ego of it. He'd produce something that was art only at its conception, until its acceptance by the client . . . at which point it became the symbol and avatar of something else, something that antedated the art but that the art would have a role in shaping.

Walter Landor—and this is why, much as I marveled at Ogilvy, it was his houseguest I subsequently fixed on—had found a way to inscribe his egomania in invisible ink.

Which, this time I promise, brings us back to the walldogs of Cincinnati . . . and to one in particular.

Until World War II, say, it would have been almost inconceivable for a sign painter to affix a signature to his (or her) work. To name oneself would be to claim the status of art for these ads, and that would both violate the code and, potentially, annoy the client. There's an interesting parallel with medieval art here. Artists of that time almost never signed their work, as they considered themselves conduits through whom God created. The first known signed work is the capital of a church column in the village of Chauvigny, France—as it happens, just eight miles from Ogilvy's chateau—that says "*Gofridus me fecit*": "Godfried made me." Gofridus pretty clearly didn't inscribe those three words of ecclesiastical Latin to promote the glory of God; he had a glory nearer by to tout. Which makes Gofridus virtually unique among the anonymous artists and artisans of Romanesque architecture. But why *shouldn't* he be proud of these wonderfully strange creations, of his life's work? Couldn't God accept his glory *by way of* a little shout-out to the conduit? And indeed, signing artworks would gradually and inexorably become a convention.

For artists, that is—not for artisans. But postwar, especially in a hollowed and hollowing city like Cincinnati, the calculus changed. The population was decamping to the suburbs or the Sunbelt; other media and other modes of advertising were emerging, flourishing, and asserting their supremacy; the hazards of lead paint—the material that had made such signs durable—were becoming apparent. The age of the ghost sign was beginning. That phenomenon has from its beginning been entangled with nostalgia, and it's not hard to imagine sign-painters being especially susceptible to this as they saw previous generations of signs outlast their creators, the businesses they'd once touted, in many cases the viability of the neighborhoods they'd adorned. Some signs were lost to the bulldozers of urban renewal, or simply to wear and to sun-bleaching. Others were painted over, blocked out, or enshrouded in graffiti (whose great underpinning has always been "Hey, I'm *here*"), and the conflation of ghost signs with wall-tagging led some city leaders to equate them, and to decry ghost signs as just a quainter form of blight.

I imagine that walldogs heard the moans and clanking chains of ghost signs well before the rest of us, and were probably more attuned, too, to the message those signs sent that both the city they'd represented and the vocation they'd made possible were imperiled. Those painters would also have discerned, again far ahead of the rest of us, what kinds of legacy tended to remain. Many of the signs around town by the 1960s were for long-gone businesses, brands, and establishments. Whole neighborhoods had been left behind or plowed under. The city's growth had slowed, then stopped, and now the hemorrhage had begun.

For the first dozen years I lived in Cincinnati, I enjoyed and mentally cataloged the ghost signs I passed—glimpses of an older city beneath the palimpsest of the present—and thought I was paying close attention. But three years ago, as I passed an old Paramount Vodka sign on Elm Street in the rapidly (and for reasons of gentrification and displacement, somewhat controversially) reviving Over-the-Rhine neighborhood, I noticed at the bottom left a little nameplate in black and white, just two bricks high and five or six wide: GUS HOLTHAUS. (In a way, I should say, gentrification—much as I might like to deplore it—had made the discovery possible; this was a neighborhood I'd often passed through while driving, but I could only have noticed the signature on foot, at old-city pace rather than with the automobile rush of *Learning from Las Vegas*.)

My experience with ghost signs, as with certain graffiti tags, has been that after a long stretch of dim, almost unconscious awareness, my notice at some point—in my case spurred by a writer friend who photographs vanishing traces of paint—turns self-aware, and once that happens I'm shocked to discover that these signs, once they swim up into vision, turn out to be *everywhere*. That experience was replicated when I saw that first signature. As I walked the city now I noticed ads signed by friends or rivals of Gus Holthaus . . . and several more featuring his name.

From the first time I saw it, the practice of attaching a signature—begun who knows how, and under circumstances I can't guess—struck me as having a rueful tone. This wasn't self-assertion of the braggadocious type, not at all. It seemed to announce on the way out, more in sorrow than in anger, that "This is art, and we were here, and likewise the generations of painters before us." That's not to say that such signatures didn't assert the artisan's pride, or even that they weren't—in a small-scale, at-the-margins way—a bid for a piece of immortality: a bet that these signs might last, and that in lasting they might, eventually, gain the prestige that longevity can confer. But to me those signatures read as small gestures of farewell, illegible except to those who slowed their approach and trained their eyes, from a profession on the way out.

I suspect they read in a similar way to graffiti artists, too. Therein lies the kinship between graffitists and pros like Gus Holthaus, who might otherwise be thought of as rivals or enemies: his signatures, like their tags, are an acknowledgment of evanescence—this both their point and their essential irony—that hopes to linger anyway. As I hinted earlier: I've noticed that though graffiti artists are attracted to the abandoned buildings and big canvases that ghost signs provide, they tend to spray their tags not across the old images but next to them. I want to think that's a professional courtesy, respect for the guild they both belong to.

I noted the signatures and moved on, and for two years I thought no more of Gus Holthaus.

But one morning last year, as I pondered what part of the cemetery to explore on my walk, I noticed—it was November, and the foliage had begun to thin—the stained glass along the back of a hulking building near the front gate.

I generally stay away from Spring Grove's street-facing southeastern corner, where the cemetery offices are, so as to avoid pestering the bereaved or getting in the way of employees. I'd known a building was nestled in those trees, but I'd thought it was one of several funeral chapels on the grounds. Now I saw that it was far too large for that, and sure enough, my map designated it as "MM"—Memorial Mausoleum. Spring Grove has several partially covered mausoleums, gardens, groves, and fountains, but until then I'd never known about this fully indoor section. I asked a groundskeeper passing on his golf cart whether it was OK to explore it, and he let me in with his key.

Near the entrance was a little room that looked like an alumni-club lounge, filled with étagères, their shelves lined with cremains-holding art pottery (often Rookwood, this being Cincinnati), a discreet plaque in front of each. At the end of the long hall on the left I found a bay-windowed solarium, complete with plashing water feature, and to one side what looked like a bank of lockers in an executive gym. But most of the building consisted of little side halls off the main one, each with upholstered benches and a stained-glass window at one end.

On the reflective marble walls of one of these, a name jumped out at me: *Gustav Holthaus*. How did I know that name? Wait ... was it? It had to be—yes, the great Cincinnati walldog, now out of the elements once and for all.

Holthaus died in 1970, at seventy-two. I learned via an internet search that there was no public hoopla—just a modest funeral notice produced by the family. The death certificate informed me that Holthaus had lived (and died) just a few blocks from my house, on a modest two-block-long street that now overlooks a school playground.

My interest was reignited, so I began digging.

It turns out that there's a thriving subculture of ghost sign fans in Cincinnati. From Ronny Salerno's book *Fading Ads of Cincinnati* (and from Bill Rinehart's blog "Writing on the Walls," which Salerno's book introduced me to), I learned that Holthaus's company has continued—as Holthaus Lackner—and that when the company won the rights to create the signage at the Reds' new Great American Ball Park in 2003, they smuggled in a hand-painted tribute to Gus Holthaus and his forebears: a flying pig, Cincinnati's symbol, daubed onto the brick exterior of a "vintage" tavern called Bootleggers.[8]

The story doesn't end there, quite. In 2005, Tod Swormstedt founded the American Sign Museum, and he has invited contemporary walldogs to town to show off their skills. Meanwhile, as part of its renaissance, the city—mainly through the labor of ArtWorks Cincinnati—has commissioned and executed over a hundred large-scale murals (with almost every one of the city's fifty-two named neighborhoods included).[9]

The best-known mural in my neighborhood, located barely a quarter-mile from the Holthaus residence, is a likeness of Nobel Peace laureate Aung San Suu Kyi by Shepard Fairey. In 2010, Fairey and his crew—it included, the press noted, Spencer Elden, the swimming baby featured on the cover of Nirvana's *Nevermind* back in 1991—placed sixteen murals around town. These are not painted, but produced in strips at his studio, then aligned and assembled on site and affixed to the wall using a method that harks back all the way to the nineteenth century: with wheat paste.

All this is to suggest that Gus Holthaus's legacy extends far past his nameplate on those few remaining walls around town. I'd contend that his unconventional decision toward the end of his career to sign some works, discreetly but visibly, contributed in a small but crucial way to the appreciation and preservation of ghost signs as art in this city, and thus to the explosion of murals and public art around town—a development that culminated (for now) in the Blink Festival of 2017, which drew a million people downtown over four nights to see those works.[10] Indirectly, at least, his determination to ignore or elide the old distinctions between commercial work and art prefigured the founding, and the thriving, of the American Sign Museum. Gus Holthaus lives on not only in the sly tribute at the ballpark but in all of his namesake firm's design work, too, and perhaps even in that of Landor, Inc.—which opened a Cincinnati office in the 1990s.

I'm reminded of that kitsch classic of short fiction, O. Henry's maudlin, wonderful "The Last Leaf." In that story, as fall staggers toward its end, a desperately ill girl is fading in tandem with the patch of ivy visible from her window. One by one, the leaves on the brick wall opposite flame out, parch, shrivel, and drop, until only one remains. But it, improbably, hangs on all winter long, providing the example the sick girl needs. Gradually her deathbed sheds that cruel prefix, the girl recovers, and come spring she goes outside . . . to discover that the last leaf was painted on by her friend, the elderly artist next door. He has saved her with his walldog masterpiece. (In the story, the artist has since died—O. Henry was not noted for artistic restraint—from a pneumonia contracted by painting outside in the cold and wet.)

Which is to say, with a pithy O. Henry–style message, that there are many ways to chase immortality, which is after all a lasting advertisement for the self. Immortality is capricious, a shape-shifter, and there's no guessing what our legacies will be, if we are lucky enough to have them. We might leave behind *Slaughterhouse-5*, or She Skips to Her Loo; might survive in memory on the basis of directing either *Fight Club* or the video to Jermaine Stewart's "We Don't Have to Take Our Clothes Off." Maybe we'll design the Barack Obama Hope poster, or possess the most famous underwater infant penis of the grunge movement.

The Man in the Hathaway Shirt; Levi's batwing logo; a fading ad for a cheap well vodka. Who knows what will outlast us? All we can do is our work, and hope the memorials we leave inspire someone.

Gus Holthaus left tombstones all over town, and he made them himself, save the last.

INTERLUDE
THE CRYPTO AUTO-OBITUARY

<hr />

THE ARGENTINE WRITER JORGE LUIS BORGES once invented a sect called the Histriones, who believed that no evil act could ever be exactly replicated. Once an atrocity occurred, all possibility of it occurring again vanished. So the Histriones set out to commit, under laboratory conditions as it were, every iniquity they could dream up. It was how you spared others from error or horror.

I was a childhood Histrione of a kind. Mom late to pick me up? Quick, Michael, imagine in awful detail the accident that's befallen her: *She's speeding down Broughton Street, beneath its high canopy, and that massive branch that's been groaning for days overhead begins calculating—five, four, three— the proper instant to plunge.* The principle behind these grisly imaginings was that I believed God wouldn't stoop to doing any harm to my mother if I had beaten Him to it. To imagine a horrific accident, then, was to prevent it. The game cost me dearly, but when Mom arrived safely and shoved open the passenger door and smiled, it gave me the chance to feel heroic. I had, after all, *saved her life.*

Put another way: I reduced potential tragedies to cheapo ironies, ironies no worthwhile God would indulge in, and vanquished them that way.

There came a point—bitter-cold winter walks in the cemetery, with no one and nothing around, no Canada geese honking overhead, the twisted semaphore of bare hardwoods everywhere, the ponds browned and iced over like dead occluded eyes, will do this to you—when I started questioning again why I was writing this book. Why these weird obituaries? What to make of the slender but persistent strand of autobiography underneath, which in the "Ghosts of the Walldogs" essay especially had pushed its way into the foreground and might rudely do so again?

Was I up to old tricks? Did I imagine that patrolling the graveyard would somehow—by the Inviolable Law of Two-Bit Irony—keep *me* from dying? That it would keep my parents and friends safe? One day I saw a cemetery prowler car parked, still running, and behind the nearby crypt its driver taking a piss that couldn't wait. His expectation of privacy was so strong that he wasn't even glancing around—why would anyone be here on an iron-gray ten-degree morning?—and I was close enough to see the steam. I ducked behind a tree so as not to be seen, or so as not to see any more? It felt almost like a panic attack, those few seconds of cowering.

But what was I afraid of? Had my childhood faith waned so far? It had. I went to the doctor for my every-other-year physical, and as I sat in the waiting room, I discovered that I half-expected Fate, that lazy hack, to give this book the plot of a medical thriller, just to spite me, in which case a) every *literary* value I'd ever believed in or treasured would be betrayed and b) (more important?) I might not make it out alive.

Thankfully, Fate had no interest in me. I was ushered promptly into an exam room, had my blood pressure taken, and then sat reading a book for fully seventy-five minutes before I summoned the nerve to click open the floor-to-ceiling door that had intimidated me into patience and ask if they'd forgotten me. Which they had. Soon the sheepish doctor came in, tapped here and there, told a few (pretty great) anecdotes about his Alaskan malamutes and the wheeled street-sled he'd bought to mush them through his city neighborhood for exercise, and then told me I didn't even need bloodwork this time. Clean bill. You're walking *how many* miles a day, you say? Keep it up.

The only thing worse than paranoia is the fear that *no one* is watching, that no one cares enough even to plot against you. You are unloved and invisible, and soon that invisibility will turn pure and permanent. Thus my interest in all the things we leave behind to mark—however vainly or futilely—our (former) places. Graveyards and obituaries and funeral ceremonies provide, of course, at least a momentary rebuke to the notion that when you're gone, the world instantly heals over the rent you've left. The newspaper obituary—even more so the variety that begins in empathy and seeks to avenge the dead—may not, by the rules of the form, include itself in any list of your survivors, but it's an important one. It is the wake of the wake, the last bit of you that might rock another's boat.

Obituary-writing, of course, numbers among the crafts praised in the last essay, those that must be practiced invisibly. The obituary writer who vies for the stage with his or her subject is (mea culpa!) a special breed of monster. And yet, implicit in every obituary ever written is a furtive hope based in the golden rule: honor others' lives as you would have your own be honored.

Like Gus Holthaus, the obituarist leaves a nameplate, and with it a hope. Every obituary is, in small and cryptic ways, an auto-obituary.

Please ignore this little block signature in the bottom left corner of the book.

"AND THEY DID KILL HER BY INCHES"

THE STRANGE CASE OF CARRIE ELDER

ON FEBRUARY 28, 1882, the *Cincinnati Enquirer*'s deaths log included Carrie Elder, "daughter of J. C. and S. L. Wagner, February 25th, at 5:30 P.M., aged 17 years 11 months and 20 days." The funeral, the entry vaguely noted, had taken place "from the residence" on the 27th. All was past.

The specificity with which Carrie's age is nailed down in this notice may strike the twenty-first-century observer as peculiar, but it didn't diverge much from the norm of such announcements. Certainly it was common, when infants died, to give them—or rather to give their grieving parents—credit for every day of the life together they'd been granted. A little odder, perhaps, for such precision in the case of a young woman of nearly eighteen. But an adored daughter, snatched away from her family abruptly, in the bloom of youth—of course one can understand.

From the cynic's point of view, though, the math was the opposite of odd. The family had been performing punctilious calculations about Carrie's age long before she fell ill that winter. Carrie Elder's father died young, and her grandfather had bequeathed her $25,000 (over half a million today). She would gain control of the money upon reaching majority—a milestone Carrie fell just ten days shy of.

After Carrie's father's death, her mother married John Charles Wagner, and the family settled first in Shelbyville, Indiana, and then, in the wake of unspecified "trouble," moved on to Cincinnati. The year before Carrie died, with the family apparently in financial straits, her stepfather made inquiries about selling off his daughter's inheritance, but the court informed him that to dispose of the fortune on his say-so, before his daughter came into it, was impossible.

We have no way to know what Carrie thought of these legal forays. The role the newspaper assigns her through the ordeal of her last days is passive sufferer, blank slate, white canvas for others' machinations—this last in a terrifyingly literal way we'll get to later. No one ever quotes her, and she remains enigmatically silent throughout, except for the "unendurable" screams that would haunt her caregivers.

By the time Carrie's name appears in the newspaper again two weeks later, on March 15, she's evidently become a cause célèbre; scurrilous rumors have caught fire. The paper's report that day is simultaneously splashy and controversy-dampening. The reporter means to end the sordid talk, and embarks on that task straightaway: "A mystery surrounded the death, and like many another mystery, it should never have existed." But he doesn't stint on the details that sparked suspicion in the first place: the heiress's impending coming-into-fortune, the attempted sale of the inheritance by a stepfather in his (this noted oh-by-the-way) third marriage, and so on. The tone keeps insisting "Nothing to see here, please move along," but it does so in a way that pumps a bellows at the embers of gossip. What to make, for example, of the simultaneously discreet and provocative mention of the "trouble" that drove the family from Shelbyville? What of the assertion that where the Wagners lived in Cincinnati was "not material"—a bit of tut-tutting righteousness followed just paragraphs later by divulging the family's address at the time of Carrie's death, then noting in a sidelong way their having moved to new lodgings almost immediately afterward? Moral dudgeon requires one tone, hawking papers another, and this reporter's strategy, deftly executed, is both/and.

The crux of the newspaper story is its reframing of a mystery that has blown up into a scandal in the public imagination. Yes, the reporter allows, a misdeed was committed, and yes, it explains the family's shady-looking secrecy, the delay in the death notice, and the lack of funerary ceremony. But the subterfuge—this "foolish . . . and reprehensible piece of action"—served to cover up not the "heinous crime" some leapt to imagine but a small offense against public health. The true villain (in the paper's version knowingly but forgivably abetted by the family) was Carrie's physician in her final days, Frederick Ehrmann, who on her death certificate listed the cause as typhoid fever.

In fact, the *Enquirer* now revealed, smallpox killed Carrie Elder. At first the family—terrified that their beloved daughter would be taken to the pesthouse to die anonymously amid filth and stigma—hushed up her disease so she could be cared for at home, and then, postmortem, continued the pretense to prevent panic and to evade prosecution for failure to report the case. "Of course this clears away the mystery," the reporter concludes, noting that while some have been clamoring to dig up Carrie's corpse, the combination of a statement from Carrie's hired nurse, testimony from the girl's loving and bereaved mother, and confirmation from the doctor has—fortunately—made such a desecration unnecessary.

Or, again, not. Three days later, the *Enquirer* resumes its coverage with a story whose first lurid subhead reads "The Body Exhumed!" Again the article's tenor and aim is to calm the outrage, to reassure readers that no nefarious fate befell the girl and to redirect blame to the doctor who failed to report smallpox, thus endangering the Wagners, their fellow tenants and neighbors, the hired nurse (and the nurse's family, as the dead girl's unfumigated sick-clothes had been given to her as partial payment), the public at large, and the sexton and his team of diggers at Spring Grove (these men, the newspaper reports, were "loud in their denunciation" of the skullduggery surrounding their skulldiggery).

The exhumation, undertaken at the insistence of an Elder relative from Indiana, did confirm smallpox. As the paper put it, "And on the hands were found pustules of *the most malignant type.*" The posthumous diagnosis should have been the end of the commotion; certainly it would scotch any whispers about cold-blooded murder for money. All that remained was for the doctor to give his apology for missing the diagnosis or covering it up, and the curtain could come down.

But the March 18 article ends with a troubling dialog between a reporter and Dr. Ehrmann, who, when the inquisitive young man knocks at his door, leans out a second-story window—one recalls almost this exact scene in Robert Louis Stevenson's *The Strange Case of Dr. Jekyll and Mr. Hyde*, which would appear just four years later—to dispel suspicion from on high.

Only Frederick Ehrmann was, in suspicion-dispelling, no match for Henry Jekyll. In point of fact, he stunk at it. Spectacularly.

The reporter lobs his accusation, couched as a question. Why did the doctor fail to report smallpox?

Ehrmann replies, "I said it was malignant typhoid fever. What's the difference?"

Reporter: "Considerable difference, I should think, but—"

Ehrmann: "It don't make any difference to me."

The newspaper report—making clear that this has now become a serial, that the arc is not concluded and there will be a new episode tomorrow, same smallpox time, same arrogant-quack channel—contains just one more sentence, or rather cliffhanger: "And down went the window, and the interview was at an end."

Frederick Ehrmann belonged to a dynasty of medical men. His father had been a well-regarded allopathic practitioner in Germany. Frederick and his four younger brothers took up the profession as well, mostly in the New World (two of them in practice just a block down Seventh Street from him), and all as homeopaths. The most illustrious was probably Benjamin Ehrmann, who had come to Cincinnati in the 1840s and begun a partnership with Joseph Hippolyt Pulte. During the cholera epidemic of 1849, the two reported stupendous results—perhaps too stupendous, as they would be arrested and charged with misreporting or miscategorizing deaths. A subsequent investigation may or may not have vindicated them, as their supporters would later claim, but in any case they emerged from the epidemic with their reputations, and that of homeopathy, enhanced.

Nineteenth-century homeopathy can seem like the veriest hocus-pocus today, but it's important to recall that Hahnemannian practice, the dominant strain in Cincinnati, a hotbed of alternative medicine, began as a reaction against bloodletting, leeches, and other dubious "therapies." Samuel Hahnemann wanted nothing less than a universal key to disease, and his mode of inquiry was as much philosophical as it was pragmatic—harking back to Paracelsus and the Greeks as models rather than to the trial-and-error heuristic slog favored by more conventional medicine. Initially, around 1803, Hahnemann fingered coffee as the likely culprit, but that beverage's durable popularity and attractiveness made it a hard sell as a villain. Hahnemann moved on to miasmas, especially the Psoric miasm, which he adjudged to be responsible for 85 percent of diseases; later still, in the 1820s, he would identify scabies as the fount of most human illness.

Meanwhile, though, Hahnemann was developing principles that would hold enormous sway, and that continue to influence alternative medical practice. The most famous of these was *Similia similibus curentur,* "Let likes be cured by likes." This theory, with some kinship to the ancient notion of sympathetic magic, held that substances that produce a disease's symptoms in the healthy will cure the same malady in a sick person. Hahnemann—theory already in hand, in search of buttressing for it—had experimented on himself, taking repeated doses of cinchona, the Peruvian bark that when stripped, dried, and refined into quinine was (and still is) used to treat malaria,[1] and he discovered that it produced in him the shivering and fever characteristic of that disease.

The second basic principle of Hahnemann's homeopathy may also—again, peering through the cynic's lens—be traced to a practicality: Treating people with harshly toxic substances (with poisons, in a word) may incite controversy, not least by killing or maiming the patient. So Hahnemann developed the "law of infinitesimal doses," which held that when these toxins were diluted in water or alcohol—and diluted again and again and again—they would *increase* in potency. This was especially the case if the medicine was vigorously shaken—"succussed"— before being administered, which would "activate" it and concentrate its effect. The practical result of the law of infinitesimal doses, in some cases, may have been to make homeopathy effective as a placebo . . . and to be fair, often as better than a placebo, since homeopaths, also trained in practical-minded medicine, were providing attentiveness and solace and the confidence of expertise. After being watered down, a solution of belladonna might well eventually contain no molecules of belladonna; it wouldn't do much *good*, perhaps, for a sufferer of Parkinson's or whooping cough or earache (right ear especially!) or menstrual cramps, but it also wouldn't violate the Hippocratic injunction to "first do no harm."

One appeal of homeopathy for patients was its focus less on the cataloging and alleviation of symptoms than on the underlying causes of disease, even if some of these root causes were unscientific or even chimerical. In practical terms, the holistic emphasis made for less embarrassing exams; less obsession with sores, tumors, and other markers of pathology; and less invasive therapies—all these innovations understandably popular with patients. Another element of homeopathy's flourishing in the United States, especially its good reputation in epidemics of contagion, was that for most of the nineteenth century, traditional medicine's treatments for such diseases were often useless or even harmful. Homeopathy might not cure cholera, but it did less damage and caused less distress than turpentine enemas or calomel (mercury chloride) or being rubbed down with cayenne pepper.

In Kurt Andersen's 2017 book *Fantasyland: How America Went Haywire*, homeopathy and quack medicine (water cures, exorcisms, snake oil and other rostrums) feature as examples of America's five-hundred-year history of susceptibility to, even embrace of, hokum, flimflam, and wishful thinking, what Andersen calls our "promiscuous devotion to the untrue." As Hanna Rosin put it in her *New York Times* review of the book,

> The country's initial devotion to religious and intellectual freedom, Andersen argues, has over the centuries morphed into a fierce entitlement to custom-made reality. So your right to believe in angels and your neighbor's right to believe in U.F.O.s and Rachel Dolezal's right to believe she is black lead naturally to our president's right to insist that his crowds were bigger. Andersen's history begins at the beginning. . . .

[The Puritans] were zealots and also well-educated British gentlemen, which set the tone for what Andersen identifies as a distinctly American endeavor: propping up magical thinking with elaborate scientific proof.[2]

One may see this as a dark underside of the American dream, which encourages innovation by creating a space that allows for, and rewards, self-invention. The problem is that making our new identities work requires genuine faith in them, and once we come to believe in our own myths, the boundaries between self and world have to give. Having invented ourselves, we insist on inventing the world that contains us, and on requiring its underlying laws to conform with our own.

In *Bech: A Book*, John Updike wrote about "those self-made men who have paid the price (for not letting God make them) of minor defects like inner deafness and constant neuralgia."[3] In Andersen's view, possibly without that qualifying adjective "minor," that's essentially the case with America—with the proviso that we insist not only on making ourselves but also that God did it, and that His principles are thus universally discoverable through us. Inner deafness is a particularly tenacious condition for us, it seems.

Of course inner deafness or self-delusion afflicts all of us, and not just the pursuers of eccentric systems that posterity may agree to find risibly in error. Practitioners like the Ehrmanns and Benjamin's partner Joseph Pulte did plenty of good, and not only in their partly serendipitous therapies for cholera sufferers. Pulte, for example, founded a medical school in 1872. . . .

Wait—Pulte? That name was tantalizingly familiar. I'd seen it, I was sure, in one of the tonier precincts of Spring Grove. So I set out walking again to refind it. Sure enough, the obelisk I recalled, almost obscured by the foliage of a giant oak, belonged to Pulte and his wife, Mary Jane.

Joseph Hippolyt Pulte emigrated from Germany in 1834, at twenty-three. Soon after his arrival in the United States, he was introduced and converted to homeopathy, and he became an important early proponent. On the journey by riverboat to join his brother in St. Louis several years later, he encountered his wife to-be, Mary Jane Rollins, and Pulte never made it to Missouri, stopping off instead at Cincinnati, where the couple would remain for forty-five years. Pulte embraced Hahnemann's intellectual grandiosity, writing—among several books—one with the formidable title *Organon of the History of the World*. Published in German in 1846, translated into English in 1859, the book derives its title most immediately from Hahnemann's *Organon of Medicine*. Hahnemann, in turn, had adopted the term *Organon*, meaning the underlying

The Wagner family marker, about twenty feet away from Carrie's

Students at the dissecting table of the Pulte Medical School.
(Note the stogey-chomping Stan Laurel lookalike in the bowler hat
who's peering from behind the skeleton's spine and ribcage)

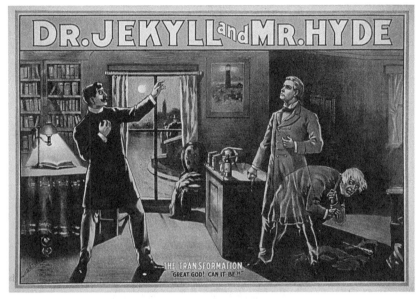

Theatrical poster, Chicago, circa 1890

Robert Louis Stevenson, 1887. His last words: "Does my face look strange?"

set of principles behind a philosophical or scientific system, from Aristotle. Pulte did not lack for ambition.

Nor for energy. He was, it seems, a man of booming enthusiasm, intellectual zeal, and public-mindedness. In addition to his thriving private practice and his contributions during the 1849 cholera outbreak, Pulte would help create a free dispensary to serve Cincinnati's poor, and later the medical college that bore his name. A technophile and a patriotic believer in American dynamism, Pulte became one of the first and most ardent advocates for the potential of the telegraph to bring the world together. Less than a decade after Samuel Morse's successful demonstration, Pulte was lobbying Congress to lay a cable to Europe—though his preference, on practical grounds, was to shun a transatlantic link in favor of one that would cross the Bering Strait and then Russia—10,600 miles, but mostly overland. Pulte was also an inventor, including a shared patent for a roof that combined clay, quicklime, tar, and a painted-on coat of dextrin—the biological sugar derived (by the action of saliva, for instance) from starch. That protective biochemical coat would prove to be an important innovation, and related patents were still being issued more than a half-century later.

Mary Jane Pulte was no less remarkable—in fact, her 1862 patent for "improved composition for cleaning gloves" was the first ever granted to a woman from Cincinnati. It antedated, and may have been the catalyst for, her husband's spate of inventions later that decade.

In 1882, Frederick Ehrmann was seventy-four years old. He would soon be the last surviving Ehrmann brother. J. H. Pulte would die just two years later, though the medical school would survive him. Homeopathy was beginning to lose sway, not so much because of a failing on its part as because it and more traditional practice were converging . . . though thanks to advances in science, they were converging mostly on traditional medicine's terms and turf. Old-time adherents were complaining by century's end that the homeopathic medical schools—there were twenty-two at the height—were neglecting Hahnemann's principles in favor of an anatomy- and biology-based medicine that was determined to crowd it out, to kill it by assimilation. Indeed, just thirty years on, *all* the homeopathic medical schools would be gone, either shuttered or subsumed into the emerging standard system.

Frederick Ehrmann, it appears, remained an old-fashioned practitioner. Even late in his career, he was espousing theories about the therapeutic uses of color, of "charged water," and the like, as in this testimonial, which ran in an advertisement after his death: "I have used blue-charged water in my practice with very gratifying results. In cases of diphtheria, I have found it of great service. I have not lost a single patient since. . . . The blue principle is a great antiphlogistic." That last sentence is a doozy, even if the final word means in this context merely "anti-inflammatory" or "fever reducer" rather than remover of phlogiston (the substance, according to a by-then-long-discredited idea, present in all bodies and released by fire). But to cling to that word fully a century after Lavoisier's discovery of oxygen and hydrogen was to flaunt one's disregard for the prevailing terminology. Combustion or phlogiston, whatever—"it don't make any difference to me."

As to why Ehrmann might have answered the reporter as he did: Was this just tragically muffed damage control? Did he feel guilty that he'd acceded to the family's wishes and kept quiet (perhaps with a financial benefit for doing so), so he struck a defensive tone? Was he piqued at being second-guessed by some dolt layman, representing a mob of dolt laymen, about the profession he'd been practicing for decades? Both these speculations are aided by the detail of his choice not to come downstairs, but to speak from on high and at distance. That decision might derive partly from self-protection, partly from the loftiness or ritual humiliation that makes bosses install low-slung wobbly chairs to be peered down on from across the expanse of their desks. Or did Ehrmann feel—one hears similar plaints from present-day doctors about the intrusions of bureaucracy—that the reporting requirements for smallpox were arbitrary and stupid? Typhoid is of course similarly deadly, similarly contagious.[4] One of the reasons smallpox sparked special terror and had special status was its disfiguring gruesomeness—precisely the sort of superficial, pathology-centric thinking that Hahnemann's homeopathy opposed. Was Ehrmann weary? Bitter that his chosen field was misunderstood and in slow-motion eclipse? Simply inclined to let the Wagners' money do the talking? There's no way to know, of course . . . but we can say for sure that willful ignorance was a terrible strategy in dealing with the press.

This might be the end of the mystery, with just the next day's story about the doctor's arrest to go. And in a way, that's what happened . . . but in a way not. The *Enquirer* article of March 19, 1882, the last major statement on the case to appear in the press, is the strangest and most fascinating of all. It begins, as expected, with Ehrmann squarely in the crosshairs, leading with an account of the doctor's perfidy or incompetence and his apparent disdain for public health. The reporter awards himself (and indignant readers) the satisfaction of a perp-walk paragraph.

But to the reporter's dismay, the acting judge releases the doctor without bail. "One might have expected this from [acting] Judge Wilson, but hardly from [usually sitting] Judge Higley," he grumbles. Worse, it becomes clear that the case will be dismissed immediately, by Wilson *or* by Higley. The accusation cannot hold because, in a sentence that oozes exasperation, "The law in the case, as laid down, is . . . absurd and meaningless." Turns out the legislature made a mistake in drafting the statute, and as a result, the threatened fine has to be recovered in a civil action rather than a criminal one. So the court has no jurisdiction, and unless another charge can be brought and made to stick, Ehrmann will suffer no legal consequence. Which seems to have been the case: the doctor is mentioned only once in the *Enquirer* after this, several months later, when he misdiagnoses another case of smallpox. But there's no subsequent report on his prosecution, no indication that his license was pulled—not even a notice of his death.

But then the article takes a weird, dark turn, into the sworn testimony— expanded and somewhat altered from her earlier statement—of Carrie's nurse, Elizabeth Jane Guy. It is Guy's unforgettably vivid account that gives Carrie Elder's story its durable intrigue. Not because her statement leads anywhere in a legal sense: if the question is "Did Carrie Elder's family murder her for her money?" the answer is certainly no. But the moral waters are more turbid, and the nurse has plenty of muck to churn up.

The details she provides are mostly transcribed verbatim, without gloss from the reporter. John Charles Wagner, Guy says, approached her at home. He offered a large sum and asked her to accompany him (when she hesitated, he "insisted") to an undisclosed place to tend an undisclosed smallpox patient. She eventually acceded to his wishes. During the nine days she sat at Carrie's bedside, Guy testified, the patient was given, per "doctor's instructions," no nourishment at all, and during that time (plus two days before Guy arrived, Carrie's mother confided) Carrie also never defecated. Carrie was fed six to eight lemons per day, squeezed but unsweetened. Many homeopaths believed that smallpox was at core a digestive disorder, brought on by the putrefaction or acidification of rich food overindulged in . . . so *Similia similibus curentur* might call for treatment with, say, citric acid. But it wouldn't, presumably, call for persisting for nine days in that treatment while otherwise starving the patient. And why, when Guy asked, was she told that the lemons were "for the purpose of making [Carrie] white"?

For the purpose of *what*? Is the implication that they—an imprecise pronoun here by design, so as not to impugn the possibly innocent—wanted to preserve her complexion *in death,* so as not to draw the extra scrutiny required for smallpox cases? It would be easier to dismiss that accusation if the nurse didn't also report that at one point the doctor incised a wound on Carrie's back, centered between her shoulder blades, with the intent "of drawing the disease to that location, in order to prevent her face from being spoiled." This sounds less like treatment than like advance work on a coverup—the coverup they would in fact undertake.

The other therapeutic measure taken, Guy said, was that every hour, Carrie was administered a dose of white powder, usually by her mother. This substance was placed on her tongue and washed down with beer or brandy. Afterward she foamed at the mouth, a white froth sometimes stringy with sputum; it was wiped away with cloths and the cloths immediately burned. That was it. According to Guy, "I objected to this treatment, and told them they were killing her, and they did kill her by inches." She complained especially to Mrs. Wagner, who replied that they must follow the doctor's orders, else what was the point of having a doctor. Guy—her demurrals being ignored, the patient's screaming becoming "unendurable"—finally tried to beg off; she couldn't take it anymore. "I have nursed many smallpox patients," she said, "but never saw such treatment before." Mrs. Wagner coaxed the nurse back to the bedside by applying, once again, the balm of cash, meanwhile reassuring her that "everything would be all right"—a haunting and jangly phrase in the context. Which *everything* does she mean?

There is in the testimony a single, passing mention of a "young physician" who visited on Carrie Elder's final Friday and lamented that they did not ventilate the room sooner—now it is too late. Who is he: an assistant to Dr. Ehrmann? An alternative to him, summoned in panic as Carrie's condition deteriorated? In the final hours, Mrs. Wagner asked Guy to cradle her dying daughter in her arms. Carrie was too heavy for that, so Guy says she rocked her in a rocking chair until, two hours later, Carrie Elder expired.

Another oddity was John Charles Wagner's abrupt and awkward appearance in the sickroom just after his stepdaughter's death, after not visiting at all during the nine days of anguish. Guy describes him as entering and remarking, "She's dead." Then he "boohooed," paced "two or three" times across the carpet, and left. Guy was instructed afterward to keep quiet, an instruction she initially followed, we can surmise, both because she too was a co-conspirator and because, as she'd been assured, "Money would hush up the whole matter." But *what* whole matter? Was it as simple as the newspaper had asserted several days before? Was the secret concealed merely Carrie's diagnosis? Maybe, but from a twenty-first-century perspective, the blandishment doesn't quite fit the sin. Where there's smoke, there's ... not phlogiston.

For its part the *Enquirer* treats Elizabeth Jane Guy's story, from the article's title on, as an indictment of Dr. Ehrmann's malpractice. The "Terrible Details of Carrie Elder's Suffering" redound, it seems, to his discredit only, and the newspaper does nothing to expand the scope of outrage. But of course there's a more sinister interpretation available, and Guy fans the flames. She implies not only neglect or insufficient help on the doctor's part but a whole course of treatment, predetermined or directed or at least approved of by the parents, that's aimed less at preventing Carrie's death than at a kind of proleptic coverup. The mother's role in any conspiracy is unclear; the nurse never questions her sincerity. But Guy is openly skeptical of Carrie's stepfather, whose postmortem appearance in the sickroom reads—her emphasis on his absence heretofore, her damning count of his "two or three" turns across the room, and especially the word "boohooed" make this unmistakable—as a charade.

Again, that does not mean that there's an infamous deed to uncover, a "heinous crime." It may be slyness on the *Enquirer*'s part to present the nurse's testimony in an unadorned way. Perhaps the paper assumes its readers will pick up a whiff of impropriety, but it does not dare libel a family that may have innocently trusted a doctor who was unworthy of their faith. Perhaps every word of Guy's testimony cannot be credited either. The reporter attests to the honesty of the undertaker and of the man who put Carrie's corpse into the coffin, but withholds any such characterization of the nurse's story. Understandably so, perhaps, as she's confessed to taking part in the conspiracy for money ... and her testimony has changed since the initial interview, in which she too claimed not to have known that Carrie died of smallpox.

The bottom line is that we can't make out intent, not from this distance—and not from the *Enquirer*'s distance, either, and probably not even from the nurse's. The accusation of murder is far-fetched, surely; even the makers of TV whodunits would balk at a script in which Carrie's stepfather killed the inconvenient heiress using smallpox as a weapon of opportunity, and then, having hired a doctor he winkingly instructed not to take heroic measures, asked his wife, the child's mother, to hunker down for nine days of attending at close range to her daughter's screaming, foaming agony. That's absurd. The truth, as usual, is more ambiguous and complex. On the continuum from perfect innocence to murder most foul, all we can safely do—in this as in almost every situation—is to eliminate either pole. It was not malice murder, and it was not pure innocence. But did the parents sincerely try to save Carrie by hiring Dr.

Ehrmann? Did Dr. Ehrmann sincerely try to save her by applying the fruits of his long experience in medicine? There's no way to answer no to either question, but the facts don't sustain a decisive yes, either. Probably. For the most part. If fate willed it. They would leave it in God's hands, and in Ehrmann's. At what point in the course of the disease does a stepfather's rooting interest become, not selfish and dastardly and a thing to be ruthlessly suppressed, but simply a wish, in no way blameworthy, for his loved stepdaughter to be released from her suffering?

Here, as usual, there's no foul beast to blame and punish and banish from the circle of human sympathy. Nor, though, is there any way to let the Wagners or Ehrmann (or Guy, or us) off the hook. Human motivation is darker and more complicated than we like to admit; psychology is a thing as coiled and pouched and involuted as the brain itself. Which was of course Stevenson's famous premise and jumping-off point in *The Strange Case*, with its tangled account of "good" Dr. Jekyll's attempt to boil off or dissociate himself from the small admixture of evil in him, which takes the twisted form of Hyde. In his typically brilliant lecture on the novella, using a strange, lovely set of Venn diagrams, Vladimir Nabokov points out that the interaction between Jekyll and Hyde is more intricate and morally ambiguous than Jekyll believes, or pretends to believe. He is not good and Hyde evil. Nabokov crosshatches a circle and projects it on the screen to demonstrate his point: "If you look closely you see that within this big, luminous, pleasantly tweed Jekyll there are rudiments of evil."[5]

Toward the story's end Jekyll, too, arrives reluctantly at a better understanding: "I learned to recognise the thorough and primitive duality of man; I saw that, of the two natures that contended in the field of my consciousness, even if I could rightly be said to be either, it was only because I was radically both."

One of the German words for "ambiguous" is "doppelbödig," which literally means "double-floored." But what's scary about ambiguity, as about irony, is that once you discover the possibility of a false floor, there's no way to step quite as surely as you did before—what's to prevent a second layer of deceit or error or unclarity, a third, a fourth, an eighty-sixth? How do you know you've reached bottom? This is the vertiginous appeal and the horror of Jekyll/Hyde, a yet stranger case, perhaps, even than Stevenson means it to be. Jekyll keeps trying to believe that he is or could be master of this fiasco. It's a chemistry experiment, after all, a matter of science, and if only he had a better supply of the salt he uses to effect the change, all would be well. Ultimately he comes (they come?) to understand, at least dimly and too late, that the problem—as in the sad saga of Carrie Elder—isn't so much medical as psychological.

The novella's plot boils down, roughly, to this: Jekyll and the string of stolid dullards trying to find or save him—all monkish and male and woefully unprepared for modernity—fail and fail again to plumb the depths of the darkness within. They just can't see how odd and how intricate the architecture of the new self is going to be. What *does* convey that complexity—this the story's triumph—is its trippy, chaotic narrative form. Stevenson stitches a crazy quilt of documents, testimonies, letters, overheard conversations, and above all an *I* being constantly contested and renegotiated: the first person's second floor . . . and all the muck beneath yet to be excavated.

Part of the mistake both Jekyll and his erstwhile London friends make is to misunderstand the genre of the story they're in. They keep thinking it's a mystery, and thus in need of a solution that will put everything back to right, if they just apply their bourgeois virtues: doggedness, logic/science, faith that the visible world is the whole world. But the book is weirder and more dangerous than that. Early in Nabokov's lecture, he urges his students to "Please completely forget, disremember, obliterate, unlearn, consign to oblivion any idea you have that 'Jekyll & Hyde' is some kind of a mystery story."

The same can be said of Carrie Elder's saga. March 19 marked the last significant media coverage. Five days later came a brief, factual announcement that Carrie's mother had claimed her estate, a day after that a notice that Ehrmann had confessed to not reporting Carrie's smallpox but would, as predicted, fight the charge because the blunder in wording made the law unconstitutional. Then silence.

The pot-stirring piece on March 18 had included the damning detail that the exhumation was surprisingly easy, as Carrie had been interred in a shallow grave in a poor corner of the cemetery; the sexton said she lay under three feet of soil, but Carrie's uncle from Lawrenceburg corrected that to two-and-a-half. Carrie's mother, Sarah Wagner, would die five years later, her husband five years after that, and they would erect a grander monument, one to reflect their (ill-gotten?) bourgeois status and wealth. Their stones are clustered together to the south of the current monument, which is topped by a piece of classical statuary, and which devotes one side each to the birth and death dates of John Charles, Sarah, and Carrie. Twenty-odd feet away and ninety degrees athwart is a gravestone that reads simply "Carrie." It's not clear whether she was exhumed again and reburied here, or whether her remains lie elsewhere.

THE SCULPTOR, HIS SON,
THE ODD FELLOWS,
AND THE WEIRD ASSASSIN
LOUIS REBISSO(S) AND OSCAR MUNDHENK

PIATT PARK IN DOWNTOWN CINCINNATI is bookended, east and west, by statues honoring the first two U.S. chief executives from Ohio, who happen to be the two presidents who served the shortest terms: James Garfield (six months) and William Henry Harrison (one). These monuments serve as reminders that before becoming the cradle of presidents, Ohio also had become the grave of them.[1]

Over the years, the statues have been moved about some, but Garfield has pride of place—figuratively, by getting the more trafficked side of the park, and literally, as the park's address is and has been Garfield Place.[2] Though Garfield died four decades after Harrison, he even beat Tippecanoe to the spot (Charles Henry Niehaus's memorial to Garfield was dedicated in 1887, nine years ahead of the Harrison statue).

There's nothing surprising about any of this: Garfield was a native Ohioan rather than a transplant; he was assassinated rather than dying of illness; he served as president for a bit longer. Yet one could hardly blame Louis Rebisso, sculptor of the Harrison memorial, if he harbored a small, private bitterness against Garfield, who now upstaged the sculptor for the second time. Complaints about martyr heroes—especially recently dead martyr heroes to whom you could object only churlishly, because they've robbed you of minor artistic glory—must remain unvoiced. But that doesn't mean that they don't rattle around the brainpan. I'm reminded of Robert Coover's ribald retelling of *Casablanca*, "You Must Remember This," in which the horny Rick, frustrated that his rival, Ilsa's husband Laszlo, cuts such a dashing, noble figure, keeps wearily referring to him in monologue as "that heroic sonuvabitch."[3] Coover's is probably a phrase Rebisso wouldn't have wanted engraved in marble, but who could fault him for whispering it into his fist from time to time in the late summer of 1892? That August, the sculptor's bronze tribute to Harrison, slated to become Cincinnati's first equestrian statue, was consigned to a warehouse in Chicopee, Massachusetts, while a display site was sought. As the *Enquirer* headline summarized the conundrum, "Poor Tippecanoe: Nowhere Can He

Rear His Proud Form." It must have been a relief to Rebisso when a permanent spot was found . . . but did it have to be in Garfield Place?

Part of the trouble in finding a suitable setting arose because Rebisso had had to make a major course correction. The super-sized pedestal designated for his statue would have made it, in its original proportions, look like the rock-opera model of Stonehenge in *This Is Spinal Tap*, which, thanks to a goof when it was sketched on a cocktail napkin, descends among guitar din and pyrotechnics only to be "in danger of being trampled by dwarves." Rebisso successfully—but amid controversy and grumbling, mainly from a selection committee member still bitter that Rebisso had been awarded the contract— petitioned for an extra thousand dollars to buy metal enough to pump up the statue's scale. But this pushed back the completion date, and even after it left Massachusetts for Cincinnati, Rebisso's memorial to Harrison would languish for three years in the basement of the National Guard Armory before being dedicated. The statue stood sentinel at the Vine Street end of the park until 1988, when it was displaced by Garfield.

Much of the little I thought I knew about William Henry Harrison turns out to be wrong. Almost the first thing I would have told you, had you asked— most people I encounter tend to ask me about William Henry Harrison; is it not the same for you?—was that Harrison died of a pneumonia he contracted because, in a show of machismo, he forwent a coat and hat on the blustery cold day of his inauguration. But that turns out to be only partly true.

The Whig party, seeking to exploit Martin Van Buren's unpopularity following the Panic of 1837 (they tagged him "Martin Van Ruin"), chose the war hero Tippecanoe as its 1840 nominee as a kind of non-ideological caretaker figure—a proto-Eisenhower. During the campaign, Van Buren's Democratic allies ridiculed Harrison as the "petticoat general" (because he'd resigned his commission before the end of the War of 1812) and as a weary old dotard: "Give him a barrel of hard cider and. . . a pension of two thousand a year . . . and . . . he will sit the remainder of his days in his log cabin," one newspaper sneered. And in fact Harrison, sixty-eight when inaugurated (and thus the last American president to have begun life as a British subject), would remain the oldest person elected until Ronald Reagan in 1980.[4]

What's true in the story I'd heard is that Harrison did decide to show off his hardiness by going hatless and coatless on Inauguration Day, which was cool but, at fifty degrees, not quite the icebox that myth has made it. Harrison's other stratagem for showing strength was more dubious yet; he delivered what remains, at 8,445 words and close to two hours, the longest inaugural speech in American history. The oration had been trimmed, heroically but perhaps not quite heroically enough, by Daniel Webster, who later joked that in pruning the text he had "killed seventeen Roman proconsuls."

Harrison's younger Whig rivals, chief among them Henry Clay, seem to have bought into part of the Democrats' argument about the elderly president. They thought he would be docile and easily co-opted. On this score Harrison, in his short time in office, proved tougher than expected, resisting both the machinations of Clay and a tide of eager office-seekers. But his physical resistance wasn't as stout as his moral. Three weeks after inauguration, on March 26, 1841, Harrison fell ill with a cold. He couldn't find a quiet room to rest in at the White House, which was still besieged by people pleading for spoils positions, and his condition steadily worsened, either despite or because of the treatments his doctors tried—opium, castor oil, leeches, Virginia snakeweed. (This makes Harrison Garfield's precursor in yet another way: a president whose death was hastened, arguably, by his doctors' failings.) When Harrison died early on April 4, his chief physician attributed the cause to pneumonia, and the Marlboro-Man-gone-wrong myth began ripening into received wisdom.[5]

The truth is crueler even than the unglamorous version in which Tippecanoe succumbed to his own long-windedness. A 2014 study of his doctor's notes suggested that Harrison most likely died of enteric fever or typhoid he contracted because . . . well, because the White House's water supply came from the sewage-filled Potomac. Daniel Webster couldn't have saved him if he'd killed off a whole legion of Roman proconsuls; nor could a time-traveling Eddie Bauer goosedown parka have spared his life in navy, wine, or hunter green. President Harrison succumbed to the sanitary and medical practices of his time. He provides a painful reminder that our vocabulary of political abuse only gradually becomes figurative, and only long after it becomes figurative can it take on even a tinge of the jocular. Meanwhile, back in the sad literality of 1841 in swampy Washington, Harrison ate shit and died.[6]

By contrast, Rebisso's memorial to Harrison has the impregnable dignity one expects of such sculptures—that is their reason for being. The culture whose memorials are built of popsicle sticks or aluminum foil glued to Styrofoam cannot abide. (Coincidentally, this is the idea undergirding the alleged "deep state" that so roiled the news in 2017; the nation whose bureaucratic structures and norms of behavior are built of popsicle sticks cannot abide, either.) The implied premise of nineteenth-century statuary is that continuity is provided by myth, and myths are by God too heavy—metaphorically, sure, but also literally—to change. In service of that ideal, Rebisso's piece depicts the future president—here with imposing military headgear, before foolish-fond old age seduced him into hatlessness—astride a horse that, it was said, the sculptor modeled on the symbol of an early insurance company. The horse's left front hoof is off the ground, signifying, in the lexicon of equestrian sculpture, that the subject was wounded in battle. There seems to be no sad-dle, so the stirrups appear magical—which I think we can safely ascribe to mythological license rather than sculptor's error.

But this essay is less about the second upstaging of Rebisso than the first, and about Rebisso's son and namesake, who became an "Artisan of the Pipes"—a plumber, if we translate from nineteenth-century newspaperese to plain prose—rather than following his father into his more glamorous field.

Louis Rebisso was born near Genoa in 1837. At twenty, he took part in one of Giuseppe Mazzini's futile attempts to found an Italian republic—a movement that would, under the leadership of Giuseppe Garibaldi, finally yield fruit in 1871, in the Risorgimento that created modern Italy. Rebisso was among the small band of revolutionaries who captured Genoa's hilltop Forte Diamante briefly in 1857—an attempt to overthrow the king that, as an American news-paperman would dryly put it decades later, "was attended with indifferent success." Pursued by decidedly un-indifferent authorities, Rebisso was forced to hide belowdecks on a barque, the *Osman II*, that was headed for the United States.

After a stay in Massachusetts, Rebisso—who in youth had trained in sculpture—landed in Cincinnati, where he decided to make a go of it as an artist. By 1869 he had taken a post at the Art Academy, then part of the University of Cincinnati, and over the next three decades he would teach a long list of distinguished pupils including Charles Henry Niehaus (sculptor of the Garfield monument), Mary Chase Perry (best known as a ceramic artist), Solon Borglum (brother to Gutzon, chief architect of Mount Rushmore), Janet Scudder (feminist sculptor and Paris friend of Gertrude Stein and Alice B. Toklas, best known for her fountains and garden fauns for the mega-rich), and Clement Barnhorn (who would succeed Rebisso at the Art Academy, eventually, besides creating the remarkable hearse sculpture discussed in another essay in this book). In 1876 Rebisso completed the Washington, DC, memorial for Union general James McPherson, who died at the Battle of Atlanta. It is recycled art of a kind, made from a melted-down Confederate cannon captured in the war, and it still occupies its spot in McPherson Square at 15th and K Streets.

Rebisso's most celebrated work, both in his lifetime and afterward, is his massive equestrian statue of Ulysses S. Grant in Lincoln Park, Chicago. That work, at the time the largest ever forged in the United States, remains the most prominent memorial in Lincoln Park (in an Alanis Morisettian irony, Augustus Saint-Gaudens's *Seated Lincoln* is the most prominent in the city's Grant Park). Paid for by a hundred thousand public subscriptions that were collected—such was Grant's popularity—even before the ex-president's burial in 1885, Rebisso's sculpture, depicting the general astride a Kentucky thoroughbred on his way into battle, was dedicated before a crowd of two hundred thousand, including twenty brass bands competitively blaring "The Star-Spangled Banner," on October 7, 1891.[7]

But the Rebisso sculpture I love most dates from a decade earlier, and resides—of course—at Spring Grove Cemetery. It was a commission for the Odd Fellows, a civic organization founded in Britain in the early eighteenth century and in the United States in 1819. The "Beautiful Rebekah Decree" of 1851 made the Odd Fellows the first American fraternal organization to become a sororal one as well, and by the latter part of the century it was the largest such American group, bigger even than the Masons. Nonsectarian and politically neutral, The Odd Fellows devoted themselves to service under the unthreatening aegis of "Friendship, Truth, and Love."[8] The movement's prehistory is murky, but the name is said to have derived from the old guild system, with the Odd Fellows constituting a miscellany that united all the professions not specifically represented by other guilds. Certainly the list of celebrity American Odd Fellows covers the gamut of jobs: aviator (Charles Lindbergh), gunslinger (Wyatt Earp), president (Grant, McKinley, FDR), Tramp (Charlie Chaplin). And sculptor (Rebisso). The Odd Fellows continue to exist, but—as with other such organizations—in a much attenuated form. (Like many of my generation, I first heard of them through REM's anthemic "Oddfellows Local 151," in 1987: a song about a street preacher and drunk that makes punning use of the number in its title.)

I first saw Rebisso's name on a small brass plaque—eye-catching mainly because it's encased in a layer of bright blue-green verdigris—that's screwed into the base of the Spring Grove Odd Fellows' Monument (1881). The statuary grouping above it is among the biggest and most embellished in the cemetery. At the pinnacle, topping out at thirty-four feet, stands a nine-foot-figure of

Moses mounted on a fluted column against which, below, three slightly smaller female allegorical figures are braced. There are little brass reliefs below, two depicting biblical scenes (the Covenant between David and Jonathan, Rebecca at the Well) and the third a bit of Oddfellovian bafflegab, the "patriarchal encampment." One can also read injunctions to "Relieve the Distressed," "Visit the Sick," and—most to the purpose here—"Bury the Dead." There's a clearing of turf around the monument, and beyond it, in serried circular arcs, hundreds of graves, blessedly not standardized, that memorialize Odd Fellows and Rebekahs from all over the region—another miscellany gathered under the three twined rings of the Odd Fellows. The monument distinguishes itself from its surroundings not only in scale but in color—that copper carbonate crust on the brass glows a brilliant blue in the sunlight—and in the way the graves are oriented, in another kind of "patriarchal encampment," toward the central cynosure of all eyes. No other monument in Spring Grove draws attention to itself in quite this worshipful way.[9]

The monument was the first major project of what would be a short-lived partnership. August Mundhenk was born in Hanover, soon-to-be Germany, in 1848, and by the late 1870s had established himself not only as a skilled artist but—perhaps more to the point for Rebisso—also as an entrepreneur: Mundhenk had established in Cincinnati one of the best fine-arts foundries in the country, and the first outside the Northeast.[10] It had rivals only in Philadelphia, New York, and Chicopee, Massachusetts. When Mundhenk's erstwhile partner retired in 1879, he and Rebisso threw in together. They would part in 1884.[11]

Rebisso & Mundhenk's usual method was to design in damp clay, then to pour over plaster of Paris and let it dry. Then they'd neatly divide the plaster in two, remove the wet clay from inside, and ready the molds for molten metal. In the case of the Odd Fellows' commission, there was great anticipation as the dedication date, Tuesday, September 20, 1881, approached. This was the culmination of ten years of fundraising by individual lodges all over the country, of preparation, design, and execution. The unveiling would take place during the fifty-seventh national convention of Odd Fellows' lodges, and in the month leading up to the gathering, the city was abuzz with this chance to show itself off. The *Enquirer* ran several long anticipatory articles about both the conclave and the Cincinnati-designed, Cincinnati-made memorial. Twenty thousand out-of-town visitors were expected—a huge influx of visitors in a city of a quarter million.

But the party would be spoiled by an odder fellow yet.

Fifteen months earlier, on June 11, 1880, that odder fellow had at last received the proof, long and ardently sought, that God had marked him for a higher purpose. He was standing on the deck of the paddlewheeler *Stonington* that fogbound night in Long Island Sound when it plowed into its sister ship *Narragansett*, piercing her side. The *Narragansett* quickly and catastrophically caught fire, trapping many passengers in their staterooms. Fifty passengers and—this latter number would ignite controversy—a single crewman died. The *Stonington*, though, was able to limp back to port, damaged but afloat, thus confirming the young man's destiny.

Charles Guiteau had been, till then, a stranger to good luck—even the pallid kind that consists of being present for a calamity but unkilled by it. He'd been a failure at college, at the law, at theology, at evangelism. He'd even been ridiculed, shunned, and run out of a utopian religious sect; the members of the Oneida Community had decided that if they were to achieve sinless perfection on the Earth, they would first have to banish the man they nicknamed "Charles Git-out." So Guiteau turned to politics.

Shortly before his ill-fated (or triumphal, as he may have seen it) trip on the *Stonington*, he penned a pamphlet called "Grant against Hancock" and arranged for its distribution to fellow Republicans in New York State. The 1880 Democratic convention in Cincinnati would indeed select Winfield Scott Hancock as the party's nominee, but just three days before the shipwreck, Guiteau's Republicans, after thirty-six grueling ballots without a winner, ended up choosing not Grant but a surprising dark horse, James Garfield. Guiteau hastily revised his pamphlet, dropping specifics about the general and substituting "Garfield" for "Grant" in most places (but not in all). When Garfield ended up defeating Hancock in the closest popular vote in American history, by a national margin of 1,898 votes, Guiteau felt certain that his speech-writing had delivered the contest to the Republicans.

Destitute, bedraggled, but certain of his destiny, Guiteau kept showing up at the White House to demand a consulship—Vienna would be a good post, he said, and then switched his preference to Paris—and he kept being turned away. Finally, in May 1881, Secretary of State James Blaine threw him out and banned him from ever returning.

But God would brook no such opposition, it turned out. He told Guiteau to assassinate the ungrateful president, thus to elevate Vice President Chester Arthur of New York, who would bring back the cozy spoils system of old. Guiteau borrowed fifteen dollars from an in-law and headed to shop for a large-caliber gun. Confronted with the choice between a wooden grip or an ivory one, Guiteau chose the latter because, he said, it would look grander, afterward, in a museum exhibit. He couldn't afford the extra dollar that weapon cost, but Destiny—its finger again on the scale—helped him haggle down the price.

On July 2, 1881, acting on a newspaper report, Guiteau lay in wait for Garfield—who was headed to his twenty-fifth college reunion in Williamstown, Massachusetts—at the Baltimore & Potomac railroad station in Washington. He shot the president twice from behind, then was quickly taken into custody outside, where he announced, "I am a stalwart of the Stalwarts. Arthur is president now!"

One bullet struck Garfield's arm. The second and more grievous wound was to his back; the bullet had entered his lumbar region, missing the spinal cord but lodging behind the pancreas. These injuries would be eminently survivable now, and wouldn't have been fatal even a few years later—but at the time, just as the benefits of sterilization were becoming evident, gunshot wounds were more dangerous. Worse, the doctors couldn't locate the bullet—and their vain quest for it resulted in all kinds of probings, with unsterilized hands and instruments, into the wound, which turned septic.

During his work developing the telephone, Alexander Graham Bell had discovered a way to detect hidden metal. Now the thirty-four-year-old scientist contacted Garfield's chief physician, Dr. Doctor Willard Bliss (no no typo typo—Bliss's parents seemed to have a preferred profession for their son from the get-go), to offer the assistance of his "induction balance." On July 26, the frustrated Bliss summoned Bell to the White House. But the inventor couldn't get any sort of decisive reading—there was an odd sputtering in the receiver, and the sounds he heard were indeterminate. He went back to the lab to tinker with his device, and then—Garfield's condition was deteriorating—returned on August 1 with the now-improved tool. This time Bliss had him test only Garfield's right side, and when Bell heard a faint sound, Bliss took it to mean that the bullet was, as he suspected, lodged there. The skeptical Graham seems to have suspected interference in the signal, and sure enough, an inquiry the next day revealed that the president was resting on a bedstead made of steel coils, which had skewed the readings. But Bliss had reached his conclusion.[12] Which would hasten Garfield's.

Guiteau's trial was one of the most bizarre in American history. His lawyers fought to offer one of America's first capital-case insanity pleas, but then muddied the water by arguing—as their erratic client had—that he wasn't guilty

Daguerreotype of an oil painting of William Henry Harrison

Nameplate, Odd Fellows' Monument, Spring Grove

Stones gently arcing toward the Odd Fellows' Monument

TERRIBLE COLLISION BETWEEN THE STEAMBOATS STONINGTON AND NARRAGANSETT,
AT 11.30 P. M., OF FRIDAY, JUNE 11TH, 1880, OFF CORNFIELD LIGHT, LONG ISLAND SOUND.

Currier & Ives, *Terrible Collision between the Steamboats STONINGTON and NARRAGANSETT*, hand-colored lithograph. Their grisly and beautiful prints of disasters (note the dangling Giacomettian figures near the prow!) presage, it seems to me, Weegee's crime-scene photographs

The "induction balance" of Alexander Graham Bell

Sculpture by Oscar Mundhenk and Eugene Schoonmaker

of murder because Garfield's wounds had been survivable. "Yes, I shot him," Guiteau said, "but his doctors *killed* him." The defendant further complicated matters, and caused dissension among his counsel, by insisting that insanity be claimed only for the time of the murder, God having taken away his free will; *now* he was right as rain. Guiteau's lawyers adopted the strategy of letting their voluble client talk and talk and talk, on the premise that the more the jury heard from him, the likelier they'd be to adjudge him mentally unfit. Guiteau bolstered this strategy in all sorts of unwitting ways. He declaimed his testimony in the form of epic poetry; he more or less publicly planned the triumphant lecture tour and 1884 presidential campaign that would inevitably follow the proceedings; he dictated a newspaper autobiography that ended with a personal ad for a nice young Christian lady (under thirty!). When the jury returned its verdict, he had to be restrained as he denounced them: "You are all low, consummate jackasses."

Guiteau is said to have "danced" his way to the gallows, where he shook the hand of his executioner and then recited a poem he'd written for the occasion called "I Am Going to the Lordy." The condemned man's request to have a full band play accompaniment, so as to show off his composition to its greatest effect, was denied. (The valedictory poem, which is built on the childlike repetition that characterizes ad jingles or nonsense verse, was adapted by Stephen Sondheim for his musical *Assassins*. "The Ballad of Guiteau" begins with an excerpt before finding the lyrical finesse its original author lacked: "I was just acting/ for someone up there./ The Lord's my employer,/ And now He's my lawyer,/ So do what you dare.")

An autopsy was performed in an effort to identify the source of Guiteau's insanity. Some accounts say that the insistence on pinpointing a Locus of Crazy was so strong that the medical men literally chopped Guiteau's brain into cubes. Evidence indicated that he was afflicted with neurosyphilis, but the finding that many seized upon was that Guiteau suffered from phimosis, the inability to retract the foreskin. To some, here was the interpretive key that would unlock everything: For want of a *bris* . . .

Garfield lingered for seventy-nine days, finally succumbing to sepsis on September 19, 1881 . . . the day the Odd Fellows convened in Cincinnati. Until the end, much of the public believed—and was encouraged to—that he would recover. The president's death dealt an especially heavy blow in his native state, and resulted in a sparser, sadder Odd Fellows convention. Fewer than half of the projected twenty thousand visitors arrived in Cincinnati, and many who did headed immediately home. Others stayed indoors out of respect. Those who ventured out did so wearing crape streamers and with a dampened spirit. After all the rah-rah of the lead-up, the *Enquirer* didn't even mention the dedication; there was a more immediate grief that needed memorializing. The planned grand procession seems to have been scuttled. The paper's account of the Odd Fellows' conclave on the day when but for an accident of timing Rebisso & Mundhenk might have expected an account of their triumph begins this way: "The day can not truthfully be called an extraordinary one, either in point of numbers in attendance or enlivening features."

Louis Rebisso would die at the beginning of May 1899, and "The Eminent Sculptor" was buried in a plot almost underneath the monument that, the *Enquirer* reported, "he of late years had come to consider one of his masterpieces."

But that's not where the story ends. After the (oft-repeated and always-with-us) allegory of the vanity of art—our petty accomplishments always overtaken by big events, unless we're insane enough to believe, like Guiteau, that the scale is reversed, the self is the grand and the outside world the puny and the lives of all others mere shadow-play staged for us by God the

Dramaturge—there comes a gradual mellowing reassessment of the things we've done or made, and we grow comfortable with recognizing those things, puny or grand (fine, then—*puny*), as our identities.

Makers of massive outdoor sculpture in particular have the long game always in mind. They have to cultivate a patience that exceeds their own life spans. Rebisso's biography, as I told it above, concludes with the swelling violin and the vaguely upbeat message that the artist belongs, in the end, to or in or at least under his work. But *does* he? It's a vexed question.

Of what does posterity consist? Do those who leave durable works behind, of whatever kind, survive mainly through those works? Public sculpture is a vivid example, since out in the world and physically stable, but what about composers and carpenters, architects and seamstresses, painters and arborists, printers and smelters of steel, the writers and storers of family-recipe troves, the designers of the kitsch of childhood (that Partridge Family lunchbox will outlast us all), actors, kids who press their prints into sidewalks not yet set? (Or, sure, scribblers too.) Does "immortality," in the pale and fractured form available, come from other human beings' continued interaction— unwitting or not of the names and contributions of the dead who built these bridges, laid these floors, latticed these pies, played these henchmen, bottled these Billy beers, shaped Moses' nose and sandals in wet clay—with the things that we have *made*?

Or as another theory, to me more congenial but sadder, has it, do we live on through the impressions we leave in the thoughts and memories of those we've loved and who've loved us, and then, in an ever fainter, more attenuated way, in the thoughts of those who've heard about us from the ones we've loved and who've loved us, until, not far down the line, we vanish altogether?

Rebisso hadn't quite entered eternity yet, in other words. He hadn't even been delivered into the subset of it that relies on the artifacts one leaves. He had remaining earthly allegiances, and nine months after his death (as soon, it seems, as winter's thaw allowed), his widow, Elizabeth, had the body disinterred from its plot near her husband's masterpiece—a grave donated by the Woodward Lodge of the Odd Fellows—and moved to the one where, later, she and her husband could be reunited. It was no dispute between the widow and the Odd Fellows that changed her mind: indeed, a newspaper item fifteen years later tells of a procession to dedicate a new lodge being diverted through the community of Norwood so the dignitaries could serenade the now housebound Elizabeth Rebisso, beloved founder of the Norwood Lodge of Rebekahs. But she had a prior claim to her husband, and she asserted it.

Also sharing the Rebissos' plot is Louis's son and namesake. I started to write that Louis Rebisso Jr. lived an eventful life . . . but the strangeness of the implied comparison with his father's now occurs to me. The sculptor father led a life that was lively in the limelight but that seems to have been privately quiet and happy; the son's life, as recorded in occasional newspaper glimpses, seems to have been privately tumultuous but lacked the public drama of his father's. Both ended up with long legacies, though of different kinds. Which of these lives is "eventful"? More to the point, what life is not?

The first glimpse I caught of Louis Rebisso Jr. came in a surprisingly vague and sidelong newspaper reference a week after his father's funeral. The *Enquirer* published a sidebar article saying that Elizabeth Rebisso had been named "administratrix" of her husband's substantial but not grand estate of $5,000 (around $140,000 today). The article concluded with the datum, left there to dangle, that "He had one son." But who was this enigma? Did the past-tense verb suggest that the child was dead, and unnamed because to speak the name would open old wounds? Had he run off to escape his parents' connections, his father's local fame? Did the vagueness suggest a family breach?

I'm loath to venture a guess at that last question (except to say that if there was a breach, it seems to have been repaired over time), but the others have more straightforward answers. Louis Thomas Rebisso was in his early twenties when his father died, and living in the same neighborhood as his parents, where he would remain for more than a half-century. He died in 1952. Rebisso the younger—he would name his own son Louis Thomas Rebisso Jr., which suggests, not surprisingly, that his Italian-born father's middle name wasn't Thomas—did not follow in his father's footsteps, at least not in the conventional way of thinking, and his private and professional life, especially early on, were messier, at least messier in the ways that make the papers. But ultimately he too was a successful artisan, and one who left a longstanding—and still extant—legacy. Louis the elder left art statuary, of course; Louis the younger left both pipework galore (residential plumbing, sewering, and more, much of it still in place) and a business, Rebisso Plumbing (Ohio Backflow License #806). The company website indicates that it began in 1892, when Rebisso was just sixteen, and in those days—in the tradition of the Odd Fellows—young Rebisso would have done all sorts of miscellaneous jobs, not just plumbing but coal-stove stoking, heating work, and other tasks. His father's leavings are more glamorous, perhaps, but what the younger Rebisso built may contribute more to Cincinnatians' daily lives, though his works are by nature and design unseen—at least unseen when they're working right.

His artistry is less obvious, but it's there. One thing this project has reminded me of often: never scoff at durability, and take your little sliver of immortality where you can get it.

It can't have been easy to be the Eminent Sculptor's child, and the younger Rebisso had his share of scrapes. On July 4, 1906, Louis T. nearly lost an eye when he mishandled a Roman candle. Later in his career, Rebisso would wrangle with a bankrupt supplier (1921); settle a wrongful death claim with the family of a laborer killed in a dirt-tunnel collapse (1925); advertise in the paper for a lost wallet (1927); and suffer a fire that burned down three buildings he owned (1929). But his two strangest and most noteworthy appearances in the paper took place in a two-year span about a decade after his father's death.

In January 1907, Rebisso was arrested. It seems he'd been infatuated with a young stenographer at the plumbing firm (the daughter of an employee). That winter Bessie Nichols married a traveling salesman named Cutter, and as soon as the couple returned from their honeymoon, the younger Rebisso—by this time long married to Annie Eliza Whitehead Rebisso (1877–1938)—mounted a campaign of persuasion (presumably of Bessie) and intimidation (of the husband and of Bessie's father). His pursuit of Bessie Cutter was so intense, and so unsurreptitious, that when the affronted husband went to the authorities, they swore out a "lunacy warrant" and arrested Rebisso on what amounted to a charge of romantic insanity. The embarrassed young plumber/swain was released on his own recognizance when he promised never to bother Bessie again . . . but not before the scandal hit the papers both in Cincinnati (under the headline "Annoyed.") and—here there was a price to pay for his father's notoriety—as far away as Washington, DC. (So far as I can tell, the chastened Rebisso was able to hold his marriage together; Annie stuck with him until her death, not only as a spouse but also as a financial and management partner in his business.)

Two years later, Louis got embroiled in an even weirder story. One spring morning in 1909, as he worked in his office in Norwood, he noticed a persistent dripping leak from upstairs. He'd recently rented the apartment up there to a pair of newlyweds, Otto and Etta Miller. Etta had until months earlier been married to one of Rebisso's father's former colleagues at the Art Academy, the internationally successful painter Vincent Nowottny. The previous summer, while on vacation in West Virginia, Nowottny and Etta had acquired a buggy and gone out into the countryside to paint and to picnic. A horse got spooked, and in the ensuing wreck Nowottny was killed and Etta grievously injured: broken hip, mangled knee, shattered nerves. The artist's death was covered widely in the press, and he left his heartbroken widow—who would have been in her forties—extremely well off.

Etta was a brilliant and eccentric woman, an "omnivorous reader" and collector of books about mysticism and ancient esoterica from the East, an adherent of Theosophy—"the synthesis of science, religion, and philosophy," as its founder, Madame Blavatsky, characterized it. The Cincinnati reporters seemed not quite sure how to convey their combination of admiration and bewilderment. Etta Nowottny-Miller "did not dabble in the occult," they settled on saying; no, she was *serious* about occultism.

In fall 1908, on the mend but still in considerable pain both physical and emotional, Etta came back to Cincinnati to recuperate, and there Otto Miller—the hospital's elevator operator—struck up an acquaintance with her. Or, actually, a reacquaintance. They'd been friendly decades earlier, when Etta had been a school chum of Miller's first wife. Etta Nowottny's friends seemed shocked by the brief, grief-fueled courtship, and they were leery of Miller. But the worst they could accuse him of was opportunism; the rest was the kind of meet-cute coincidence and unruly chemistry that rom-coms are built upon.

This was headed for a different genre, however. Rebisso would later report to the police that, alarmed by the leak, he went upstairs to knock several times. When there was no answer, "he took it for granted that Mrs. Miller had gone away for the day." Her husband returned in the afternoon and informed Rebisso that she should be at home. So the nimbler, younger plumber shinnied up a banister, forced a hallway window, and entered the apartment. He found a welter of blood. On her bed lay Etta Nowottny-Miller, already in rigor mortis, with two gaping throat wounds and two deep wrist lacerations. A red-daubed straight razor lay on the floor, and a trail of crimson traced the route from the bedroom to the kitchen, where the tap was running.

The coroner ruled suicide, a decision Miller (cleverly, if one suspects murder) cast doubt on by saying that his wife's chronic pain had been somewhat better lately, and by reporting that a thorough search of the apartment had revealed no note or sign of planning. The coroner's perhaps-not-*CSI*-proof theory was that Mrs. Nowottny-Miller, intending to kill herself, had sliced her wrists, but found that they bled too sluggishly, and that death by those cuts was going to be slow and agonizing. So she went to the sink, washed out the wounds (?!), and distractedly (or perhaps to arouse attention?) left the tap on. Then she headed into the bedroom and finished her task, and her life, with two deep throat incisions, either of which would have been quickly fatal.

We're not in a position to second-guess the coroner on the basis of today's cynicism and today's science. There would have been pressure, presumably, for him to resolve the case quickly, and if possible without suggesting that a maniac was on the loose; Mrs. Nowottny-Miller was grieving and unusual and in unremitting pain, so she seemed a candidate for self-destruction; and there was little prospect of finding evidence to sustain a murder charge. Best to be done with it.

But the deputy coroner *was* in such a position, and did question his boss's verdict: he could not be sure it was homicide, but he was dubious about the conclusion that Etta Nowottny-Miller had done herself in. Why were there *two* fatal wounds, and why did neither cross the throat's center line, as he would expect? "If Mrs. Miller made these incisions herself," he said, "she was a most dexterous woman."

Suspicion mounted because, as the paper put it, "Miller has been extremely unfortunate in his matrimonial alliances." His previous wife had died under peculiar circumstances—from, it was discovered later, the ingestion of strychnine. But there'd been no way to link Miller, or anyone else, to the poison, and charges were never filed. This coincidence was too much for the public, though, and resulted in headlines like "Funeral Held at Crematory/ Her Wealth Willed the Husband."

There's no reason to believe that Louis Rebisso played any role in this spectacular crime or non-crime besides eyewitness and athletic neighbor, but the episode provides yet another proof—one Rebisso didn't need, I'd guess—that you don't get to control what you'll be known for. Will it be as moon-mad pursuer of stenographers? As a fireworks-safety cautionary tale? The defendant in a landmark workplace safety suit? For a feat of Kato Kaelinesque proximity to a crime, which you were destined to discover in part because, for professional reasons, you've cultivated the ability to climb and snake yourself into confined or inaccessible spaces? Or would you be known, happily but among a narrower swath of people, for the long haul of a successful fifty-year career in plumbing, a long and prosperous marriage, two children successfully conducted into adulthood?

Furthermore, will everything you do, even into middle age, be interpreted first of all as a postscript to or commentary on the story of an Eminent Parent? His father was the shadow Louis Rebisso the younger would always labor to escape. But we have no choice but to live—to the (ever greater) extent that we must do so in public—with the image others allow or accord or saddle us with. As Robert Coover put it in his novel *The Public Burning*,[13] narrating as a

bitter but triumphant Richard Nixon who's learned to embrace the devious-
ness everyone has always seen in him: "So everybody liked Ike, that casual
straightforward bumbler—me they called Tricky Dick. I hated this at first, it
was a brutal thing to fight, but eventually I discovered it won votes. Uncle Sam
probably didn't like being called Yankee Doodle at first either, but eventually
he stuck a feather in his cap and called it macaroni."

Sure enough, the initial *Enquirer* story about Etta Nowottny-Miller's death
did invoke the name of Rebisso's famous father. By the next day, though,
thanks to a slew of sordid revelations, that angle had disappeared (and Louis
had been, in one instance, redubbed "Robison"—how quickly fame fades).
One can only imagine what might have happened had the coroner reached
a different conclusion; had Rebisso been called as star witness for the prosecution; had there been more excavation of the history between Nowottny and
the Rebissos; had there been more questions that would surely have innocent
explanations, but the very answering of which would incite suspicion among
those hungry for scandal (Why didn't the two men use Miller's key to get into
the apartment, for instance? Why didn't the professional plumber go into the
apartment earlier, in a building he likely owned, to investigate/resolve the
leak?); had the public imagination—as the public imagination is wont to do—
gone hunting for alternative suspects and found in the discoverer of the body,
himself a Lunatic Annoyer of Women, an alluring option?

But the story faded, and Rebisso didn't get sucked into fictive intrigue or
rumor-mongering. From that point forward—Rebisso was thirty-three—he
mostly managed to stay out of the limelight. His marriage continued. His business thrived. He became a pillar of the community of Norwood. Wars inter-
vened; the city and the country changed irrevocably. And Rebisso's father's
public memory receded some, which gave his son room both to build his own
identity and, later, to re-embrace—one imagines—his father's legacy.

Oscar Mundhenk, son of Rebisso's old partner, had his biggest brush with
notoriety that same year, 1909. The younger Mundhenk's story is in some ways
a mirror image of the younger Rebisso's. Oscar, five years younger than Louis
Thomas Rebisso, did follow his father's career path. He was a precocious and
gifted artist, and soon took on work as an itinerant sculptor, accepting commissions from churches and other clients around the region. In the winter of
1908–09, just as the Nowottny-Miller romance was ripening, Oscar Mundhenk
was in Marietta, Ohio, working on a sculpture of the Virgin for the Basilica of
Saint Mary of the Assumption.

Years ago, on a completist tear, I read Vladimir Nabokov's correspondence, and was dismayed and surprised—I was young, in defense of my dismay—to discover that many of the magisterial stylist's letters were devoted to wheedling dollars out of editors. In researching this essay I've been similarly struck by how much of the public sculptor's life is devoted to winning commissions, fending off interference from sponsoring committees, pleading for advances so as to obtain materials and make molds and so on, negotiating or upgrading display spots, and wrangling over hyperspecific contracts (for instance the one for Rebisso & Mundhenk's monument to General McPherson in Clyde, Ohio, which stipulates stone "free from wind shakes, sand holes, or imperfections of any character or kind"). The right to do one's art is won through a dull, enervating, life-long campaign of venal commerce.

Which is where things went haywire for Oscar Mundhenk in Marietta. He was working on the kind of project that may be trickiest of all when it comes to tension between funder and artist: a church commission. There's bound to be strain. The artist is producing not just imaginative work, nor merely a likeness, but something that, from its moment of completion,[14] enters the long tradition of religious iconography. The thing is an instant holy relic, and cannot be tampered with. This strain is present even if the sculptor is a devotee of the church being worked for, even if s/he cultivates the kind of medieval faith that makes the artist a willing instrument of divine inspiration. For one thing, even God's instruments (like Gofridus the sculptor, in an earlier essay) have tastes and professional standards. For another, godly inspiration tends not to come with a manna per diem. Most of all, though, there's the bedeviling question of church hierarchy: both artist and priest will tend to consider themselves God's chosen representative.

Mundhenk, twenty-eight, had spent much of the winter alone in the small river town, preparing his sculpture. On February 12, 1909, newspapers all over the region reported—the story had to vie for space with Lincoln's centenary—that the young artist, in a monetary dispute with the presiding priest, had . . . well, had dismembered the Holy Mother, lopping off her nose, ear, and eye. He found himself now a ward of a nearby county's jail. Interestingly, the journalists' shock seemed to derive less from any theological affront than from the fact that Mundhenk, as the *Indianapolis Star* put it, "destroyed the work of art that his genius had created." In Cincinnati, August Mundhenk defended his son: Oscar had been under immense strain, struggling with cold and hunger, and the priest had flatly refused to pay him $65 he was owed. Under those circumstances, his father implied, was it any wonder that the hotheaded young man had, as the article said, "procured a hammer"?

I've long loved Gillian Welch's song "Everything Is Free," a lament that those holding the purse-strings in the music business (and perhaps consumers) have figured out artists' never-closely-enough-held secret. "Everything is free now," the song begins, "that's what they say,/ Everything I've ever done, gotta give it away./ Someone hit the big score, they figured it out,/ That we're gonna do it anyway, even if it doesn't pay."[15] It occurs to me that sculptors—especially in the Gilded Age—may have encountered this reality. If they wanted to do the work that fulfilled them, they needed the materials and the commissions . . . so it was easy to summon them to unfamiliar towns, with meager accommodations and scanty food, in bleak stretches of the year, and there to short them. If you love your trade too much, you'll do whatever you must to ply it. And when penury catches up with you, and you've been left just one available currency, what choice but to take up a tool and whale upon "the work of art one's genius had created"?

Up in New Bedford, Massachusetts, Lizzie Borden [hatchet, guest bedroom] had given her mother forty whacks;[16] Mundhenk [hammer, basilica] gave Christ's mother just a handful. And the story in Marietta had a happier ending. The next day Mundhenk repaired the damage, so deftly that the priest in charge immediately paid the outstanding debt and offered him a contract for additional work. He'd found a way, as Welch does in the song,[17] to seize control of the means of production, or at least of the narrative. In the last verse, Welch tries to find solace, at least, in making the decision to keep playing and writing *hers* rather than the moneymen's: "'Cause everything is free now, that's what I said,/ No one's gotta listen to the words in my head./ Someone hit the big score, I figured it out,/ And I'm gonna do it anyway, even if it doesn't pay." What pisses off artists, it seems to me, is that they know that in economic terms, at least, the money people's calculus is *right*. In a capitalist system, we're not owed a living—thus, for many, the hobbification of the thing that feels most like a calling. The list of people who take literary or visual art seriously and make a living wage from it is short, and ever shorter. But what can you do? You figure it out. Are you going to do it anyway? Even if it doesn't pay? Don't fool yourself.

Oscar Mundhenk had made his decision, and he followed the work where it took him. He settled in New York, where he worked steadily until his death, at seventy-seven, in 1956. His siblings were all buried in Spring Grove alongside his parents, but not Oscar, who grappled with his father's legacy by choosing the same profession and achieving escape velocity—whereas the younger Rebisso, who's interred alongside his parents, chose to rebel in place. Mundhenk's art was his tribute to his upbringing, as Rebisso's proximity was.

So what does the elder Louis Rebisso's transient grave tell us about posterity and the artist? I for one am glad that Elizabeth Rebisso had him moved, not only because humanity always ought to get the nod (there's some dissension on this point, but I believe it) but also because there's something superfluous about being buried beneath one's artwork. You already *have* a headstone there, and may as well plant as many as you can. Posterity is always a both/and proposition. The sculptor—and not just the sculptor: the gardener, the mason, the assembly-line floormat-stamper, the plumber—leaves markers all over the place. Rebisso's are more monumental than most, and some of them are also, modestly or trickily (is the artist a slyboots, a parasite?), contributions to the legacies of more famous others. But isn't that true of all of us?

SIX DEGREES OF
JONATHAN CILLEY

NOWADAYS, "SIX DEGREES OF SEPARATION" IS a parlor game of the post-parlor era.

There's Six Degrees of Kevin Bacon—a version so popular that it spawned an internet "Oracle of Bacon," which can trace any actor's link to the prolific Mr. Breakfast Meat instantly and in very few steps. In fact, in order to find someone with a "Bacon number" as high as three, I had first to make twenty failed tries, ranging from earlier screen icons like Myrna Loy and Mary Pickford; to TV character actors like Stuart Margolin (Angel on *The Rockford Files*) and Marcia Strassman (Mrs. Kotter) and the entire cast of *Hogan's Heroes*, to stars who died young and with few roles under their belts (Anissa Jones, James Dean, Dana Plato); to foreign-born stars of the interwar years (Paul Muni, Hedy Lamarr, Peter Lorre). Finally I hit a few: Fatty Arbuckle and Leni Riefenstahl; Wallace Beery and Greta Garbo.

An early version of the game featured bare-knuckle boxing champ John L. Sullivan: "I've shaken the hand that's shaken the hand that's shaken the hand..." Recently, I've seen a variation involving Falco's 1981 Europop hit "Der Kommissar."[1] But the phrase came into common parlance thanks to playwright John Guare's *Six Degrees of Separation* of 1990, in which it's no parlor game, and where the tone is not jocular reaffirmation of our small-world interconnectedness. The *concept* of six degrees traces back to Hungarian writer Frigyes Karinthy's 1929 "Chains," a short story that reads mostly as a thought experiment, and Karinthy—or his narrator—finds the idea of the ever-tinier world as much terrifying as it is exciting.[2]

One salubrious effect of the "six degrees" idea, from our perspective—though this wouldn't have been the case in Central Europe in 1929, the year in which Hitler,[3] seizing upon the crash of the stock market and the death of the *Reichskanzler*, emerged from his "quiet years" and began to consolidate power—is that it disdains/transcends boundaries of class, race, ethnicity, and religion. If your sense of security is built upon being insulated from those who don't look or act or believe like you, there's no comfort in the unpredictable promiscuity of such connections. Such links are leveling; they throw you into uncomfortable company. Note the odd couples just in the acting examples above: the Swedish Sphinx and the guy who played Sweedie in drag; the louche comedian[4] and the gifted Nazi propagandist. It's hard to cling to the idea of social superiority when the formerly bright lines between high and low are dimmed, blurred, or effaced altogether. The Oracle of Bacon doesn't care whether you're linked by *Jules et Jim* or *Starsky et Hutch*.

An even earlier, more salacious enactment of the concept came in the Viennese writer Arthur Schnitzler's *Reigen*, a play so scandalous that the version he printed for friends circulated for two decades before the work could finally premiere in 1920. *Reigen*'s awkward English translation is "roundelay" (in French, "la ronde"), meaning a circle dance, and Schnitzler's drama consists of a daisy chain of ten couplings, starting and ending with the same prostitute. She engages first with a soldier, and in the final scene with a nobleman—in between, crossing the boundaries of profession and marriage and class, we travel the intermingling by-ways of respectability and smut (and syphilis).

In 2018, in a world radically shrinking, six degrees may be too many. Now when we cite the number, we may do so less to invoke quick connectedness— which is ubiquitous, inescapable; just try to imagine the person who's fully half a dozen steps away from you on social media—than to deny or delay that link. We do so to keep at bay the idea that in most cases, we're only one or two intermediaries away. Or zero. That's the kind of six degrees *this* essay is about, anyway.

DODGE #1: KEVIN BACON

I met Kevin Bacon once, at a cast-and-donor party for the 1988 Broadway revival of Eugene O'Neill's many-houred comedy *Ah, Wilderness*. Bacon's fiancée, Kyra Sedgwick, starred as the ingénue, and I remember thinking her swell in the role, though I now see that Frank Rich, writing for the *New York Times*, was less susceptible to dewy-eyed innocence than I was. I had no business being at the celebration; it's the only such party I have ever attended, or likely ever will. But an old college roommate was working for the New York International Festival of the Arts, which was underwriting the production, and he invited me, and I was starving for culture (and canapés) that I couldn't afford. So I found myself lurking near the buffet table, far from anyone else, and scarfing down finger foods at a rate I hoped was one tick below humiliating.

I should have been more aware, but I'm afraid that at twenty-three, once you accounted for *self*-consciousness, I had precious little energy left over for any consciousness of others. Bacon and Sedgwick would be married in less than three months. Kyra Sedgwick was (and is) three months younger than me—though at the time I would have guessed that she, like everyone else who had accomplished anything enviable, was approximately ten years older, which calculus would leave open the possibility, however remote, that given the right series of breaks I might catch up. The point is that she was just getting started, and there was nothing like inevitable success ahead; that *New York Times* review must have stung. Bacon, meanwhile, was seven years older, already a star. He was alone like me, waiting for his betrothed to make her way from the dressing room so that he could greet her, congratulate her, praise her, reassure her. He was in the wings, preparing for a role. Yes, I should have been more aware. But I wasn't, and I was drunk—did I mention the open bar, or how nervousness and thirst and no one to talk to kept draining my glass faster than I would have liked?

And so, when Bacon broke from a knot of well-wishers, came over to sample some food, looked up at me hovering near the fruit bowl next to him, and nodded, and after I mumbled hi and he dutifully did the same, did I really follow up with this little conversational gambit: "My friends say that if we averaged your nose and mine, we'd both be normal"?

Everything about this was false. No friend had ever said anything of the kind, for one thing. The few I had didn't really go in for nose-averaging. And Kevin Bacon didn't *need* my nose tip, by God—his upturned retroussé unschnoz had won him millions of fans, that time he danced to a bitchin' soundtrack against the wishes of all those grown-up prudes. Besides, age would only make his handsomer and mine more dewlappy, as we—students of gravity, both of us—were aware. I was the one who wanted the trade. Who was I kidding?

And I didn't want a trade, truth be told. The beak was mine, always had been, and I was fine with it: not least because being handsome might have required me to be less terrified and awkward. This was protective coloration, and I was—when not in a rare moment of idly envying the young and famous— grateful for it. Grackles only envy swans on crystalline spring days; mostly we wonder how the hell you ever *hide*, looking like that.

God help me—had I, encountering a movie star among the cocktail shrimp, actually proposed instantaneously that we go out and get a team rhinoplasty?

That question is genuine. I've told the anecdote many times since, but I honestly can't be sure now whether I said it or not. I was tipsy, nervous, alone, insecure. I would certainly have had the thought. But was my impulse control so poor that I would actually blurt it out? I hope I didn't. Still—though ne'er was our nose-flesh united—the incident gives me a modified Bacon number of zero.

DODGE #2: JONATHAN CILLEY—NO, NOT *THAT* JONATHAN CILLEY

I don't think I could have said what drew me, one winter morning, to the gravestone that read "Jonathan Cilley." I'd hiked to the cemetery through the woods, just after a wet snowstorm, and been amazed at how blindingly white the old-growth, tumbledown forest was, with branches and stumps and fallen behemoths crossing at every angle. The flocked sycamore branches looked like veins trying to convey the snow back upward to the sky for recirculation. Meanwhile robins—shockingly numerous, shockingly fat, shockingly russet—hopped from ground to root ball to fallen log like a virus looking for a vulnerable spot to invade the snowstream. Maybe it was something about the starkness of the monument in that landscape: the straightforward typeface, first and last name crammed together almost without space, so that it looked like the jersey-back of an NFL player with an especially long name, a Houshmandzadeh or Gbaja-Biamila; the upright stone that somehow managed to convey both modesty and pride. The name was familiar; that much I could have said. But where did I know it from?

Back home I fired up Google and discovered that Jonathan Longfellow Cilley had been a congressman from Maine. A member of Bowdoin College's stellar class of 1825 alongside Henry Wadsworth Longfellow and Nathaniel Hawthorne, Cilley was admitted to the bar, served in the state legislature, and in 1836 was elected to the U.S. House of Representatives. It was a bitterly partisan moment, just after the panic of 1837, when Cilley, a Democrat, gave a fiery speech in which he accused the publisher of a prominent Whig paper in New York, James Watson Webb, of essentially having taken a bribe. Webb persuaded Representative William Graves of Kentucky to deliver to Cilley his challenge to a duel. Cilley refused to accept the letter, and did so in a way that the emissary felt gravely injured *his* honor. When Graves, a peer rather than (as Cilley must have seen it) a corrupt blowhard of the press, then dropped the gauntlet, Cilley felt duty-bound to accept.

As challenged party, Cilley got to pick the weapon. Warned about Graves's pistol marksmanship, he made the rather unusual choice of rifles; Graves didn't own one, and had to use a loaner. Because dueling was illegal in DC, the aggrieved parties made their way across the bridge to the Bladensburg Dueling Ground in Maryland. They paced off eighty steps. (The distance would later be measured at ninety-four yards, and a quick calculation indicates that the average male's stride at the time would have been less than two and a half feet . . . which means that somebody was long-stepping that day, stretching his stride. As I would have been.) The duelists missed on the first volley, not surprisingly at that distance. Their seconds urged them to let that be fate's final word on the dispute, but both men insisted on moving closer and firing again. After that round yielded no wound, either, the seconds pleaded with the congressmen to quit. But both insisted on a third volley, in which Cilley was hit in the thigh, transecting the femoral artery and killing him almost instantly.

Cilley was memorialized soon after by his classmate Hawthorne in "Political Portraits with Pen and Pencil." His death resulted in a law that forbade congressional duels, and it almost resulted in Graves's removal from office. Its most important legacy, however, was the dramatic deepening of hostility between northern and southern factions in Congress, a split that would lead not only to more intra-legislature violence (most infamously the caning on the Senate floor of Charles Sumner of Massachusetts by Representative Preston Brooks of South Carolina in 1856) but also, eventually, to the Civil War.

But my Jonathan Cilley's dates were 1791–1874, not 1802–1838, and the article concluded with the note that Dueling Jonathan Cilley was buried not in Cincinnati but in Maine. The Jonathan Cilley buried in Spring Grove, it turned out, belonged to a branch of the family that had moved west to Ohio just before it achieved statehood in 1803. There, replicating Yankee grit and family names—Greenleaf, Joseph, Bradbury, Benjamin, Jonathan—they had set out to build a western dynasty. It was a prolific family; Ohio Jonathan was one of ten siblings, and he would father at least six children, five of whom are buried alongside him and his wife, Sarah.

Cincinnati's Jonathan Cilley, eleven years older than his cousin, had until shortly before the latter's death lived a public life in parallel, but afterward he contrived to keep himself not only out of the graveyard but very nearly out of the newspaper. Admitted to the bar at twenty-one, this Jonathan entered politics, too, and was elected to the Ohio House in 1828 as a Jacksonian Democrat. Four years later, he resigned to become a judge in the Hamilton County Court of Common Pleas, a position in which he served for nearly a decade. (He served as a presidential elector for Martin Van Buren in 1836, which presumably would have put him in political opposition to his cousin.) Cilley married Sarah, began a family, and entered the coal business, in which he thrived. His obituary brims with anodyne praise, offering no chink or foothold for scandal or even, truth be told, for much interest. He seems to have been a good man and a poor biographical subject. Sober as the judge he was, he lived to be an octogenarian, alongside a vibrant wife (two decades his junior) and surrounded by dutiful and apparently thriving children. The end.

DODGE #3: NAMESAKE

Or not. There's one child of Jonathan Cilley who's *not* buried in Spring Grove.

Jonathan Longfellow Cilley was born, presumably in Cincinnati, the same year that his namesake uncle died. The outlines of this Jonathan Cilley's life are also impressive. An 1858 graduate of Harvard and a Civil War veteran, he became one of the country's most eminent anatomists, and was said to have been the first scientist ever to describe accurately "the main fissure of the lungs." Having left Ohio for Brooklyn in the last two years of his life—chiefly for access to distinguished medical relatives and the treatment they could offer—he inaugurated there a popular lecture series that united science and painting, "Anatomy for Artists."

But Jonathan Longfellow Cilley wasn't as adept as his father at evading publicity, and his reputation would be tainted—in a strange, behind-hand way—even after his death. When this Jonathan Cilley died in 1903, the *Enquirer* obituary touted the departed as "one of the greatest anatomical professors in the world," and the body of the notice never stints in its praise. But above it the paper included a sensational subhead—not one word of it picked up or even alluded to in the article—that reads, "Bodies of Ex-President Harrison's Father and Three Murdered Victims Also Found in College." Oh, that weird "Also": never let the mavens of style tell you that adverbs are *infra dig*, not if they're as poignant and devastating and sidewise-mordant as this one. Here, the obit seems to say, is a life told straight and blameless, the way the deceased would want. *Also*, we'll just rig this lamp up here for you to read it by.

Cilley was an anatomist at the Ohio Medical College at the time of the John Scott Harrison bodysnatching scandal of 1878 (detailed earlier in "Accidental Charon"). He was never directly implicated, but he was the person whose awkward task it was, afterward, simultaneously to repair the medical college's reputation . . . and to keep acquiring cadavers for research from a public the controversy had made warier. This job required him to deal with unsavory characters, and in 1884 it may have made him become one.

On a mid-February Friday evening, an Avondale dairy farmer named Louis Mills noticed that a remote tenant shanty on Blachley Farm, which he ran, was aglow on the horizon. He'd rented the log cabin to a man named Beverly Taylor and his wife, Elizabeth, and they were caring for an eleven-year-old granddaughter, Emma Jean Lambert. By the time Mills arrived, flames had engulfed the house. He found no sign of the three inhabitants. Which was surprising, given that Beverly Taylor—a man born into slavery who scraped together a living in old age by taking in neighbors' washing and mending—was so afflicted with rheumatism that he'd been a shut-in for months. In the light of morning, Mills searched the environs, but found nothing. On Monday, with a crew of four hired men, the local marshal combed the ashes for remains. One of the searchers, Allen Ingalls, irritated the others by plucking up virtually anything he saw that was phalange-size or larger and asking, "Is this a bone? Is this a bone?"[5]

After a couple days of mostly fruitless investigation, the police decided to do a sweep of medical schools to see if resurrectionists might be responsible. At the Ohio Medical College, Dr. Cilley could shed no light . . . but fifteen minutes after their visit he realized that, well, on second thought he *did* have three recently delivered African American bodies that might fit the bill. He contacted the authorities and told them that during their first visit he had misunderstood the timeline. Now he led police to the family's bodies, naked and in bags—and showing obvious signs of trauma. Cilley reported that the cadavers had been brought in by two people he didn't know well, "Harrison" (a ghoulish connection, given the college's painful notoriety in that case?) and "Jack," who had told him that these three people were victims not of bludgeoning but of a train accident. He described the men. One was short, thick-set, bug-eyed—and immediately put the police in mind of the overeager searcher, Ingalls.

The key to unraveling the case turned out to be a wagon driver, Robert Dixon, who—as he often did—had delivered the cadavers to the college. He identified "Harrison" as Ben Johnson, a relative and roommate of Ingalls. He also reported that on Friday night, Ingalls had approached him with a note from Dr. Cilley asking him to deliver some corpses for dissection. He met them at the last lamppost on the Avondale Road, he said, and Ingalls and Johnson clambered over the fence, disappeared into the dark, and returned with the canvas bags.

In court the next day, a guilt-wracked Johnson—sleepless, rumpled, tear-streaked, breakfastless, in a "seedy broadcloth suit with an extravagance of collar and cuff"—would confess. Ingalls, meanwhile, claiming to have slept well and fortified by a steak breakfast, entered a plea of not guilty. Johnson's tale included previous instances of grave-robbing with Ingalls, who dug into resting places "like a demon." It also included the detail that Ingalls had had a long-term arrangement with Dr. Cilley to supply cadavers. Their euphemism of choice for acquiring a body was "making a point"—and in this case, Johnson said, Cilley had been so desperate for specimens that he'd told Ingalls, "Get points if you have to hit someone over the head."

Ingalls eventually came clean, too, though he pinned most of the blame on Johnson, whose locust-wood cudgel he identified as the murder weapon. Ingalls's telling was coldly matter-of-fact. Mrs. Taylor, he reported, had fought back, and so had suffered a drubbing; meanwhile, "About one blow settled the girl." Ingalls reported, too, that Beverly Taylor had in earlier days been a resurrection man, and had introduced Ingalls to the business.

But as his accomplice had predicted, Ingalls never accused Jonathan Longfellow Cilley of having prior knowledge of the crime, and charges were never filed against him. From this distance, there's no reliable way of judging Cilley's responsibility. That he was in cahoots with the unsavory Ingalls, and that he recognized Ingalls's lack of scruples—even cultivated it—seems clear. But to Cilley, I suspect, engaging such suppliers seemed just a distasteful condition of his job. He—or rather medical science—needed specimens for dissection; every student paid a per-semester fee for access, and there were doctors to train, lives to save. If people, for reasons of squeamishness or superstition or religion, were reluctant to donate bodies to the cause, it was his solemn though unpleasant duty to acquire them by whatever means necessary. In such a situation, one might have to deal with rough customers—and there was no benefit in asking questions.

Did he really say, "Get points if you have to knock someone over the head"? Impossible to know. He does on the one hand seem to have been sincerely appalled, after that first visit from the authorities, and his description of Ingalls did direct the police his way. It's likely that Cilley, a pillar of the community, a man proud of his standing and a firm believer in his own rectitude, would have drawn an unbreachable line at murder. And what incentive would Ingalls have had to leave his accomplice out of the accounting, if he considered him culpable?

"We are of course extremely anxious," Cilley was quoted as saying, "that if a murder was committed the murderers should be brought to justice." Yes, certainly. But isn't there something weaselly and damage-controlly in that statement: the royal *we*, the sniffy "of course," the careful subjunctive "if"? The most compelling fifteen minutes of Cilley's life, from our perspective (note the weaselly royal *we*), is the stretch between the police's first visit and his decision to recontact them and cooperate. He had lied—I see no way around this—about not knowing Ingalls; he had likely deceived the police, too, about his understanding of the crime's timing. He may have examined the bodies earlier and tried to set aside any concerns that a train accident would result in the pattern of blows Mrs. Taylor suffered; he may have avoided examining the bodies so as not to have to consider that. He may have remembered expressing desperation to Ingalls, even if not in the terms Johnson claimed to hear, and may have thus felt compromised or implicated. He surely understood that a bright line had been crossed, a vicious crime—"the Avondale Horror," as it would come to be known—committed. The truth would come out, it was clear, and the Ohio Medical College—its chief anatomist, too—was about to suffer, at minimum, another public relations catastrophe.

I should note here that almost every principal in this sordid story, Cilley excepted, was African American: victims, murderers, wagon driver. Black people were wildly overrepresented among cadavers ending up at medical colleges. "Colored" cemeteries were remoter and less zealously guarded. Sextons in those graveyards lived closer to the bone, and might thus be more susceptible to bribes. African American families were less likely to have the wherewithal to hunt down loved ones' remains once they disappeared from graves and landed on the dissecting table, and police were less likely to search; perhaps for Cilley that had been one lesson of the John Scott Harrison debacle. And white doctors and medical students were less likely, I would think, to identify with black citizens, and thus to pose questions—who *was* this, and what was her life like, and how did she come to be here?—that had only discomfiting answers.

Dr. Cilley weathered the storm, kept his job and his freedom, but his esteem in the community—as seen, anyway, by that obituary subhead, and by similar notes in other obituaries (including the one in the *Brooklyn Eagle*)—sustained permanent damage. Cilley would suffer one more public blow, an emasculating one, shortly before ill health drove him east to Brooklyn. In August 1901 he had a dispute with a tenant, a Mrs. Williams, who had had a bathtub delivered to the house for installation in her upstairs quarters. After "hot words in his parlor," the argument moved upstairs, where, the sixty-three-year-old doctor declared, he went to retrieve shades and a mirror that belonged to him. Both disputants "secured little hammers"—a puzzling but unexplained development—"and the trouble was on in earnest." Mrs. Williams reported that she thought the doctor was going to hit her in the head (a phrase calculated, perhaps, to dredge up in some minds the Avondale affair of seventeen years earlier?), so she got a stranglehold on him, and down he went. Mrs. Williams then pinned Cilley, planted a knee on his abdomen, and waited for the police.

The famed anatomist was charged with assault and battery. The judge censured him for not leaving her rooms when asked, but the charge was immediately dismissed, as the *Enquirer* trumpeted, because "WOMAN DEFEATED DR. J. L. CILLEY."

DODGE #4: WILLIAM KIRK

Six weeks after the Avondale Horror murders, the Cincinnati jail and courthouse were attacked by rioters intent on lynching a killer, a teenaged German immigrant named William Berner. Over the next two days, hundreds would be wounded or die in the streets surrounding the courthouse.

Cincinnati in 1884 was a rough-and-tumble place. A crime wave was cresting; the city had tallied nearly a hundred murders the previous year. A recent Ohio River flood had disrupted lives and worsened already poor labor conditions. And the city government and the court system it supported were shot through with corruption.

The immediate spark for the Courthouse Riots was the murder of a downtown stable owner named William Kirk, who on Christmas Eve 1883 was robbed, cudgeled, and dumped onto the verge of the befouled Mill Creek in Northside. The evidence led police immediately and, thanks to a loose-tongued defendant, incontrovertibly, to two of Kirk's young employees, William Berner and an accomplice named Joe Palmer. Palmer (not incidentally, of mixed race) was sentenced to hang. But Berner's lawyers, after winnowing a massive jury pool of five hundred to twelve, were able to secure a verdict of manslaughter—this despite the testimony of seven people to whom Berner had confessed his cold-blooded planning and execution of the crime. The judge who pronounced sentence was appalled, and said so. The *Enquirer* fanned the flames, editorializing on March 9 that "Laxity of laws gives the Queen City of the West its crimson record. Preeminence in art, science, and industry avail nothing, when murder is rampant."

The Berner verdict sparked mayhem. Jurors who were identified lost their jobs, had their homes vandalized. One hid out in a police station, then was roughed up by a mob when he ventured home and had to rush back to protective custody. The foreman went into hiding. Rotten eggs and dead cats were flung through the windows of someone who turned out to be the wrong L. Phillips. The situation deteriorated, fueled by rage, copious drink, unemployment, and the muckraking media. A protest at Music Hall on Friday, March 28, drew eight thousand, and afterward the riled-up crowd moved en masse to the jail, where they hoped to drag Berner out and lynch him.

But Sheriff Morton Lytle Hawkins, anticipating trouble, had already spirited Berner, dressed in drag, out and up toward the state prison in Columbus. (Ironically, Berner escaped his captors during the train trip, and during much of the bloodshed in Cincinnati he was holed up in suburban Loveland, playing cards. Recaptured a day later, he resumed the journey to Columbus, where he

Drawing of Allen Ingalls smoking in his cell, *Cincinnati Commercial Gazette*, February 24, 1884

Barricade, Cincinnati Courthouse Riots, 1884

"A Murderer Hung in Time Saves Nine," by legendary editorial cartoonist Thomas Nast (who gave us both the modern version of Santa Claus and the Republican Party elephant)

The three young men killed in Orangeburg, February 8, 1968:
Delano Middleton, Samuel Hammond, and Henry Smith

Pee-wee football team photo, circa 1975, Orangeburg, SC. The author, #85, is at left

served almost a decade of his sentence before being released and disappearing into private life in Indiana.) Hawkins had only thirteen deputies to help him stave off the mob. The rioters managed to enter the jail through the sheriff's apartment, but were persuaded to leave when it became apparent that Berner was gone. Meanwhile, the crowd outside grew larger and more restive. When a worried Hawkins sounded the alarm, it had the effect of drawing even more people—many of them, on this payday evening, wrathfully drunk. The First Regiment of the Ohio Militia, billeted just half a block away, was called in, and they reached the jail by way of a tunnel from the courthouse. The fighting worsened. The fusillade of brickbats and stones continued, and when a rioter was killed by militiamen, someone used kerosene to try to set the jail on fire.

The next morning, the papers crowed about the turmoil they'd encouraged. For example, the *Enquirer*: "At Last the People Are Aroused and Take the Law into Their Own Hands; Enraged Community Rises in Its Might." But as Saturday wore on, it became apparent that this was no controlled burn. The governor had been slow to call in the reinforcements the sheriff sought. When he did order soldiers to muster, 80 percent didn't show, and some who did took the side of the rioters. That Saturday, makeshift ramparts and fortifications were rigged, and looting grew widespread, resulting in additional deaths when shopkeepers opened fire. A gunfight raged for hours, killing dozens. Late that evening, a militia force of 425 men, armed with a machine gun, arrived from Columbus and was finally able to clear the streets. As the *Daily Times Star* would tout it later, finding civic pride wherever it could, "The deadly Gatling gun, the product of a Cincinnati inventor, yielded its thrumming voice to the yelp of the pack, and that weapon, more than any other single agency, was responsible for the return to sanity of the thousands who had been swept off their feet by the fiendish desire to kill."

There would be sporadic fighting on Sunday, too, but Secretary of War Robert Lincoln, the former president's eldest son, had called in federal troops, and order was restored.

The mood amid the wreckage and death on Sunday was more circumspect. The *Enquirer* struck a somber tone: "Fire and Fury, the Reign of Terror: Awful Scenes in Cincinnati." But many observers still expressed sympathy for the rioters. In the aftermath, a *Harper's Weekly* cartoon by Thomas Nast showed a jury box full of jackals, geese, and asses, with the caption "A Murderer Hung in Time Saves Nine." A *Commercial Gazette* editorial—understating the carnage, which would end with fifty-six dead and three hundred seriously wounded— lamented the loss of life this way: "First, we have saved our jailful of murderers.

We have killed 45 innocent men and wounded or maimed 45 more, all to save our jailful of murderers."[6]

Among the murderers saved were Ben Johnson and Allen Ingalls. Ingalls was by every account despondent—rattled by the days and nights of threat and clashing uproar, by the mob baying for revenge; depressed, too, by the death watch for the prisoner in the cell opposite his. Just a month after the riots, he dictated a note to a trusty who wrote for illiterate inmates. Ingalls knew he'd be hanged inside a month, the note indicated, and didn't want to end up in the hands of his old friends at the medical college, so it was necessary to spoil the corpse. Which he did, beating the hangman to the drop with a knotted bedsheet. His body was dispatched to a nearby funeral home, whose windows the curious soon pressed against for a glimpse of the infamous killer. The police soon gave up any idea of keeping them out, and allowed for an impromptu version of the state funeral; gawkers were allowed inside to file past and see the corpse, with one eye stubbornly open, as it lay in state in a zinc icebox.

Repentant, newly baptized, Ben Johnson was hanged in September 1884. His execution was overseen by Sheriff Hawkins, who had to chase off a "cheeky cuss" who tried to climb the scaffold and nab a souvenir length of rope. Johnson, too, took pains to steer clear of Dr. Cilley's table; he arranged for burial in a family plot well out in Indiana.

DODGE #5: SEARCHING FOR EDMUND PERRY

Intriguing as it was for me to trace these convolutions, all the foregoing was a dodge. When I saw the name Cilley, I immediately recognized it. It sent me back thirty-five years.

In 1982, at seventeen, I left my Deep South town and went away a thousand miles. I was desperately unhappy in the school I attended at home, a segregationist academy (though that was a term I had never heard at the time, a badge of shame I would discover only when I left). So I told my parents—both of whom had blazed the trail by skipping a grade, my mother the first and my father the twelfth—that I wanted to jump to college a year early. They acquiesced, reluctantly, but since I was a clueless, sheltered, socially hapless kid, they insisted that I attend, at least for the first year, an in-state college. If I wanted to venture farther, they suggested, I should try to get into prep school instead.

Which, for the three of us, meant one place: Phillips Exeter, in New Hampshire—a state I'd never visited in a region I knew nothing about. My mother and I had both read *A Separate Peace*, by alumnus John Knowles, which featured Exeter in the kind of ultra-light disguise that only made it more eye-catching; and my visions of a wider world than the one I knew (one more antic, more just, and more strange) had lately been stoked by the novels of another Exonian, John Irving. Back in the real world my father preferred, a boy from his town in yet deeper Dixie, a generation earlier—an older kid whose smarts he admired—had gone there, too.[7] So I applied.

One spring day my parents showed up in tandem at my typing class—a madhouse presided over by Miss P., a sweet-tempered woman from the deep country who wore home-sewn dresses, and who tried to keep order without ever enforcing a rule or even meeting an eye—to share the news that I'd be going north in September. Miss P. seemed puzzled; I agreed with her. I attributed Exeter's decision to their pursuit of geographic diversity, and I invested precisely zero racial self-awareness in that last noun. Now Exeter could claim to have students from forty-nine states instead of forty-eight. So far as I was concerned, *I* was diversity.

But what would these sophisticates make of my drawl, my redneck tastes (boiled peanuts, field peas) and narrownesses? I'd never seen a bagel, never even heard of sushi or biryani or falafel or pho; the only "ethnic" cuisine I had any awareness of was Chinese, which we had to drive an hour to get as my birthday treat, in a place with dragons galore and gold wallpaper flocked with red velvet. What were crew and lacrosse and water polo? Was I hardy enough to survive a rhymingly frigid Robert Frost winter? Most crucial: how, once I was there, to disappear? I recall that spring, as research, reading Lisa Birnbach's *Official Preppy Handbook*,[8] trying to translate its parody and baffling anthropology into practical advice. Buy Docksiders and observe, it basically boiled down to. Avoid the first-person singular, *Aaah*, which will mark you as both a hick *and* an egoist.

At Exeter, after we unloaded and said our goodbyes, I stood and watched the taillights of my parents' blue-and-beige van—suddenly, here, a skunk among the daisies, if Volvo diesels may be called daisies and if skunks may have captain's chairs and a tiny pump-operated sink—wink off as they pulled away from the stop sign in front of the giant new gym complex. I lingered for probably two minutes afterward, in the middle of an empty residential street, just because I had nowhere to go, nothing to do. The previous six months had led to this moment. But what happened when the script abruptly ran out?

I found that I didn't *mind* isolation, mostly; it provided time to think. That fall, in ways I mostly failed to see at the time, made me reckon with race for the first time in my life. Who moves to a redoubt of wealth and whiteness in a state more than 98 percent Caucasian to start pondering race and racism? A kid of thoughtless privilege. A few weeks after I landed in the North, trolling the ultramodern library's South Carolina holdings in a fever of homesickness, I was shocked, as my gaze flicked over a low stack, to spot the name of my hometown. It felt for an instant like an affirmation: my little homeplace, here in august Oz. Until I noticed that the spine's full title, in bold black set off against a blazing orange binding, was *The Orangeburg Massacre*.[9]

I opened the book, imagining it would tell of a clash centuries back between European settlers and Native Americans, and discovered for the first time— this sounds impossible, but it's true, an index of just how racially unaware I was, how unaware I and white kids like me were allowed to be—that just fourteen years earlier, in February 1968, three unarmed young people at South Carolina State College, the larger of the two side-by-side HBCUs in my majority-black hometown, had been killed when police, mostly from the state highway patrol, fired into campus following a protest bonfire. (An officer had been struck across the bridge of the nose with a thrown wooden porch balus-ter, which prompted cries of "Officer down," unleashing the flurry of shots.) Among the dead was a high-school student from Orangeburg, Delano Middle-ton, who was sitting on the steps of a freshman dorm, hundreds of yards away, waiting for his mother's work shift to end. Twenty-seven people were injured, most shot from behind as the rally dispersed. Several of the wounded hadn't even attended the rally; they were just looking on from the distance.

The protest had begun as an attempt—the modesty of its aim seems now almost the stuff of satire—to desegregate a bowling alley, so that students didn't have to make the same hour-long drive to Columbia that I made with my mom to eat hot-and-sour soup. The All-Star Triangle Bowl—the same alley where my mom sometimes took us on rainy Saturdays—was next to our tiny bus station, across from the Dairy-O, down the way from the Confederate memorial square. The principals in the tragedy included several people I knew, at least by sight: the president of SC State, who served with my mom on the county mental health board; my brother's friend's father, by 1982 the town's police chief, who'd been on the scene, and who was later identified as the only local officer who'd fired into the crowd; and even the proprietor of the bowling alley, a reedy, nervous-seeming older man who lived in the neighborhood, and whom I now saw in a photo from the time, standing outside his business in a cardigan, pointing a bony justifying finger to the door sign that said—that heart-sinking euphemism—"Privately Owned." Furthermore, I was alive and in Orangeburg at the time, though just two years old. How was it possible that I didn't know this before?

Twenty years ago I wrote an essay about all this, "Home Truths," in which I reexamined, in the light of the Massacre, some things it turned out I'd noticed—but failed to notice that I'd noticed—in 1975, when my Pee Wee football team was coached by three South Carolina State students, the youngest coaches in the league and the only black ones.[10] Unlike me, they—and my black teammates, and every black person in town—didn't have the option of not knowing, and thus of being able to imagine or pretend that racism was a relic of bygone generations, like the fading signs on the shuttered cotton mills. Only private-school whites like me had that option.

But I won't rehearse what I said in 1998. My focus here isn't 1968 or 1975, either, but 1982, and my delayed "discovery" (those quotation marks sting) about my own racial blindness. It wasn't that I'd failed to see "Founded 1964" on the sign outside my school, but I had utterly and conveniently failed to consider what that datum implied. Had it occurred to me that there were, among the mascots of the schools we played against, two sets of Rebels (one of them my school's), plus Generals, War Hawks, and Patriots? It had. The old people who'd founded these schools seemed ridiculous. But did I take any step bolder than private sarcasm? No.

Most damningly, had I failed to notice that I had no African American classmates, teammates? Of course not. But until 1982, my sense—compromised and suspect as it seems now—was that my parents were ponying up their $700 a year for a college-prep curriculum and a five-minute commute. This essay is not about questioning their decision to enroll me, after the free-spirited public "Demonstration School" I attended early on lost its funding, at Wade Hampton Academy. They wanted to give their kids the best education they could, parochial, private, or public. Do I think they would have preferred an integrated school? I do. Racial exclusion—which wasn't long for the world, I thought, or even for the South, that side world or underworld or Confederate-frigate-in-a-bottle world, and which was already getting nibbled away at in the independent schools of Columbia and Charleston—was an unfortunate side effect, temporary and caused by lingering ignorance. That the school was all white was a bug, not a feature. But no one was eager to fix the bug.

It's hard to blame parents, when it comes to educating their kids, for making decisions based in expediency or self-interest rather than sociological principle. Moral perils abound for white people who want to judge: Did you (or your parents, or theirs) choose a religious school, or move to the suburbs, or buy a house based on school district, or squall about busing? The public school system we have now, as is often pointed out, features far more racial segregation—paired with far more moral self-congratulation—than the one of thirty years ago did. My wife and I, too, have made an uneasy compromise between our belief in public schools and our desire to have our child sheltered and challenged, and so we've enrolled our daughter in a series of public magnets rather than in the neighborhood school. Years down the road, will that decision hold up to my daughter's scrutiny? Will prevailing notions about how privilege perpetuates itself make the choice look fishy? I can't say I have perfect confidence that we'll be cleared of all charges. Thanks to Martin Luther King Jr., we all know which way the arc of justice bends, but how many of us are willing to try to throw full weight behind bending it farther, faster? Mightn't it break? Mightn't we?[11]

During my year at Exeter, my parents gave me a subscription to Orangeburg's paper, *The Times & Democrat* (not *that* kind of Democrat, some locals immediately explain). Tight-coiled copies arrived, three or four days behind, in my campus mailbox, and I vividly remember how it reassured me to peer through the tiny window above the combination lock and see a rubber-banded baton that would bloom, back in my room, into a translucent windowpane of news that no one here but me could make a lick of sense of. The *T&D*, that fall especially, was a weird religion with but a single adept. I recall seeing a story on SAT scores that identified South Carolina as having the nation's lowest average, a hundred points below the national mean, and Orangeburg County as ranking forty-fifth among the state's forty-six, another hundred points below. That story has stuck in my head for thirty-five years now, which suggests that I used it—again, not in any way I acknowledged consciously—to justify not only my enrollment at Exeter, but the fact that my siblings and I had been sent to private rather than public school. It's a hell of a lot easier to *check* one's privilege, perhaps from the safe vantage of decades later, than it is to chuck it.

Twenty years ago, my friend and teacher Fred Hobson wrote a book called *But Now I See: The White Southern Racial Conversion Narrative*.[12] He identified the striking similarity between the conversion stories of American Puritanism and a certain subgenre of twentieth-century southern white writing. The commonalities Hobson noted included the omnipresence, in southern works about racial awakening, of traditional religious terminology; recurrent metaphors of blindness and vision, sin and repentance; the movement from confession of error or ignorance, to reluctant moral reckoning, to the kind of salvation that grants a clean slate—and that can, afterward, make one impatient with those traveling the same path more slowly.

The genre is *spiritual autobiography.* Though such works might offer an exposé of racism, any account of the conditions people of color face is contained within and subsumed under a white personal narrative. Southern racial conversion narratives provide not an exploration of black experience but an in-depth view of what it's like to be *white* in an unjust situation. There's something self-aggrandizing in this, of course[13]—that's part of the rap against navel-gazing memoir in general. It's also reminiscent of those movies, especially common in the 1980s and 1990s, that focused on racial injustice, but not through black subjects and protagonists. Instead, these films centered on white journalists and law officers and sympathetic souls, characters who marked the far edge of where empathy could be expected to take the white audience—or, in business terms, the far edge of what Hollywood believed it could risk without tanking at the box office. See for example *Cry Freedom*, of 1987, which managed to be about the white journalist played by Kevin Kline (such movies tend to have big-name stars opposite black up-and-comers, in this case a young Denzel Washington) rather than Steven Biko; and *Mississippi Burning*, of the following year, which was about Willem Dafoe's eyeglasses and Gene Hackman's accent, as I recall, and only secondarily about the Freedom Summer murders of James Chaney and Andrew Schwerner and Michael Goodman—which killings came to galvanize America's attention in the first place in part because two of the victims were white northerners and not poor, native Mississippi blacks. Almost the same thing, by the way, can be said of the Orangeburg Massacre. Why is it so much less well known than the shootings in 1970 at Kent State? Yes, well, that would seem to be *one* reason, anyway.

Another feature of racial conversion stories has to do—in the terms of fiction writing—with their collapsed timeline. The conversion almost always gets told as if it occurs in an instant, á la Saul on the road to Damascus. But that's artifice. Conversions don't occur spontaneously and without context. Instead they are often grueling, fitful, resisted, only half-perceived processes, which may unspool over half a life. Narrative convention requires that they be *told* this way, but it's psychological necessity that requires them to be *thought of* as occurring in a trice. We often approach unpleasantness at an angle, or come upon it too suddenly and so avert our gaze or back away or file it for future contemplation. We waver, we postpone, we backslide. But when we get to the other side, when our minds have changed, it spares us anguish to imagine that we responded decisively as soon as we saw injustice. You think of yourself as reformed or redeemed, and then—self-savingly, self-vauntingly—take a backward look and decide that . . . hey, I was already on the side of the angels in 1982.

I don't want this essay to be a racial conversion narrative. For one thing, I haven't reached any destination—and it seems to me folly to think that one's reckoning with racial privilege can have a declarable endpoint. White people may think of themselves as only temporarily or intermittently having a race; people of color can't. Here, conventional narrative form can make it seem as if one's former racism or the advantages systemic racism conferred are a barrier safely passed over, a burden cast off, an evil renounced. *Was* blind, sure, but *now* I see. So get off my back.

That scene in the Exeter library, and those I'll tell of later, aren't instants of aperçu, I realize. They're not moments when I *did* anything, but moments when I glimpsed something and had it singe my retinas for a second before I looked away. Such moments are quick-opening and quick-closing cataracts of vulnerability, brief episodes of sun-gazing that leave you dazed, stunned. Writing about them—and maybe this is why racial conversion narratives take the form they do, and why this is one whether I like it or not—is a kind of penance, undertaken out of the need to examine yourself, though you'd mostly rather not.

But the legacy of racism isn't past, and—more to the point—this essay won't, I hope, ultimately be about me. I need to get to Cilley, and from there to Edmund Perry.

In a roundabout way, as you will have guessed.

I considered myself as much an outsider as anyone I met at Exeter. I know how ridiculous this sounds, and is. But the African Americans I encountered every day in class and at practice (gregarious B., effervescent F., quiet A., brilliant bespectacled C.) seemed to me at the time to belong to the prep school world as much or more than I did. That I felt this way is a shameful analog to my failure to consider that black folks might not be able to satisfy themselves, as I did, with the thought that racism was ebbing or thinning or passing away, and all we had to do was wait for our generation's turn. This was the kind of thinking that empowered the "moderate" southern stratagem of "all deliberate speed," to quote the most abused phrase of the *Brown v. Board* decision, the one that allowed for sixteen years of foot-dragging before Orangeburg's schools were finally fully integrated in 1971, my first-grade year.

I cop to my failure of empathy. But wasn't it also predictable that the few one-year seniors at Exeter (a dozen or two, not counting postgrads honing their athletic or academic credentials) would feel like isolates? We were late transfers in, late exiles from home—and an awkward interbreed of old hand and newbie, of senior and prep (as ninth-graders were known). Even within this group, I was an outlier. Unlike almost anyone else I encountered—including my roommate, from Caracas, Venezuela, who had arrived on campus with a close pal from home and who seemed instantly to find a community of Spanish speakers, hard-rock enthusiasts, and oglers of the *Playboy* centerfolds he lined the walls with—I had no family here, no history, no ties, no friends, no models who weren't fictional characters.

There was among Exeter's African American students a distinct exception to my rule, someone whose outsiderdom yielded to no one's. He was a sophomore (or, to speak proper Exonian, a lower), and a resident in the big, raucous dorm—Cilley Hall, dear reader, Cilley Hall—next to the spot where, when I could remember to, I went to drop off and fetch my laundry. The dormitory was named for one of the New Hampshire Cilleys, Bradbury, who was appointed professor of classics at Exeter in 1858–59—the same school year in which the school admitted its first black student, a local named Moses Uriah Hall. Bradbury Cilley had graduated Harvard just months earlier, alongside his cousin and classmate Jonathan Longfellow Cilley.

Our laundry went out in ever-dirtier canvas bags that bore our scrawled first initials and surnames—which is how I came to know that he was E. Perry. Edmund (friends called him Eddie) seemed somehow both the most and the least relaxed person I'd ever seen. He had an easy smile, but behind it lay something he wanted to make clear was untouchable. He was thin and gangly; his clothes—according to the academy's dress code, boys had to wear coats and ties to class—might on the one hand be called ill-fitting (I'm reminded of the description of Cincinnati burker Ben Johnson: Edmund's "extravagance of collar and cuff" I recall vividly), but everything about his look was intentional, was owned. I knew and know absolutely nothing about clothing: I couldn't say whether Edmund's coats were tailored on Savile Row or, like Johnson's, "a seedy broadcloth." But whatever the case, they were *self-bespoke*. He carried an unmistakable aura of cool—some of it, no doubt, projected upon him by me and by others, white kids with a limited vocabulary to account for black confidence, black self-possession, but he cultivated, too, a swagger that he virtually demanded you call streetwise. He left no doubt at all that he was not only from the city but from The City—from Harlem, I was told when I asked.

But it was clear, too, that this confidence was an import to Exeter. Everything about Edmund Perry said that though he was in this place—and he appeared to be thriving in it, seemed determined to make it his own—he was not *of* this place.

Here I must interrupt, apologetically, to confess the lifelong inferiority complex of the small-town kid, and particularly to my intimidation by those not only snazzily dressed, but dressed in some way that indicated *intent*, an identity not accidental. To my mortification, the point requires two examples, only one of which I can tell in the chipper tone of anecdote:

#1: At the end of one youth football season—it's hard to overstate that sport's cultural importance in 1970s Dixie, and in towns like mine city-league athletics were that rarity, an integrated realm where "voluntary" segregation wasn't an option on offer—an Orangeburg all-star team got to go to Charleston to play in a tournament. We were outfitted in castoff tees from the high school, plain orange with maroon numbers (the color scheme a clashing mess occasioned by the merger of the white school, Orangeburg, with the black, Wilkinson). The teenagers' shirts were big enough to stretch over our shoulder pads, and we wore them with our own grass-stained pants, mismatched cleats, varied socks (as seen in the photo reproduced here, my favorite pair was forest green), and our rainbow coalition of helmets, some of them home-spray-painted (and many featuring stickers for wacky products like "Weakies, the Breakfast of Chumps," and "Killy Putty, the twenty-megaton toy that scrambles your eggs"), plus the scuffs we made, trying to look tough, by whacking our headgear against everyone else's on the sideline at practice. Two of our best players came in over the weight limit of ninety-six pounds, and so, an hour before kickoff, the rest of us congregated on the bleachers' top row to watch them put on garbage bags and run laps around the stadium. One of them sweated his way down to the limit, but he looked peaked and spent. We took the field, started our ragtag warmup . . . and then our opponents arrived. They ran through a paper sign (a paper sign!?) held by cheerleaders (cheerleaders!?), and they wore not only matching black helmets, jerseys, pants, socks, and shoes but also ponchos—the kind we'd seen only on NFL Films—emblazoned with the name of their suburban titletown. As they fanned to their places in military-looking lines and began doing calisthenics, shout-counting every rep, a black-clad manager snaked down the rows, Batman's valet, scooping up the cowls they'd shed. Team Orangeburg didn't *go on* to lose; we lost right then.

Edmund Perry's effect on me was similar. That his cool might be a mask never occurred to me, wouldn't even have been conceivable; the appearance of perfect confidence *was* perfect confidence. Around him, I felt like I was jogging in a Hefty bag with a raggedly cut neckhole and having to hitch up my ill-fitting pants every three strides along the way.

#2: Though I didn't like coats or ties, which I'd almost never worn at home, I did like the near-invisibility conferred by Exeter's dress code. But as basketball season began, my magical thinking about clothing exacted its price. By the time our first game rolled around we'd had tryouts, then several weeks of practice, putting in plays, experimenting with lineups, and so on. But for some reason, uniforms had not been distributed. I was not only a newcomer, but— at 5'11" and 150 pounds—suddenly a point guard rather than the baseline-roaming extra-small forward I'd been at home. I wasn't going to be a crucial cog in the team. I was mostly just happy to have made the roster, and my lack of status made me even less likely to ask questions. So I didn't. By our first game, which as I recall was a cross-state road trip to Cornish, the village best known in the prep-school pantheon as J. D. Salinger's hermitage of choice, I was mildly anxious about my lack of a jersey, but not worried; I hadn't seen anyone else in uniform, either. I didn't know any teammates well enough to risk the embarrassment of asking whether they already had their gear. So I held my silence, assuming that Exeter—a place of tradition, of class, of mystique, an avatar of the cosmopolitan glamor I'd seen the South Carolina version of back in kiddie football—used the Distribution of the Vaunted Uni as a way to fire up the team for that first game.

But uniforms weren't handed out at the last practice before our opener, nor as we climbed onto the bus, nor when we arrived at the away gym. By the time we filed into the locker room for Coach Hamblet's low-key motivational speech, I'd begun to collapse into myself like the rained-on cake in that Jimmy Webb song. His instructions given, coach left the locker room, my teammates started plundering their gym bags, and I remember sitting there, unzipping my duffel and peering inside as if, somehow, a miracle, it might now contain something more than socks, shoes, and a jock strap. That first game, I sat on the end of the bench wearing a maroon Exeter warmup suit someone had lent me, with nothing underneath it but an athletic supporter. My teammates kindly averted their eyes from the disgrace. I will, too.

All this is offered as a kind of explanation for why Edmund Perry stuck out to me. It was in part just the way he wore his clothes, the way he sat on his laundry bag, knees up and wrists draped over them. This guy, an outsider like me, had made this foreign place his own. Now, as I think back, there's far more ignominy in my misreading of Edmund Perry than there ever was in the visitors' locker room whose drain I wanted to seep down. Bizarrely, I thought that being southern conferred upon me a kinship with him. We both had racial worlds to return to that bore little resemblance to the placid progressive microcosm of Exeter.

Deciding to envy Edmund Perry surely had to do, too, with tamping down the racial guilt that my late encounter with the Orangeburg Massacre had made bubble up. And that my abrupt immersion in southern literature—my year in New Hampshire was also the year I discovered Flannery O'Connor, Eudora Welty, Carson McCullers, Robert Penn Warren, and William Faulkner—kept making me reconfront. I tried to use the cushion of a half-century to deny that I was implicated in the South they described. Most of what we were reading was pre–Civil Rights Era, and of that group only Welty and Warren, septuagenarians both, were still alive. I knew the truth, but still I labored to believe in my status as a stranger in a strange land. But what kind of idiot—I wish this question didn't qualify as rhetorical—tries to make Straight Outta Compson the equivalent of Straight Outta Compton? Part of the unbridgeable distance between Eddie Perry and me, it would turn out, was that if I made a mistake about how compatible my alternate worlds were, about how to negotiate the border crossings, I got embarrassed; if he did, the stakes were far higher.

I don't mean to suggest that I spent much time thinking about Edmund Perry. I had my own dramas, and I paid no attention to his. I heard his up-from-poverty story and filed it, lazily, under Inspiration; I counted him as blessed to be at Exeter and Exeter as lucky to have him. This was an obviously flawed, shopworn narrative, but my infrequent interactions with him—in front of Cilley with a laundry bag on my shoulder, jockeying a tray at the Elm Street Dining Hall, maybe a time or two playing pickup basketball—never required more than a handful of words. I kept my head down, worked hard, had a year that changed my life. I graduated in June 1983, and for two years, until I saw his name in the newspaper, I didn't think of E. Perry.

In June 1985, Edmund returned home to Harlem for the summer before heading to Stanford in the fall. He'd just graduated from Exeter with honors, and had also entertained scholarship offers from Berkeley, Yale, and Penn. He'd landed a summer messenger gig on Wall Street to help earn spending money. But mainly he was hanging out near home, reconnecting with friends and family, enjoying—one imagines—being back in a place where he had the invisibility that can come from being part of a majority. (There were barely forty black students at Exeter at the time, in a student population of nearly a thousand.) Now he'd shed coat and tie, shed his status as Representative Black Man.

On June 12, Edmund and his brother Jonah played pickup basketball at the Wadleigh pit on West 114th Street, next to his junior high school. My dim recollection is that Edmund was not a very good player, all awkwardness and bravado, and one of the few details that day about which reports were unanimous is that he lost, either to his brother or playing on a team with his brother. Then they went out.

A few hours later, at 12:55 A.M., seventeen-year-old Edmund Perry would be pronounced dead from a single gunshot wound in the belly—a shot fired by a young undercover officer named Lee Van Houten.

We've heard stories before that begin with this same awful datum, in recent years with terrifying frequency. Dead young black man. Baby-faced white cop, in this case just two years on the force, and on plainclothes detail as a kind of bait pedestrian, part of his precinct's response to a rash of thefts from doctors' cars near Saint Luke's Hospital, hard by Morningside Park. There's the distrust that attends the fact of a police force, in a majority-black neighborhood like Harlem, in which whites are massively overrepresented. It's easy to see bias, too, in the policing priority that put Van Houten on the sidewalk that night, in civvies. Given scarce resources and high crime, did it make sense for the NYPD to devote undercover officers to stop petty theft from (mainly white) physicians' cars? What else? Era of the thin blue line. Procedures not followed that would have kept Van Houten within sight of his backup. A black teenager fired upon and killed—startlement and adrenaline playing their part, as in Orangeburg—and then discovered to be unarmed.

All this context makes clear why the community's response right after Edmund Perry's death—a response echoed by much of the press coverage— was either outrage at the NYPD or mistrust of them. Nor did it help that the shaken, frightened-looking Van Houten, in the days afterward, was photographed wearing one of those donut neck braces that were in those days virtually the trademark of fraudulent injury. This extremely successful, promising young black man had been killed in cold blood, then. Surely a young man with Edmund Perry's gifts and prospects wouldn't participate in a street mugging.

But the tragedy quickly grew more complicated, the brutality narrative more vexed. Van Houten wasn't a hothead. There had never been a civilian complaint about him in his two years on the force. He seemed genuinely broken up about the events of that night. Most of all, his story of being attacked checked out. His version was that as he turned a corner, two young men leapt out at him. One knocked him down and got him in the yoke grip, arm tightly around the neck from behind, a common m.o. for two-person street assaults. There was a shouted demand for money, and the accomplice started rifling through Van Houten's pockets. They then started pummeling him. Before losing consciousness, Van Houten extricated his revolver from an ankle holster and fired three times, with one shot hitting the second young man, the one in front of him—Edmund Perry.

More than twenty witnesses were able to confirm or buttress Van Houten's version in one detail or another. Meanwhile, Jonah Perry's account of his whereabouts wasn't persuasive, and several people reported that he told them he'd been involved in a mugging. In the end, a grand jury would decline to bring charges against Officer Van Houten, who was found to have acted within departmental guidelines on the use of lethal force.

Many in the community still believe that Edmund Perry's death amounted to murder by cop. For support they can point to Jonah's acquittal on assault charges a couple of years later. And New York did settle the family's $145 million wrongful death suit . . . but for $75,000, which figure suggests that neither party felt the city had much chance of being judged liable by a jury. Of course, even the determination that this was "justifiable homicide" wouldn't exculpate the police entirely. The fatally wounded teen was handcuffed, put in "shock pants" designed to force blood to his vital organs, then left for a time on the sidewalk before being moved to the emergency room where he was pronounced dead. Did the delay contribute? Was it intentional? Did Van Houten, in a moment of panic, clearly identify himself as an officer, as he claimed? Might he have reacted differently, in a way that wouldn't have escalated the confrontation? Still, the facts that dribbled out—and subsequent revelations about Edmund's sale and use of drugs at Exeter—had the effect of blunting the initial broader indignation.

Once a consensus emerged among white observers—if, understandably, not as strongly among African Americans—that Edmund and Jonah Perry had ambushed Van Houten, the discussion's focus shifted. *Why* would this young man, who'd accomplished so much already and was poised to do much more, risk it all on a low-reward crime, on what amounted to a vicious prank?

Robert Sam Anson's account, first in a *New York* magazine profile and later in *Best Intentions: The Education and Killing of Edmund Perry*,[14] proved tough for me to read. The facts of Edmund's life put the lie to all the false analogies and equivalencies I'd dreamt up at Exeter. This was the era of the "Just Say No" campaign, which seemed to me sincere but also ridiculous. The slogan pretended to be based on the invocation of a simple moral code: *Just say no because that's the right thing to do.* But abstract ethics, treated as if its tenets are universal, can't snuff out experimentation among teenagers—especially among those with reason to doubt whether staying within the lines is designed to benefit *them.* At its core, "Just Say No" addressed itself to the would-be drug user's self-interest, to his or her understanding of the social contract—an appeal that made sense if you were, say, an upper-middle-class white kid. *Just say no . . . and you will avoid jail or scandal, and in time be rewarded with a college degree, a good job, public respect, the trappings of success, and with these the complacent sense that you have fairly earned everything you have and that you live, with your own status as evidence, in a just world.* The calculus would make less sense—or not add up at all—for a kid growing up in the ghetto, where risks were far greater, moral conflicts knottier and more numerous, peer pressure stifling, and rewards for compliance much harder to see. *Just say no . . . and, well, on second thought, just say no about covers it.* As I read Anson's article, I couldn't help noticing that I was guilty of the very same blindness I wanted to sneer at Ronald and Nancy Reagan for.

I read Anson's *New York* profile with intense interest and intense shame. While I'd been at all-white Wade Hampton, Edmund had been enrolled in a program for academically promising inner-city children called—note how modest the name is, how intent on not overpromising—"A Better Chance." Its motto and rallying cry? "Fight Back with Merit." The program had placed more than two hundred students in top-tier boarding schools. After Edmund's death, Anson interviewed the director, Edouard Plummer, who—talking philosophically about what the program could ensure and what it couldn't—said, "I could have reunions of my graduates at both" Harvard and Rikers Island.

Some details Anson reported were heartbreaking: for instance Edmund, as a boy aspiring to be a surgeon, building plane and ship models to develop a "steady hand." Someone had made a short documentary about A Better Chance during Edmund's time at Wadleigh Junior High, and Anson sought her out. She showed him the film, including the scene in which Edmund Perry introduced himself to the camera: "My age is thirteen and I will be going to Phillips Exeter in the fall. It is located in Exeter, New Hampshire. Since the first or second grade, I told myself I would be coming to this school. I don't have any more goals yet, but I'll put some up there soon."

I couldn't help noting the stiffness in this, not only in the syntax of "My age is thirteen" or "It is located" but also in the way Edmund's speech seems translated into the narrative cliché white America demands of the so-called talented tenth. At thirteen, he has to cast his life as a Horatio Alger story, and Exeter must be a lifelong dream, framed when he was six or seven. This fortunate child of the ghetto is required, already, to be thinking in terms of the conventional goals of white-defined "success" . . . goals whose specifics he knows little enough of that he has to postpone naming them. Or, rather, not naming them but—this the most relaxed, real-seeming phrase of the clip—"putting some up there"? Putting them up where? On some kind of scoreboard? For whom to see?

And, too, the picture of Edmund steadying his hands by constructing kit models, perhaps of 1950s Chevys or sailing vessels—a pastime my friends and I thought of as kids today might of Rubik's Cube or board games like Risk or Monopoly: a barely surviving relic of the quaint, "innocent" childhoods of our parents? True or not, that detail read to me as reassurance to an older generation of white people of the young black man's shared values, of his nonradicalism.

The documentarian—Anson, respecting her desire for anonymity, gives her the pseudonym "Carolyn"—spoke eloquently of the predicament Edmund and his fellow alumni of A Better Chance faced at places like Exeter. To be black, she said, was to grow up with full knowledge of your powerlessness. Admission to an elite prep school doesn't offer, at least not in the short term, access to power of one's own; first must come the full reckoning with just how entrenched those elites are, with just how many ways the dice are loaded. "You are caught up," she told Anson, "in a situation where everybody says you should be happy, where you think you should be happy, and instead of being happy, you find that there are tears in your eyes because you are so angry. That was one of Edmund's tragedies. He was in an environment where he was constantly being reminded how powerless he was."

Yes, Edmund and I were both outsiders, but of wildly different kinds. When I went home at Christmas I felt mild pressure to prove I hadn't turned into some kind of egghead Yankee. But giving my accent a little boost and drinking a beer or two around an open car trunk at the dead end of "Two-Minute Road" (named for how long it was said to take certain speedsters to drive it) were the furthest cry from the code-switching required of Edmund Perry. Negotiating the gulf between home and Exeter was for him, in the pungent phrase of Mark Anthony Neal, "like a version of W.E.B. Du Bois' theory of 'double-consciousness' on crack." As Carolyn put it, "You've got a week to prove you're black, because you're on that bus [back to New England] Monday morning."

Was it any wonder that by the end of his senior year Edmund Perry had grown disillusioned, resentful, angry? In his yearbook entry, Edmund skipped the typical quotes from philosophers or poets or rock stars. His quote was signed, in capital letters, "ME (Eddie Perry)." "Good-bye, Exeter," he wrote, "you taught me many things. God bless you for that. Some things I saw I did not like, and some things I learned I'd rather not know. Nevertheless, it had to be done because I could never learn not to learn. It's a pity we part on a less than friendly basis, but we do. . . . Work to adjust yourself to a changing world, as will I."

During the winter of Perry's senior year, Exeter put on a symposium called "The American Dream Deferred," and to the surprise of many, Edmund—to this point not very politically active—took a major role. He seemed pissed off about the sparse attendance, hostile (in ways that read to some African American visitors as histrionic, as performative) to the white students who did come. The crucial event of the symposium for him was an assembly to mark MLK's birthday, at which Edmund was slated to give a speech to the student body. He said this:

> I am the new black. I am at Exeter not to be like you, nor to enter your society. . . . Assimilation is no longer the solution. . . . My most effective role in tomorrow's society will be to lead the advancement of Black power; and I, the new black, dedicate my life to that role. . . . We are at Exeter to obtain knowledge of ourselves, and when we become leaders, we will derive our strength not from your friendship, or your brains, or your money, but from ourselves.[15]

Then Edmund announced that he'd taken the text of his stirring declaration of rage and independence not from "ME" but from a prior Exonian, Theophus "Thee" Smith, who'd written it back in 1968, immediately after MLK's murder (and less than two months after the Orangeburg Massacre).[16] "These words were written seventeen years ago," Perry said. Again the performing mask, then, but it was clear that Edmund was growing into the role he'd chosen. He closed with three words of his own: "Nothing has changed."

After Edmund's death—Anson's evenhanded, mystery-respecting book is especially good on this point—people vied over what narrative to assign him. The history of police brutality? Another victim of the tenacious claims of poverty and "the street"? The evils of peer pressure? The follies of affirmative action? The awful burdens of double consciousness, which Du Bois had defined in his 1903 book *The Souls of Black Folk* as "this sense of always looking at one's self through the eyes of others. . . . One ever feels his twoness, an American, a Negro; two souls, two thoughts, two unreconciled strivings; two warring ideals in one body, whose dogged strength alone keeps it from being torn asunder"?[17]

Edmund Perry's story is irreducibly complex, and I am as guilty as anyone else, I can't help seeing, of co-opting him for my own ends, much as I want to respect the unknowability at his core. A family friend of the Perrys, Bill Perkins, warned Anson early on of the folly of looking for an *answer*, for some truest version of him. "You're not going to have an easy time finding Eddie Perry," he said. "The real Eddie is elusive. He is like smoke." You can't, after requiring double consciousness of black people, declare that you have pushed aside all the masks and identified the one inmost single identity.

This essay began with Jonathan Longfellow Cilley of the Ohio Medical School, another upper-middle-class white abuser of the African American dead, and one I felt inclined to judge harshly. Now I must admit a bitter kinship with Dr. Cilley, whose aggressive incuriosity about the source of those specimen corpses read to me as a self-indulgence, if not as a crime. But how was I different, really? "I had no idea, officer," Cilley had told the police, and that was enough to indemnify him, or not.

When it comes to Edmund Perry, reader, I had no idea.

DODGE #6

What of the sixth degree of separation? It is an extra convolution; it can lead almost anywhere. Maybe to Kevin Hooks, the prolific TV director who made the movie *Murder without Motive: The Edmund Perry Story* . . . and who a decade earlier, in the role of fast-talking point guard Morris Thorpe on *The White Shadow*—in which a white ex-NBAer takes over as coach at a predominantly black LA high school—played a big part in my own racial conversion narrative?

Or Michael Jackson, another tragic performer of split racial identities, whose song "Bad" he based on the story of Edmund Perry?

Or, by way of the epic eighteen-minute video for that song, director Martin Scorsese, or producer Quincy Jones, or scriptwriter Richard Price (later one of the principal writers of *The Wire*, which features several plotlines that seem inflected by Edmund Perry).

Or perhaps Wesley Snipes, who earned one of his first significant roles, in that video, by beating out another aspirant named Prince?

Or, really, anyone. That's the thing about the sixth degree, in a world as interconnected as ours. It's cruel to those who'd like to opt out, hide, hover above the fray. The net gets ever wider; there's no staying out of its mesh.

THE PERMEABLE EARTH

"THE MAGIC OF THE STREET IS the mingling of errand and epiphany," writes Rebecca Solnit in her wonderful *Wanderlust: A History of Walking*.[1] She's talking about urban jaunts like Virginia Woolf's winter-evening excursion across London in "Street Haunting" (1927). Woolf insists in that essay that the errand she sets herself, the purchase of a pencil, is pure artifice, an excuse to get her into the streets, into her own head, and into glancing collisions with others. The ramble itself is the goal. Walking allows her, and all of us, to think associatively, discursively, on the move. It may do even more, Solnit argues: "Walking, ideally," she writes, "is a state in which the mind, the body, and the world are aligned, as though they were three characters finally in conversation together, three notes suddenly making a chord."

Whether I was watching pale-purple spider lilies sprout overnight under oaks, then wilt over weeks; or relishing the frequent sight of couples staging wedding photos where the camera angle could exclude inconvenient *memento mori* (till *what* do us part?); or chasing after a woodchuck as it waddled into a storm drain and turned to taunt me; or just drifting, whim-blown, from grave to grave . . . my year exploring Spring Grove has felt, at least in a few ecstatic moments, like the three-part conversation Solnit describes.

In this book the streets are necropolitan rather than cosmopolitan, and errand and epiphany mingle unequally. There's no shortage of the former: the project evolved from an errand that resembles Woolf's both in its substance ("Why don't I nip out to sharpen the pencils I'll need to write my novel?") and in being a pretense (what I needed, I knew, wasn't finer pencil-points but finer thoughts). By way of epiphany, though, I have little to offer.

Perhaps it was inevitable, given Spring Grove's scale and all the haphazard miles I logged, that one spring morning, wet-footed and preoccupied, I'd sidestep a knot of roots, fail to slip cleanly through a beaded curtain of foliage, and get a faceful of dew, and I'd remove and wipe and replace my glasses, and when the world swam back into focus I'd find myself beside a stone that bore my surname. It didn't mark the grave of an ancestor or even a distant relative, so far as I know. Still, that was my name incised there, in a medium and a font I'd seen now thousands of times but failed, perhaps purposely, to imagine could accommodate this set of letters in this order.

And when I broke the rule I'd apparently made but never realized the existence of until then, when I reached across and touched the granite, I felt the sun's warmth lodged there. That living heat could of course be explained away, by sun-angle and reflectivity and all the tiresome rest of physics, but for a moment I found it hard to believe anymore even in the one degree of separation that had always seemed most obvious and unbridgeable. Maybe a human lifespan was just the errand a soul sets out on, some winter evening of eternity, as an excuse to haunt and ponder and mingle. Maybe Laura Pruden and the Doyles were right after all, and the earth, a permeable membrane, can be passed through from either side. Maybe what I'd been up to all along was staging a belated party that Leon Van Loo *could* attend.

I'd never wanted a grave before, but as I lifted my hand and stepped back, I found myself thinking that it might, you know, it might be *nice* to have a stone—small, inconspicuous, overgrown, rain-worn, glade-hidden—for people to stroll past, and a modest one-word inscription on which, once in a while, some passerby's eye or mind might alight.

Acknowledgments

This kind of book can't happen without a generous, obsession-tolerant community of friends. I am deeply grateful to all those who have helped, collaborated, and encouraged along the way.

First readers/editors: Brock Clarke, Trenton Lee Stewart, David Stradling, David Kirby, and Chris Bachelder; Leah McCormack, Dietrik Vanderhill, and Brian Trapp; Elizabeth McKenzie, Susann Cokal, Keith Lee Morris, and Laura Micciche.

Magazines that published earlier versions of or excerpts from essays: *Chicago Quarterly Review*, *Broad Street*, *South Carolina Review*, and *Composition Studies*.

For their encouragement at the start: Bess Winter, Jamie Quatro, Inman Majors, Kelly Grey Carlisle, and Adrianne Harun. My fabulous students at the University of Cincinnati and the University of the South, and colleagues including Gary Weissman, Jennifer Habel, Leah Stewart, and Kristen Iversen. Photographers Maya Drozdz, Ronny Salerno, and Derek Goodwin. Those who graciously allowed me to use images from their collections: Richard O. Titus, Gene Gill, and Barry Delk; South Carolina State University; the Metropolitan Museum of Art; the Smithsonian Institution; the Springfield Museums; the Dittrick Medical History Center at Case Western; *Ohio History*; the Film Music Society; the Ohio County Public Library (Wheeling, WV); the Hett Art Gallery and Museum; the University of North Carolina at Asheville; the University of Cincinnati; and Landor. For other appreciated help: Robert Swartz, Jay Jennings, Mike Levine, Greg Hand, and Richard O. Jones.

Emily Williamson, for heroically trying to fly an anvil.

Sarah Muncy and especially Liz Scarpelli at the University of Cincinnati Press, for their hard work, kindness, and belief in the project.

Marilyn Campbell, Meghan Krausch, and Kathie Klee, for graciously and expertly rescuing me from error.

Jonathan Z. Kamholtz, without whose advice and photographer's eye this project would be immensely poorer.

The Charles Phelps Taft Center at the University of Cincinnati, for a generous rights and indexing subvention, and (bless you!) for the semester of leave from teaching that made this book possible.

And to Nicola and Bix, first and last.

Notes

A STATE OF UNGRESS

1. Marilyn Johnson, *The Dead Beat: Lost Souls, Lucky Stiffs, and the Perverse Pleasure of Obituaries* (New York: HarperCollins, 2006).

2. A cartoon character who was drawn so as to resemble, uncannily, the man who voiced him.

3. The full lyrics, per the internet: "Beyond the rim of the star-light/ My love is wand'ring in star-flight./ I know he'll find in star-clustered reaches/ Love, strange love a star woman teaches./ I know his journey ends never,/ His star trek will go on forever./ But tell him while he wanders his starry sea/ Remember, remember me." If you can suss out the song's point of view, you're a better critic than I am. Is Captain Kirk Roddenberry's/the speaker's platonic love, maybe, and Roddenberry/the speaker has dispatched the character into the vortex of space to find the weird interspecies love that "a star woman teaches"? Your guess is as good as mine. But who's the *you* who's supposed to tell the star trekker not to forget the speaker who loves him? A Vulcan's probably not the right person to convey this message.

4. Or the lawyers of his heirs and assigns, anyway: Roddenberry died in 1991.

5. Thanks, Caitlin and Martha, for the use of your saw, and sorry to have to tell this tale of unneighborly tool abuse.

6. Through much of the 1960s, because he found it hard to find a manufacturer to take a junior upstart like him seriously, Fogarty would end up hand-making and hand-tying catheters for himself and an ever-widening circle of fellow surgeons.

7. I apologize for that superfluous "much," reader. It is a psychological necessity. Kindly ignore it. (Also, for the uninitiated: a hink-pink is a miniature rhyming puzzle, and "hinkily pinkily" simply designates to the would-be solver that this one has three syllables on either side of the rhyme.)

8. Michael Griffith, *Trophy* (Evanston, IL: TriQuarterly Books, 2011).

9. Jorge Luis Borges, "Garden of Forking Paths," in *Ficciones,* trans. Anthony Kerrigan (New York: Grove Press, 1962)

10. One of the essays in this book came about when I chased two turkeys through a hedge-gap.

11. John Barth, "The Ocean of Story," in *The Friday Book: Essays and Other Nonfiction* (New York: Putnam, 1984).

THE ABSENT GUEST

1. I have found no record of whether the pet dog was booted or blackballed when his (at the time, the club admitted only males) presence was no longer needed to stave off numerological curses.

BAKE VISIBLY!

1. Schott certainly loved animals, for example her giant pampered slobbering St. Bernards, which during the years of her ownership had the run of Riverfront Stadium (and were even allowed to crap on the field, to the players' displeasure)—so her motives here may have been pure, or pure-ish. But Schott's record for loving her fellow human beings was far spottier, and she had plenty of reputation-mending to do, after her many racist and ethnic and sexist slurs and then her year-long ban from baseball after she repeatedly told the media that "Hitler was good in the beginning, but he went too far."

"A GREAT AWKWARD BUNGLEHOOD OF WOMAN"

1. I want to give thanks for and special acknowledgment to Kimberly Nichols's essay "The Red Harlot of Liberty: The Rise and Fall of Frances Wright," *Newtopia Magazine*, May 15, 2013 (https://newtopiamagazine.wordpress.com/2013/05/15/the-red-harlot-of-liberty-the-rise-and-fall-of-frances-wright/), which was an invaluable resource for this essay.

2. Frances Wright, *Views of society and manners in America; in a series of letters from that country to a friend in England, during the years 1818, 1819, and 1820* (New York, E. Bliss and E. White, 1821), 87.

3. Edmund White, *Fanny, a Fiction* (New York: HarperCollins, 2003).

4. William H. Gass, "Emerson and the Essay," in *Habitations of the Word* (New York: Simon and Schuster, 1985).

5. Norman Mailer, *Armies of the Night* (New York: New American Library, 1968), It may strain the reader's sympathy—or smash it to smithereens—to recall that the public image Mailer is moaning about centered on the fact that, after a 1960 party, he stabbed his wife Adele Morales with a penknife. As I said, he is the strangest ally conceivable for Fanny Wright. And yet...

6. I once had an undergraduate student write, memorably, about this phenomenon. The protagonist of his story was on spring break in South Padre, grooving to a live performance by Vanilla Ice, when sneering ironists started a fight. The protagonist threw in with his hero, and—as he held off the attackers in the club's cramped kitchen (ironists are poor brawlers)—was thanked from the door by an escaping Mr. Ice, who sadly confided: "All I wanted . . . all I ever wanted was to rock the mic like a vandal."

7. Flannery O'Connor, "The Life You Save May Be Your Own," in *A Good Man Is Hard to Find* (New York: Harcourt, Brace, 1955).

INTERLUDE: THE BANK-SHOT UNMEMOIR

1. Brock Clarke, *The Arsonist's Guide to Writers' Homes in New England* (Chapel Hill, NC: Algonquin Books, 2007).

2. David George Haskell, *The Forest Unseen: A Year's Watch in Nature* (New York: Viking, 2012).

"DEATH'S TAXICAB"

1. Nor would the evolution of materials end there. If Calhoun had lasted another half-century, he might have had the option devised by a Russian immigrant to Herkimer, NY, one Joseph Karwowski, who patented a glass cube burial; the corpse could be "hermetically incased" in a block of glass and thus "maintained in a perfect and lifelike condition." The first page of Karwowski's patent shows a natty cartoon corpse standing tall. He appears to be modeling a suit—he crooks his left elbow like a catalog model. An even more macabre illustration below shows a severed-head-only option, possibly suitable for display on a wide mantel or end table.

2. Mark Twain, *Life on the Mississippi* (Boston: James R. Osgood and Company, 1883), 437.

3. Allan Gurganus, *Blessed Assurance: A Moral Tale* (Rocky Mount: North Carolina Wesleyan College Press, 1990).

4. Evelyn Waugh, *The Loved One* (Boston: Little, Brown, 1948).

5. Clement Barnhorn was also a charter member and later president of the Cincinnati Art Club, mentioned in the essay "Absent Guest."

6. I remember from my childhood a later attempt to market the auto as work of art: the short-lived "Designer Series" of Mark V Lincoln Continentals in the late 1970s, which featured "designs"—color combinations, mostly—selected by fashion-house stars like Cartier, Givenchy, Bill Blass, and Emilio Pucci.

7. Collazo would be convicted and condemned, but Truman commuted his sentence to life imprisonment. He served almost three decades in Leavenworth before being released by President Jimmy Carter to return to Puerto Rico, where he would die in 1994. An odd footnote: Oscar Collazo was initially radicalized as a teenager, in 1932, when he heard of a racist letter by a resident American cancer researcher, Cornelius Rhoads. In the letter Rhoads disparaged Puerto Ricans, calling them "the dirtiest, laziest, most degenerate and thievish race of men ever inhabiting this sphere" and saying that he hoped "a tidal wave or something" would exterminate them. Rhoads then essentially boasted that he'd murdered several in medical trials, and had tried to kill others by injecting them with tumor cells. When an appalled lab assistant leaked the letter to nationalist leader Pedro Albizu Campos, it created—not surprisingly—an uproar. But Rhoads said he'd merely been annoyed at having his car vandalized and was blowing off steam by "joking" with a friend, and—I'd like to find this story harder to believe—the outrage in Puerto Rico translated, on the mainland, to a brief uncomfortable buzz. The scandal did nothing to sink Rhoads's career: In fact, he would go on to become the first director of Sloan-Kettering Institute and, starting in the same year Collazo was released from prison, the namesake of a prestigious medical award. An investigation launched in 2002 by that award's sponsor, the American Association for Cancer Research, would uncover no evidence that Rhoads actually committed the crimes he bragged about, or indeed that he engaged in any research misconduct, but it would result in the prize being given a new name.

8. Both these features, incidentally, I remember well from the one sybaritic possession my mother ever indulged herself, a metallic-flake powder-blue 1974 Eldorado she was inspired to buy, I believed, by Jim Croce's death by plane crash in 1973. To me the car, huge and hearselike in its dignity (though now it would be called a pimpmobile), seemed a permanent one-vehicle retinue for the folk singer my parents had loved. Surely, though, the link I was so weirdly sure of, Croce to Cadillac, originated not with my mom but with me—an accident of timing, aided by the imagination of a nine-year-old who was just piecing together what death was and discovering that it could come unexpectedly, even to the famous? Or maybe my belief was just a retroactive construction based on the fact that Croce's song "You Don't Mess Around with Jim," which contained a reference to a "drop-top Cadillac" (as well as a warning to the unwary that it's inadvisable to tug on Superman's cape), played constantly on Mom's eight-track.

9. It had to be Kennedy's graveside tribute that sparked the dark hilarity in *The Loved One* about "standard eternal" versus "perpetual eternal"—a bit that doesn't appear in the late 1940s novel. Terry Southern and Christopher Isherwood were at work on the screenplay by early 1964, immediately after JFK's assassination.

10. The bullet-scarred original, linchpin of a thousand conspiracy theories, may now be seen in the National Archives.

ACCIDENTAL CHARON

1. That race should be a crucial component of who counted as "decent" comes, alas, as no surprise—as the last essay in this book will make clear.

"DUE ALLOWANCE FOR FOAM"

1. Republished in 1987 by the Cincinnati Historical Society.
2. The inferiority complex attached to this remark persists among Cincinnatians. So much so that in May 2018, during the triumphant announcement—at a brewery, naturally—that

the city had been awarded a Major League Soccer franchise, Mayor John Cranley crankily alluded to Twain: no one could say that Cincinnati was ten years behind *now*.

3. Vladimir Nabokov, *The Eye*, trans. Dmitri Nabokov in collaboration with the author (New York: Phaedra, 1965).

4. The Stockyard Café, mentioned in the essay "Bake Visibly," was another bar we encountered while conducting, you know, fieldwork.

5. Richard H. Chused, "Courts and Temperance 'Ladies,'" *Yale Journal of Law & Feminism* 21, no. 2 (2009). In this essay I have relied heavily on Chused's research.

6. Is it possible that Sloane was misconstruing Dickens's tone? Why yes, yes it is. (Also, re "to blow her boy out": Dickens means to plump him up, to make sure he is properly inflated.)

7. In 2016, the presidential nominee chosen in the Prohibition Party's national, um, conference call was a tuba-playing spelunker and former county tax assessor from Pennsylvania named Jim Hedges, who would garner 5,617 votes nationally. Hedges had made his bones in the party by being a crusading figure in the schism of 2004, which unfolded after longtime leader Earl Dodge sold the party's headquarters for $119,000 with the stated intention of building a new one on his own property. Instead he pocketed the money and shoehorned the party HQ into a toolshed.

"ANOTHER WELL-PICKED SKELETON"

1. In one of my favorite grad-school bars, in Baton Rouge, someone had hung as whimsical decoration a yellowed diploma from the Cincinnati School of Embalming—not only a school I'd never heard of, but a concept I'd never considered. For years afterward, "Cincinnati School of Embalming" became, for my friends and me, the euphemism of choice for a ridiculously overmatched foe in football or basketball, a synonym for what some call a "rent-a-win" or "tomato can." *Who are the CSEs they've scheduled this year?*

2. Among these is the marker for J. W. Meal, a "commission merchant"—middleman—who was murdered during the so-called Militia Wars in Arkansas in 1868, perhaps by the Ku Klux Klan. (As a wealthy Yankee "carpetbagger" at the beginning of Reconstruction, Meal would have represented an enticing target for the Night Riders.) His epitaph has the feel of an unedited rush, a heart's cry: "J. W. Meal, born in Ohio, Feb. 6, 1822, killed on his plantation in Ark. while writeing at his desk by an unknown assassin, March 23, 1868 . . ." Note the word "killed," unusual in the epitaphs of non-soldiers; the misspelled detail about "writeing at his desk," which emphasizes the suddenness of his death and asserts that Meal was innocently minding his business; and especially that grammatically untethered, grief-stricken final prepositional phrase. I don't ever recall seeing "unknown assassin" on a gravestone before. The underlying assumption—accurate in this case—is not only that the killer is *currently* at large but that he will remain so for as long as the stone survives.

3. In spring 2019, Spring Grove landscapers trimmed an out-of-control yew hedge, and in so doing exposed a fourth petrified-log stone. It marks the resting place of Katherine Hamilton Banning, widow of a globe-trotting lumberman. On their travels together the Bannings amassed a large trove of wooden and wood-themed curios from all around the world. They also seem to have collected alligators, for some reason, one of which escaped and was apprehended on a neighbor's porch, where it seemed intent on making a meal of a pet cat.

4. As historian David Stradling notes in his terrific *Where the River Burned* (Ithaca, NY: Cornell University Press, 2015, cowritten with his brother Richard Stradling), the 1969 fire was neither the first nor the worst of the Cuyahoga blazes, but it was the one that ended up galvanizing public opinion and making Cleveland, for a generation or more, both a laughingstock and an object lesson in the costs of environmental degradation.

5. Unless we are the current (as of 2020) administration and its Environmental Protection Agency.

6. Joan Connor, "The Deposition of the Prince of Whales," *Southern Review* (Winter 1996); reprinted in *History Lessons* (Amherst: University of Massachusetts Press, 2003).

7. Stephen Dobyns, "A Happy Vacancy," *Southern Review* (Summer 1994); reprinted in *Eating Naked* (New York: Metropolitan Books, 2000).

OUTLOOK HAZY

1. A regular Van Loo, that Houdini.

2. John Updike, "Love as a Standoff," review of Knut Hamsun's *Victoria* (New York: Farrar Straus Giroux, 1969); reprinted in *Picked-Up Pieces* (New York: Random House, 2012).

3. Arthur Conan Doyle, "The Riddle of Houdini," *Strand Magazine* (August–September 1927), https://www.arthur-conan-doyle.com/index.php/The_Edge_of_the_Unknown#I._The _Riddle_of_Houdini.

GHOSTS OF THE WALLDOGS

1. Lydia Pinkham's Vegetable Compound—marketed mainly as a "women's tonic"—is perhaps the best known. Its original formulation contained five herbs (pleurisy root, life root, fenugreek, unicorn root, and black cohosh), plus a generous snort of 18 percent alcohol.

2. A popular ballad of the time, "Sammy Slap, the Bill Sticker," contained a verse in which the eponymous antihero says, "If they'd let me kiver old St. Paul's, so help me, Bob, I'd reach it." Parry's painting contains what seems a sly reference to the ballad; virtually the only thing unmarred (or unbeautified, depending upon one's point of view) is the church dome at top left, which happens to be Saint Paul's. Also, a friend has pointed out that Parry includes a playful advertisement for himself: just to the left of the painting's center one finds a bill with "John Parry" at the top.

3. Robert Venturi, Denise Scott Brown, and Steven Izenour, *Learning from Las Vegas* (Cambridge, MA: MIT Press, 1972).

4. Advertising had, not unpredictably, beaten the city planners to the punch. Burma-Shave's famously playful roadside ads, with rhyming couplets divided into six parts and set on signs one hundred feet apart to create a sort of slow-motion animation—"Does your husband/ misbehave/ grunt and grumble/ rant and rave/ shoot the brute some/ Burma-Shave," for example, or "Are your whiskers/ when you wake/ tougher than/ a two-bit steak!/ Use/ Burma-Shave."—began in 1925.

5. Marjorie Sandor, "The World Is Full of Virtuosos," *Georgia Review* 43, no. 3 (1989).

6. *This Is Spinal Tap* (Rob Reiner, 1984).

7. Barney Keeney, on the episode of *What's My Line?* originally aired June 1, 1958. Another job created by Marilyn Monroe.

8. I'd like to express my gratitude for Ronny Salerno's *Fading Ads of Cincinnati* (Charleston, SC: History Press, 2015), an invaluable source of information for this essay. His photographs— several reproduced here—are gorgeous.

9. In 2017, ArtWorks published *Transforming Cincinnati: How a Decade of ArtWorks Murals Changed People and Communities Forever* (Wilmington, OH: Orange Frazer Press, 2017), an excellent resource for those interested in these beautiful large-scale works.

10. A second Blink Festival, in 2019, attracted even more—the crowds were estimated at 1.25 to 1.5 million people.

"AND THEY DID KILL HER BY INCHES"

1. Quinine is of course a key component of tonic water's "Schweppervescence," too.
2. Kurt Anderson, *Fantasyland: How America Went Haywire* (New York: Random House, 2017); Hanna Rosin, "Fake News: It's as American as George Washington's Cherry Tree," *New York Times*, September 5, 2017.
3. John Updike, *Bech: A Book* (New York: Knopf, 1970).
4. How deadly might be suggested by this: typhoid is now suspected in the deaths of two mid-century presidents who died in office, Zachary Taylor and (see "The Sculptor, His Son, the Odd Fellows, and the Weird Assassin" essay) William Henry Harrison.
5. Vladimir Nabokov, *Lectures on Literature* (New York: Harcourt Brace Jovanovich, 1980).

THE SCULPTOR, HIS SON, THE ODD FELLOWS, AND THE WEIRD ASSASSIN

1. The latest ranking of "Presidential Greatness" by American political scientists was released in February 2018. It got a lot of attention, mainly because the current occupant of the Oval Office supplanted poor James Buchanan as the caboose of chief executives. To me, the surprise was that Garfield (now #34) and Harrison (now #42) each fell three slots. I would have thought, in these times, that a kind of Hippocratic "First, Do No Harm" principle would obtain, a standard that would reward these two.
2. Until the early 1900s, Garfield got the special honor of holding up traffic in the middle of the avenue, but when it became obvious that annoying streetcar riders and motorists stuck in traffic wasn't the tribute most ardently to be desired, he was moved.
3. In Robert Coover, *A Night at the Movies; or, You Must Remember This* (New York: Simon and Schuster, 1987).
4. The record would be broken again in 2016, and in 2020.
5. Harrison's wife, Anna, stayed home in the Cincinnati area (North Bend). She was packing for the journey to join her spouse when word came of his death. A sad, flabbergasting side note: the Harrisons had ten children, only two of whom lived to see forty. Seven survived to adulthood and then died in their twenties and thirties.
6. And not only the vocabulary of abuse. For instance, Harrison's campaign is said to have given rise to the idiom "Keep the ball rolling." Supporters built a giant tin ball, decorated with slogans and campaign planks, and rolled it from event to event . . . a stunt that would later be adopted by Harrison's grandson Benjamin in the 1888 campaign. "Gallant Ben" had a metal and canvas sphere about twelve feet in diameter, resembling a gargantuan beach ball, that supporters dribbled some five thousand miles.
7. Tragedy would follow just eight months later, when lightning struck the statue in a late-spring storm, killing three people who had sought shelter beneath it and wounding seven others. It's said that a bluish streak still shows the path of the bolt.
8. "Unthreatening" is important. Even today, some of the wilder conspiracy theories about the Illuminati and the New World Order derive from a fear of these secret organizations and their (usually benignly silly) rituals. In "The Cask of Amontillado" (1846), Edgar Allan Poe's loopy, hilarious tale of revenge, the doomed and drunken Fortunato, down in the cat-acombs with the man who's about to wall him in forever, makes an elaborate flourish with a wine bottle, then seems aghast that his companion doesn't recognize it as a secret gesture. *Aren't you a Mason?* he asks. Montresor defensively retorts that of course he is. Fortunato presses him: if so, then show a sign. So Montresor, now at a loss . . . reaches into the sleeve of his cloak and unveils the trowel he's about to use. Screw you, obscure Masonic symbology. To the thirty-third degree.

9. The price tag for all this was $20,000, roughly half a million in 2018. The Odd Fellows didn't stint on such things. A decade later they commissioned Samuel Hannaford, Cincinnati's most eminent architect, to design and construct a beautiful headquarters downtown, close to his City Hall. The Odd Fellows building, now considered one of Hannaford's lost gems, lasted less than a half-century; it was sold in the 1940s to Western & Southern, the mortgage holder, at a fire-sale price, and subsequently razed. The grim parking garage that succeeded it has now survived twenty-five years longer.

10. Mundhenk, too, may have been present at the dinner honoring the late Leon Van Loo with which this book opened. He was certainly a member of the Cincinnati Art Club, and he lived until 1922.

11. Rebisso's role in the firm was taken over by Conrad Walther, who had accompanied the Tyler Davidson Fountain—Cincinnati's most enduring civic symbol, in part thanks to *WKRP in Cincinnati*'s opening credits—from the Munich foundry where it was made. Walther left in 1885, leaving Mundhenk to go it alone for several years until his son Oscar became a partner for a time.

12. Not only did the metal detector work, but Bell's further refinements would result in a device to find bullets and ballistic fragments in wounds, and also the mine detectors that came into wide use in World War I. The failed attempt to save Garfield would, peculiarly, lead the way to two *other* breakthrough inventions. Attempts to keep the president's fever down in the brutal DC summer resulted in an ingenious device involving fans, ice, and fabric that was a precursor of modern air conditioning. Toward the end, Garfield asked to be moved to Ohio, but the long, bumpy journey across the Appalachians wasn't feasible. Instead, he was transferred over flat ground to Long Branch, NJ. One of the contrivances worked out for the train trip, this one by the Corps of Engineers, was a water-filled mattress that absorbed the shocks of the journey, keeping Garfield comfortable: an early version of the waterbed.

13. Robert Coover, *The Public Burning* (New York: Viking, 1977).

14. In several southern states, it may be conception.

15. "Everything is Free," written by Gillian Welch and David Todd Rawlings, *Time (The Revelator)*, Acony, 2001.

16. Or, if our poetic license is revoked, her stepmother eighteen whacks. (Or none—she was acquitted, after all.)

17. Along with her co-lyricist, David Rawlings.

SIX DEGREES OF JONATHAN CILLEY

1. A writer friend tells me there's a Wikipedia game called "Degrees to Hitler," the premise of which is that you can get from virtually any Wikipedia page to Hitler's in just a few steps.

2. Frigyes Karinthy, "Chain-Links," 1929, trans. by Adam Makkai. https://djjr-courses.wdfiles.com/local--files/soc180%3Akarinthy-chain-links/Karinthy-Chain-Links_1929.pdf.

3. Our degree of Hitler here: one, apparently. Less than a paragraph.

4. Or worse than louche, if you adjudge him guilty of the rape and manslaughter of Virginia Rappe. Arbuckle was tried three times on those charges, the first two ending with hung juries and the third in an acquittal—and, weirdly, a formal statement of apology to the defendant.

5. True-crime podcaster Richard O. Jones's "The Avondale Horror: Cincinnati's 1884 Burking Murders," *Belt* magazine, February 12, 2015, was of invaluable assistance in researching this section.

6. Time has changed this perspective, I am glad to report. In 2000, a plaque was erected behind the present courthouse to commemorate Sheriff Hawkins's heroic work to preserve

the rule of law during the riots. Hawkins had been a journalist at the *Cincinnati Enquirer* before running for sheriff, and soon after presiding over the third conspirator's, Joe Palmer's, execution in 1885 (the job was bungled, and Palmer—the last person to be executed in Hamilton County—died hard), he left law enforcement to return to journalism, first in St. Louis and later back in his hometown, as managing editor of the *Enquirer*.

7. My father was cagey about what had become of this friend, whose first name was Miles. I discovered only years later that he had committed suicide, an example my parents wanted no part of mentioning to me. I already knew about conniving classmates who might rattle you off a tree, and about the incompetence of bone-setting surgeons there. And about the perilous undertoad.

8. Lisa Birnbach, ed., *The Official Preppy Handbook* (New York: Workman, 1980).

9. The book was a collaboration of the journalists Jack Bass and Jack Nelson (*The Orangeburg Massacre* [New York: World Publishing, 1970]). I also recommend my friend and fellow Orangeburg native/exile Jack Shuler's *Blood and Bone: Truth and Reconciliation in a Southern Town* (Columbia: University of South Carolina Press, 2012).

10. *Oxford American*, no. 24 (1998).

11. Of course, many of these questions—especially about neighborhood schools, suburban districts, and so on—apply, too, to nonwhite parents of means.

12. Fred Hobson, *But Now I See: The White Southern Racial Conversion Narrative* (Baton Rouge: Louisiana State University Press, 1999).

13. Yes, irony noted—thanks!

14. Robert Sam Anson, *Best Intentions: The Education and Killing of Edmund Perry* (New York: Random House, 1987).

15. Robert Sam Anson, *Best Intentions: The Education and Killing of Edmund Perry* (New York: Vintage Books, 1988).

16. Smith is now a professor of religion at Emory University in Atlanta.

17. W.E.B. Du Bois, *The Soul of Black Folk* (Chicago: A.C. McClurg, 1903), 2.

THE PERMEABLE EARTH

1. Rebecca Solnit, *Wanderlust: A History of Walking* (New York: Penguin, 2000).

Image Credits

Page 2   Alexander Courage. Courtesy of the Film Music Society.

Page 7   Some radical tree-hugger. Photo by Nicola Mason.

Page 7   Dr. Thomas Fogarty with President Obama. White House photo.

Page 7   The Fogarty catheter. Courtesy of Edward's Lifesciences.

Page 8   Eisenhower Executive Office Building. White House photo.

Page 8   Louise McLaughlin vase. Courtesy of the Metropolitan Museum of Art, New York.

Page 16   Leon Van Loo stone. Photo by J. Z. Kamholtz.

Page 19   Advertising card. Courtesy of Richard O. Titus.

Page 20   Huenefeld crypt. Photo by J. Z. Kamholtz.

Page 27   Cinci Freedom. Photo by Derek Goodwin.

Page 30   Wright stone. Photo by J. Z. Kamholtz.

Page 36   Frances Wright. This drawing was used as the frontispiece for *History of Woman Suffrage*, Vol. 1, by Elizabeth Cady Stanton, Susan B. Anthony, and Matilda Joslyn Gage, in 1881. Library of Congress, https://www.loc.gov/item/2003652654/.

Page 36   *I Was a Teenage Frankenstein*. Poster by Reynold Brown.

Page 36   Wright gravestone. Photo by J. Z. Kamholtz.

Page 39   "A Downright Gobbler." Library of Congress, https://www.loc.gov/item/2002708975/.

Page 57   Fisk Coffin. Courtesy of the W. C. Brown Collection, Ohio County Public Library, Wheeling, WV.

Page 57   John C. Calhoun. Photo by Mathew Brady.

Page 57   Ad for Crane, Breed & Co. Digitized by the Public Library of Cincinnati and Hamilton County. Image extracted by Greg Hand.

Page 58   Crane monument. Photo by J. Z. Kamholtz.

Page 59   Barnhorn's hearse. Courtesy of Thomas A. McPherson Collection.

Page 59   Image from the Institute of Puerto Rican Culture.

Page 59   Blair House. Courtesy of Harry S Truman Library & Museum, Independence, MO. https://www.trumanlibrary.gov/photograph-records/59-1634.

Page 66   X-100. Photo by Robert Knudsen. Courtesy of John F. Kennedy Presidential Library and Museum, Boston.

Page 67   Hess's stone. Photo by J. Z. Kamholtz.

Page 68   Strader crypt. Photo by J. Z. Kamholtz.

Page 74   Brown stone. Photo by J. Z. Kamholtz.

Page 81   Carrie Nation. Photograph by Philipp Kester, *New York Times*, 1910.

Page 82   Woman's Crusade. Photo by Fred S. Crowell, 1873–74. Courtesy of the Ohio History Connection.

Page 90   Image from *A Woman of the Century: Fourteen Hundred-Seventy Biographical Sketches Accompanied by Portraits of Leading American Women in All Walks of Life*. Edited by Frances E. Willard and Mary A. Livermore. Buffalo: Charles Wells Moulton, 1893.

Page 91   Brown's memorial marker. Photo by J. Z. Kamholtz.

Page 92   Miller cross-section. Photo by J. Z. Kamholtz.

Page 97   A faithful mourner. Photo by J. Z. Kamholtz.

Page 97   Twins. Photo by J. Z. Kamholtz.

Page 98   Fritz memorial. Photo by J. Z. Kamholtz.

Page 98   Ernst's marker. Photo by J. Z. Kamholtz.

Page 98   Wheeler family. Photo by J. Z. Kamholtz.

Page 106 Reuben Buck Robertson Sr. Courtesy of Reuben B. Robertson Collection, Ramsey Library, University of North Carolina, Asheville.

Page 106 Longview State Hospital. Courtesy of the University of Cincinnati Libraries.

Page 116 Pruden stone. Photo by J. Z. Kamholtz.

Page 121 The Fox sisters. Library of Congress, https://lccn.loc.gov/2002710596.

Page 121 Jean Doyle. Courtesy of the George Grantham Bain Collection, Library of Congress, https://www.loc.gov/item/2014697442/.

Page 121 Pruden monument. Photo by J. Z. Kamholtz.

Page 123 Laura Pruden slate. Courtesy of the IUPUI University Library Digital Collection and the Hett Art Gallery & Museum, Camp Chesterfield, Indiana.

Page 126 Holthaus signature. Photo by Ronny Salerno.

Page 135 *A London Street Scene.* Courtesy of Alfred Dunhill Collection.

Page 135 A Cincinnati Streetscape. Library of Congress, https://www.loc.gov/pictures/item/2016800475/.

Page 135 Liberty Tire. Photo by Maya Drozdz.

Page 136 David Ogilvy. Photo by Rob Mieremet.

Page 136 Chateau de Touffou. Courtesy of the Base Mérimée, French Ministry of Culture. © Monuments historiques, 1992, https://www.pop.culture.gouv.fr/notice/merimee/PA00105353.

Page 136 Walter Landor. Courtesy of Landor.

Page 136 Collégiale St. Pierre. Photo by Jochen Jahnke.

Page 137 Paramount Vodka ad. Photograph by Ronny Salerno.

Page 137 Spring Grove mausoleum. J. Z. Kamholtz.

Page 152 Carrie stone. Photo by J. Z. Kamholtz.

Page 159 Wagner family marker. Photo by J. Z. Kamholtz.

Page 159 Students at dissecting table. Courtesy of Dittrick Medical History Center, Case Western Reserve University.

Page 160 National Prtg. & Engr. Co, and Robert Louis Stevenson. *Dr. Jekyll and Mr. Hyde*, 1890. Library of Congress. https://www.loc.gov/item/2014635954/.

Page 168 Odd Fellows' Monument. Photo by J. Z. Kamholtz.

Page 177 William Henry Harrison. Photo by Albert Sands Southworth and Josiah Johnson Hawes. Gift of I. N. Phelps Stokes, Edward S. Hawes, Alice Mary Hawes, and Marion Augusta Hawes, 1937.

Page 177 Nameplate of Odd Fellows' Monument. Photo by J. Z. Kamholtz.

Page 177 Stones by Odd Fellows' Monument. Photo by J. Z. Kamholtz.

Page 178 *Terrible Collision Between the Steamboats STONINGTON and NARRAGANSETT.* Michele and Donald D'Amour Museum of Fine Arts, Springfield, MA. Gift of Lenore B. and Sidney A. Alpert, supplemented with Museum Acquisition Funds. Photo by David Stansbury.

Page 178 Induction balance. Courtesy of the Division of Medicine & Science, National Museum of American History, Smithsonian Institution.

Page 179 Sculpture by Mundhenk and Schoonmaker. Blegen Classics Library, University of Cincinnati, circa 1929.

Page 190 Jonathan Cilley Stone. Photo by J. Z. Kamholtz.

Page 201 Allen Ingalls. Archival image extracted by Richard O. Jones, in "The Avondale Horror," *Belt* magazine, February 12, 2015.

Page 201 "A Murderer Hung in Time Saves Nine." *Harper's Weekly*, 1884.

Page 202 Delano Middleton, Samuel Hammond, and Henry Smith. Courtesy of SC State University Historical Collection & Archives.

Index

numbers in italics refer to photos

A
Adams, John Quincy, 38
Alger, Horatio, 124, 218
Andersen, Kurt, 157
Anson, Robert Sam, 216–20
Anthony, Susan B., 89
Arbuckle, Fatty, 191
Aristophanes, 86
Arthur, Chester, 175, 176

B
Bacon, Kevin, 191–93
Barnhorn, Clement, 61, 172
Barnum, P. T., 37, 107
Barth, John, 14–15, 47
Barthes, Roland, 134
Beecher, Catharine, 38, 45
Beery, Wallace (Sweedie), 191, 192
Bell, Alexander Graham, 176
Berner, William, 200, 203
Berryman, John, 144
Biko, Stephen, 209
Birnbach, Lisa, 205
Blaine, James, 175
Blavatsky, Madame, 184
Bliss, Dr. Doctor Willard, 176
Bloomer, Amelia, 38
Bly, Nellie, 110
Bon Jovi, Jon (John Francis Bongiovi, Jr.),
   41–42
Bookman, Abe, 125
Booth, Sam, 87
Borden, Lizzie, 188
Borges, Jorge Luis, 14, 150
Borglum, Gutzon, 172
Borglum, Solon, 172
Bowman, S. M., 17
Boyer, Jean-Pierre, 42
Brady, Mathew, 52
Breed, Abel, 53
Breed, Austin, 60
Breed, William James, 55–56

Brooks, Preston, 195
Brown, Denise Scott, 130
Brown, Martha McClellan "Mattie," 89–91, *90*
   headstone, *74*
   memorial marker, *91*
Brown, Molly, 3
Brown, W. Kennedy, 89, 90
   memorial marker, *91*
Burke, William, 70, 73
Burton, Tim, 61
Buttre, John Chester, 36

C
Calhoun, John C., 52, *57*
Carlisle, Belinda, 134
"Carolyn" (pseudonym of character in
   documentary), 218
Carter, Albert, 125
Cavatica, Charlotte A. (literary character), 4
Chalfant (minister), 112–14
Chaney, James, 209
Chaplin, Charlie, 173
Charles, Ezzard, *138*
Chused, Richard, 84–85
Cilley, Bradbury, 211
Cilley, Jonathan, 194, 195
   gravestone, *190*
Cilley, Jonathan Longfellow (Congressman),
   194–95
Cilley, Jonathan Longfellow (anatomist),
   196–99, 211, 220
Cilley, Sarah, 195
Cinci Freedom (cow), 26, *27*, 28–29
Clarke, Brock, 47
Clay, Henry, 33, 52, 171
Cleopatra, 90
Clines, Francis, 13
Clover, Philip K., 52
Coffelt, Leslie, 63
Coffin, Catherine, 13
Coffin, Levi, 13
Cole, Miriam, 88–89
Collazo, Oscar, 62–63
Connor, Joan, 107

Cooper, James Fenimore, 31
Coover, Robert, 169, 185
Courage, Alexander "Sandy," *2,* 5–6
Crane, Martin Hale, 52–53, 54–55
   hillside monument, *58*
Cranley, Jack, 10
Cruncher, Jerry (literary character), 86
Currier & Ives, 36, 178
Cutter, Bessie Nichols, 183
Cyclopes (mythological figure), 139

D
Dafoe, Willem, 209
Damon (mythological figure), 113
D'Arusmont, Frances Sylva Phiquepal, 44
David (biblical figure), 174
Davis, Jefferson, 52
Davis, W. C., 52
Dean, James, 191
Devin, Augustus, 72–73
Dewey, Thomas, 63
Dickens, Charles, 86
Dickinson, Emily, 47
Dixon, Robert, 197
Dobyns, Stephen, 115
Dolezal, Rachel, 157
Dos Equis "Most Interesting Man in the
   World" (advertising character), 142
Downs, Joseph, 63
Doyle, Arthur Conan, 117–20, *121,* 122–25, 222
Doyle, Jean Leckie Conan, 117, 119, *121,* 222
Draper, Don (TV character), 134
Dred Scott decision, 70
Du Bois, W. E. B., 218, 219
Duke, David, 129–30
Duveneck, Frank, 17

E
Earp, Wyatt, 173
Eaton, Joseph Oriel, 71
Edison, Thomas, 87
Edwards, Edwin, 129
Ehrmann, Benjamin, 156, 158
Ehrmann, Frederick, 154–55, 158, 161–67
Eisenhardt, Charles, 61
Eisenhardt, Charles, Jr., 51, 61, 63–67
Eisenhower, Dwight, 105, 170
Elden, Spencer, 148

Elder, Carrie, 153–55, 163–67
   tombstone, *152*
Elizabeth II, Queen, 63
Emerson, Ralph Waldo, 41
Ernst, Andrew, 100
   tree trunk marker, *98*

F
Fairey, Shepard, 138, 148
Falco, 191
Farny, Henry, 17
Faulkner, William, 214
Fern (literary character), 4
Fincher, David, 134
Finn, Huckleberry (literary character), 99
Fisher, Carrie, 3
Fisk, Almond (born Fiske), 51–53
Flaubert, Gustave, 5, 6
Fogarty, Thomas, 6, *7,* 9–11, 49
Foghorn Leghorn (cartoon character), 78
Forbes family, 52
Ford, Gerald, 51
Fox, Kate, 118, *121,* 124
Fox, Maggie, 118, *121,* 124
Fox, Margalit, 5–6
Franklin, Benjamin, 25
Fritz, Jacob, 112
   memorial, *98*

G
Gallup, George, 142
Garbo, Greta (the Swedish Sphinx), 191
Garfield, James, 169–70, 175–76, 179–80
Garibaldi, Giuseppe, 172
Garner, Margaret, 70
Gass, William, 41
George (former slave), 69
Gofridus, 145, 187
Goodman, Michael, 209
Graham, Christopher, 69
Grant, Ulysses S., 12, 17, *18,* 25, 173
Graves, William, 194–95
Griffith, Bix, *7*
Guare, John, 191
Guiteau, Charles, 175–76, 179–80
Gurganus, Allan, 54
Guthrie, William Eugene, 44
Guy, Elizabeth Jane, 163–65

H

Hackman, Gene, 209
Hahnemann, Samuel, 156, 158, 161–62
Hall, Moses Uriah, 211
Hamblet, Coach, 213
Hammond, Samuel, *202*
Hancock, Winfield Scott, 175
Hare, William, 70, 73
Harrison, Benjamin, 72, 73
Harrison, John Scott, 72–73, 196, 199
Harrison, William Henry, 72, 73, 169–71, *177*
Haskell, David, 48
Hawkins, Morton Lytle, 200, 203, 204
Hawthorne, Nathaniel, 194, 195
Heat Miser (cartoon character), 3, 4
Hegel, Georg Wilhelm Friedrich, 11
Henry (former slave), 69
Hess, Emil, 61
Hess, Willard, 51, 61, 63–67
    gravestone, *67*
Higley, Judge, 163
Hitler, Adolf, 191
Hobson, Fred, 208–9
Holmes, Sherlock (literary character), 117
Holthaus, Gus, 146–49, 151
    nameplate, *126*
    signature and mausoleum marker, *137*
Hooks, Kevin, 220
Hoover, J. Edgar, 63
Houdini, Harry, 117, 119–20, *121*, 125
Huenefeld, Ernst H., *20*, 22, 24–25, 26
    crypt, *20*
Huggins, Miller, 13
Hulseman, Leo, 3, 4
Hussein, King, 63
Hyde, Edward (literary character), 52, 155, *160*, 166–67

I

Ilsa (movie character), 169
Ingalls, Allen, 197–98, *201*, 204
Irving, George S., 3, 4
Irving, John, 205
Isherwood, Christopher, 54
Izenour, Steven, 130

J

Jackson, Andrew, 33, 34, 38

Jackson, Michael, 220
Jackson, Stonewall, 90
Jefferson, Thomas, 33–34, 37
Jekyll, Henry (literary character), 155, *160*, 166–67
Jerry Cruncher (literary character), 54
Jesus, 76, 94
Johnson, Ben, 197–99, 204, 211
Johnson, Lyndon B., 51, 65, 66, 67
Johnson, Marilyn, 3, 15
Jonathan (biblical figure), 174
Jones, Anissa, 191
Jones, Quincy, 220

K

Kaelin, Kato, 185
Kafka, Franz, 133
Karinthy, Frigyes, 191
Keckeler, Temperance, 108
Keith, Toby, 3, 4
Kennedy, John F., 64, 65, 107
Kennedy, John F., Jr. (John-John), *50*, 51
King, Martin Luther, Jr., 43, 208, 219
Kirk, William, 200
Kline, Kevin, 209
Knowles, John, 205
Kyi, Aung San Suu, *138*, 148

L

Lafayette, Marquis de, 33, 40
Lamarr, Hedy, 191
Lambert, Emma Jean, 196
Landor, Walter (born Landauer), *136*, 141, 143–45
Lang, Fritz, 122
Laszlo (movie character), 169
Lavoisier, Antoine, 162
Levinson, Max, 125
Lewis, Diocletian (Dr. Dio), 82–84, 85
Liberace, 54, *58*
Lincoln, Abraham, 17, 53
Lincoln, Robert, 203
Lindbergh, Charles, 173
Lodge, Henry Cabot, 107
Longfellow, Henry Wadsworth, 194
Lorre, Peter, 191
Loy, Myrna, 191
Luther, Martin, 128

M
Madison, James, 33
Mailer, Norman, 43
Margolin, Stuart, 191
Mary, Queen of Scots, 90
Matthew (biblical figure), 94
Max, Peter, 28–29
Mazzini, Giuseppe, 172
McCay, Winsor, 17, 19
McCullers, Carson, 214
McKinley, William, 173
McLaughlin, Mary Louise, 13
McPherson, James, 172, 187
Medusa (mythological figure), 139
Middleton, Delano, *202,* 206
Miller, Charles: in *Cincinnati Enquirer*
    archives 1872-1922, 108–10
Miller, Charles A., 108, 110–14;
    headstone, *92*
Miller, Isaac, 108, 114; Isaac, 114
Miller, Lulu, 108, 114;
    headstone, *92f*
Miller, Martha, 108
Miller, Matilda Oberdieck (afterwards
    Kiechler), 114
Miller, Otto, 183–86
Miller family stone marker, *92*
Mills, Louis, 196–97
Monroe, James, 33
Monroe, Marilyn, 43
Morissette, Alanis, 173
Morrison, Toni, 70
Morse, Samuel, 161
Moses (biblical figure), *168,* 173–74
Mr. Hundred and One (cartoon character), 3
Mullett, Alfred, 13
Mundhenk, August, 174, 180, 187
Mundhenk, Oscar, 186–89
Muni, Paul, 191

N
Nabokov, Vladimir, 28, 78, 166, 167, 187
Nast, Thomas, 203
Nation, Carrie, 76–77, *81,* 86, 87
Neal, Mark Anthony, 218
Nicholson, Jack, 99
Niehaus, Charles Henry, 169, 172
Nirvana (rock band), 148

Nixon, Richard M., 51, 105, 107, 186
Nowottny, Vincent, 183–84
Nowottny-Miller, Etta, 183–86

O
Obama, Barack, *7,* 43, 149
O'Connor, Flannery, 45, 214
Odd Fellows Monument, *168, 177*
Ogilvy, David, *136,* 141–43
Ogilvy, Herta, 142–43
O. Henry, 149
O'Neill, Eugene, 192
Oswald, Lee Harvey, 64, 65
Owen, Robert, 33, 35
Owen, Robert Dale, 35, 41
Ozymandias (literary figure), 94

P
P., Miss (author's teacher), 205
Paine, Thomas, 31
Palmer, Joe, 200
Paracelsus, 156
Parker, Theodore, 43
Parry, John Orlando, 129, 130, *135*
Partridge Family (television characters), 181
Payne, Alexander, 99
Perkins, Bill, 220
Perry, Edmund, 211–20
Perry, Jonah, 215–16
Perry, Mary Chase, 172
Philada, James Akin, 39
Phillips, L. (juror in Berner case), 200
Pickford, Mary, 191
Plato, 14
Plato, Dana, 191
Plover, Jason W. (literary character), 115
Plummer, Edouard, 217
Pontius Pilate, 90
Presley, Elvis, 79
Price, Harry, 117
Price, Richard, 220
Prickett, Vada, 12 (literary character)
Prince, 220
Pruden, Andrew, 120, 122
    grave monument, *121*
Pruden, Laura Carter, 120, 122–23, 124–25, 222
    grave marker, *116*
Pruden, Mary Powell, 120

Pruden, Thomas, 120, 122
Pulsifer, Sam (literary character), 47, 48
Pulte, Joseph Hippolyt, 156, 158, 161
Pulte, Mary Jane (neé Rollins), 158, 161
Pythagoras, 90
Pythias (mythological figure), 113

R
Reagan, Nancy, 217
Reagan, Ronald, 170, 217
Rebecca (biblical figure), 174
Rebisso, Annie Eliza Whitehead, 183
Rebisso, Elizabeth, 181–82, 189
Rebisso, Louis, 169–70, 172–74, 180, 181–82, 189
Rebisso, Louis Thomas, 172, 182–86
Rebisso, Louis Thomas, Jr., 182
Reed, Jerry, 28
Reeves, George, 13
REM (rock band), 173
Reuben (former slave), 67
Reynolds, Debbie, 3, 4
Rich, Frank, 192
Richardson, James, 35
Richardson, Tony, 54
Rick Blaine (movie character), 169
Riefenstahl, Leni, 191
Rinehart, Bill, 148
Robertson, Charlie, 103
Robertson, Grace, 103
Robertson, Peggy, 107
Robertson, Reuben Buck, Jr., 103, 105, 108
Robertson, Reuben Buck, Sr., 103, 104–5, *106*, 107, 108
Roddenberry, Gene, 5–6
Roosevelt, Franklin Delano, 105, 173
Root, Joseph Cullen, 96
Rosin, Hanna, 157
Ruby, Jack, 65
Rudolph the Red-Nosed Reindeer (cartoon character), 3
Rumford, Count (Sir Benjamin Thompson), 25

S
Sachs, Marilyn, 3, 4
Safford, William, 85–86, 88, 91
Saint-Gaudens, Augustus, 173

Salerno, Ronny, 148
Salinger, J. D., 213
Sandor, Marjorie, 140, 144
Saul/Paul (biblical character), 84
Sayers, William, 60
Schmidt (movie character), 99
Schnell, John, 55
Schnell, Lou Ransom, 55
Schnitzler, Arthur, 192
Schott, Marge, 28
Schrödinger, Erwin, 49
Schroer, John, 24
Schwerner, Andrew, 209
Scooby-Doo (cartoon character), 52
Scorsese, Martin, 220
Scovill, A. R., 60
Scudder, Janet, 172
Sean (author's basketball teammate), 113, 115
Sedgwick, Kyra, 192–93
Shelley, Mary, 35, 38, 41
Sherman, William Tecumseh, 12, 17, 25
Shiftlet, Mr. (literary character), 45
Shippen, Charmé, 90
Shippen, Edward, 90
Simpson, O. J., 28
Sloane, Ulrich, 86, 88
Smith, Henry, *202*
Smith, Theophus "Thee," 219
Snipes, Wesley, 220
Sohn, J. G., 75
Solnit, Rebecca, 221
Sondheim, Stephen, 180
Southern, Terry, 54
Spears, Britney, 43
Splitfoot, Mr. (demon summoned in séance), 118
SpongeBob SquarePants (cartoon character), 14
Stanton, Elizabeth Cady, 38
Starker, Mr. (movie character), 54
Stein, Gertrude, 172
Stevenson, Robert Louis, 155, *160*, 166
Stewart, Eliza Daniel "Mother," 84, 88
Stewart, Jermaine, 149
Sting, 134
Storer, Maria Longworth, 13
Stowe, Harriet Beecher, 38

Strader, Jacob, 69–70, 73
  crypt, *68, 71*
Strassman, Marcia (Mrs. Kotter – TV
  character), 191
Sullivan, John L., 191
Sumner, Charles, 195
Superman (TV character), 13
Swormstedt, Tod, 148

T
Taney, Roger, 69–70
Taylor, Beverly, 196, 198
Taylor, Edward, 42
Taylor, Elizabeth, 196, 198
Thompson, Hunter S., 127
Thomson, Peter, 103, 104
Thoreau, Henry David, 125
Thorpe, Morris (TV character), 220
Timberlake, Justin, 43
Toklas, Alice B., 172
Torresola, Bianca Canales, 59, 62
Torresola, Griselio, 62–63
Trollope, Anthony, 31
Trollope, Frances, 31, 35, 37, 40
Trollope, Henry, 37
Truman, Harry, 62, 63
Twain, Mark, 53, 60, 77

U
Underdog (TV character), 4
Updike, John, 124, 132, 158

V
Van Buren, Martin, 170, 195
Van Gogh, Vincent, 21
Van Houten, Lee, 215–16
Van Loo, Leon, 17, *18*, 19, 95, 222
  headstone, *16*
Venturi, Robert, 130
Vonnegut, Kurt, 139

W
Wagner, John Charles, 153, 163, 164, 167
Wagner, Sarah, 153, 163–64, 167
Wagner family marker, *159*
Walker, Kimberly, 14
Warren, Robert Penn, 214
Washington, Denzel, 209
Waugh, Evelyn, 54, 56
Webb, James Watson, 194
Webb, Jimmy, 213
Webster, Daniel, 52, 171
Weisz, Cecelia, 117, 119
Welch, Gillian, 188
Welty, Eudora, 214
West, Mae, 43
Wheeler, John Egbert, 102–3
Wheeler, John Pogue, 102
Wheeler, Margaret Culbertson, 102
Wheeler, William, 102
Wheeler family: petrified log stones, *98*
White, Edmund, 40
White, E. B., 4
Whitehead, Edward, 142
Wilbur (literary character), 4
Willard, Frances, 89
Williams, Mrs. (tenant of Dr. Cilley), 199
Wilson, Judge, 163
Wong, Tyrus, 3, 4
Woodall, F. F., 60
Woolf, Virginia, 221
Wright, Camilla, 31–32
Wright, Frances "Fanny," 31–35, *36*, 37–46,
  47, 49
  caricature of, *39*
  gravestone, *30, 36*
  on historical marker, 44, *45*
Wright, Sylva. *see* D'Arusmont, Frances Sylva
  Phiquepal

Z
Zepenrick, Phoebe, 108
Zuckerberg, Mark, 128

MICHAEL GRIFFITH'S previous books are *Trophy* (named one of *Kirkus Reviews*' Best Books of 2011), *Bibliophilia*, and *Spikes*. Griffith's nonfiction has appeared in *Southern Review*, *Oxford American*, *Five Points*, *Shenandoah*, *The Washington Post*, and elsewhere, and his work has been honored by fellowships from the National Endowment for the Arts, the National Humanities Center, the Taft Foundation, the Louisiana Division of the Arts, and the Sewanee Writers' Conference. He is Professor of English at the University of Cincinnati and Fiction Editor of the *Cincinnati Review*. He is also the Founding Editor of *Yellow Shoe Fiction*, an original-fiction series from Louisiana State University Press.